LEADING
FROM THE
EMERGING
FUTURE

**From Ego-System
to Eco-System Economies**

Otto Scharmer and Katrin Kaufer

LEADING
FROM THE
EMERGING
FUTURE

From Ego-System
to Eco-System Economies

$\overline{\text{BK}}$

Berrett–Koehler Publishers, Inc.
San Francisco
a BK Currents book

Berrett-Koehler Publishers, Inc.
1333 Broadway, Suite 1000
Oakland, CA 94612-1921
Tel: (510) 817-2277   Fax: (510) 817-2278   www.bkconnection.com

Ordering Information
Quantity sales. Special discounts are available on quantity purchases by corporations, associations, and others. For details, contact the "Special Sales Department" at the Berrett-Koehler address above.
Individual sales. Berrett-Koehler publications are available through most bookstores. They can also be ordered directly from Berrett-Koehler: Tel: (800) 929-2929; Fax: (802) 864-7626; www.bkconnection.com
Orders for college textbook/course adoption use. Please contact Berrett-Koehler. Tel: (800) 929-2929; Fax: (802) 864-7626.
Orders by U.S. trade bookstores and wholesalers. Please contact Ingram Publisher Services, Tel: (800) 509-4887; Fax: (800) 838-1149; E-mail: customer.service@ingram publishingservices.com; or visit www.ingrampublisherservices.com/Ordering for details about electronic ordering.

Berrett-Koehler and the BK logo are registered trademarks of Berrett-Koehler Publish-ers, Inc.

Printed in the United States of America

Berrett-Koehler books are printed on long-lasting acid-free paper. When it is avail-able, we choose paper that has been manufactured by environmentally responsible processes. These may include using trees grown in sustainable forests, incorporating recycled paper, minimizing chlorine in bleaching, or recycling the energy produced at the paper mill.

Library of Congress Cataloging-in-Publication Data
Scharmer, Otto.
    Leading from the emerging future : from ego-system to eco-system economies / Otto Scharmer and Katrin Kaufer. -- First edition.
        pages   cm
    "A BK Currents Book."
    Includes bibliographical references and index.
    ISBN 978-1-60509-926-2 (pbk.)
    1. Economics--Sociological aspects. 2. Social problems--Economic aspects. 3. Social change--Economic aspects. I. Kaufer, Katrin. II.
    Title.
    HM548.S33   2013
    306.3--dc23   2013013602

First edition

22 21 20 19 18 17 16 15   10 9 8 7 6

Produced by BookMatters, cover designed by Steve Pisano, photo of Otto Scharmer by Sven Nieder, copyedited by Laura Harger, proofed by Anne Smith, indexed by Leonard Rosenbaum.

To
HMS and JCS

CONTENTS

Breathing Life into a Dying System

Finance. Food. Fuel. Water shortage. Resource scarcity. Climate chaos. Mass poverty. Mass migration. Fundamentalism. Terrorism. Financial oligarchies. We have entered an Age of Disruption. Yet the possibility of profound personal, societal, and global renewal has never been more real. *Now* is our time.

Our moment of disruption deals with death and rebirth. What's dying is an old civilization and a mindset of maximum "me"—maximum material consumption, bigger is better, and special-interest-group-driven decision-making that has led us into a state of organized irresponsiblity, *collectively creating results that nobody wants.*

What's being born is less clear but in no way less significant. It's something that we can *feel* in many places across Planet Earth. This future is not just about firefighting and tinkering with the surface of structural change. It's not just about replacing one mindset that no longer serves us with another. It's a future that requires us to tap into a deeper level of our humanity, of who we really are and who we want to be as a society. It is a future that we can sense, feel, and actualize by shifting the *inner place* from which we operate. It is a future that in those moments of disruption begins to *presence* itself through us.

This inner shift, from fighting the old to sensing and presencing an emerging future possibility, is at the core of all deep leadership work today. It's a shift that requires us to expand our thinking from the head

1

to the heart. It is a shift from an *ego*-system awareness that cares about the well-being of oneself to an *eco*-system awareness that cares about the well-being of all, including oneself. When operating with ego-system awareness, we are driven by the concerns and intentions of our *small ego* self. When operating with eco-system awareness, we are driven by the concerns and intentions of our emerging or *essential* self—that is, by a concern that is informed by the well-being of the whole. The prefix *eco-* goes back to the Greek *oikos* and concerns the "whole house." The word *economy* can be traced back to this same root. Transforming our current ego-system economy into an emerging eco-system economy means reconnecting economic thinking with its real root, which is the well-being of the whole house rather than money-making or the well-being of just a few of its inhabitants. But while the whole house was for the Greeks something very local, today it also concerns the well-being of our global communities and planetary eco-systems.

This shift in awareness from ego-system to eco-system is something that we are approaching and living through not only as groups and organizations, but also as a global community. Pioneering the principles and personal practices that help us to perform this shift may well be one of the most important undertakings of our time.

Crumbling Walls

Numerous books have been written about today's global crises. Why add another one? We hope to contribute some frameworks, methods, and tools that can help leaders and change-makers understand what is going on and be more effective in helping communities shift from ego-system to eco-system economies.

The world has changed. Walls are crumbling. Tyrants are toppling. The polar caps and glaciers are melting. We have been watching these developments for years. But the two things that appear to be deeply frozen and unchanged are our *collective habits of thought* and the *actions* that they produce and reproduce in our world.

Why is that? Why do we collectively create results that nobody wants? What keeps us locked into old tracks of operating? And what can we do to transform these patterns that keep us firmly in the grip of the past?

The Blind Spot: How to Lead from the Emerging Future

We have written this book for change-makers in all sectors, cultures, and systems, including business, government, civil society, media, academia, and local communities. The book addresses what we believe to be a *blind spot* in global discourse today: how to respond to the current waves of disruptive change from a deep place that connects us to the emerging future rather than by reacting against the patterns of the past, which usually means perpetuating them.

In this book, we argue that responding from the emerging future requires us to shift the inner place from which we operate. It requires us to *suspend* our judgments, *redirect* our attention, *let go* of the past, *lean into the future* that wants to emerge through us, and *let it come.*

The ability to shift from reacting against the past to leaning into and presencing an emerging future is probably the single most important leadership capacity today. It is a capacity that is critical in situations of disruptive change, not only for institutions and systems, but also for teams and individuals. In the old days, we used to learn one profession and practice it throughout our working lives. Today we face rapidly changing environments that increasingly require us to reinvent ourselves. The more dramatic the changes in our environment, the less we can rely on past patterns, and the more we need to learn to pay attention and *tune in* to emerging future opportunities.

This book is a quest to answer three interrelated questions:

1. In the face of disruption, how do we lead from the *emerging future?*
2. What *evolutionary economic framework* can guide our journey forward?
3. What *strategies* can help us to function as vehicles for shifting the whole?

Let's start by taking a quick tour through what we call the iceberg model of the current system. Why an iceberg? Because the name implies that, beneath the visible level of events and crises, there are underlying structures, mental models, and sources that are responsible for creating them. If ignored, they will keep us locked into reenacting the same old patterns time and again.

Progressing through the levels of the iceberg, from surface to depth, will illuminate several blind spots that, if attended to, can help us rebuild our economy and society to be more intentional, inclusive, and inspired.

Symptoms: Landscape of Pathologies

Like the tip of an iceberg—the 10 percent that is visible above the waterline—the symptoms of our current situation are the visible and explicit parts of our current reality. This symptoms level is a whole landscape of issues and pathologies that constitute three "divides": what we call the *ecological divide,* the *social divide,* and the *spiritual-cultural divide.*

THE ECOLOGICAL DIVIDE

We are depleting and degrading our natural resources on a massive scale, using up more nonrenewable precious resources every year. Although we have only one Planet Earth, we leave an ecological footprint of 1.5 planets; that is, we are currently using 50 percent more resources than our planet can regenerate to meet our current consumption needs. As a consequence, one-third of our agricultural land has disappeared over the past forty years. Rapidly falling water tables are taking us on a path toward food riots. Food prices are expected to double by 2030.

THE SOCIAL DIVIDE

Two and a half billion people on our planet subsist on less than US$2 per day. Although there have been many successful attempts to lift people out of poverty, this number has not changed much over the past several decades. In addition, we see an increasing polarization in society in which, in the case of the United States, the top 1 percent has a greater collective worth than the entire bottom 90 percent.[1]

THE SPIRITUAL-CULTURAL DIVIDE

While the ecological divide is based on a disconnect between self and nature, and the social divide on a disconnect between self and other, the spiritual-cultural divide reflects a disconnect between self and Self—

that is, between one's current "self" and the emerging future "Self" that represents one's greatest potential. This divide is manifest in rapidly growing figures on burnout and depression, which represent the growing gap between our actions and who we really are. According to the World Health Organization (WHO), in 2000 more than twice as many people died from suicide as died in wars.[2]

What, if anything, have we as a society learned from addressing these issues over the past hundred years?

In the twentieth century we created ministries and UN agencies to deal with each of these divides. In addition, we created dedicated non-governmental organizations (NGOs) to address single issues; in academia we created dedicated university departments, scholarly journals, and professional career paths to combat each symptom. Today we realize that this silo-type approach—dealing with *one symptom cluster at a time*—isn't working. On the contrary, it seems to be part of the problem. We seem to have a blind spot that prevents us from seeing the rest of the iceberg, the deep systemic structures below the waterline.

Structures: Systemic Disconnects That Give Rise to Symptoms

Today's system does exactly what it is designed to do. But it is a system that features a number of significant structural disconnects. Here are some of them:

1. *A disconnect between the* financial *and the* real *economy.* The total value of foreign exchange transactions worldwide amounted to US$1.5 quadrillion (1 quadrillion is 1,000 trillion) in 2010, whereas the total value of international trade was only US$20 trillion, or less than 1.4 percent of all foreign exchange transactions. Says Lawrence Lau, professor of economic development, emeritus, Stanford University, and chairman, CIC International (Hong Kong): "The overwhelming majority of foreign exchange transactions are thus purely speculative, in effect, pure gambles, and serve no useful social purposes."[3] This disconnect between the financial and the real economy produces the

financial bubbles that keep plaguing the global economy: the Latin American debt crisis (1980s); the Asian financial crisis (1997); the dot-com bubble (2000); and the US housing crisis (2006–07), which was followed by the world financial crisis (2007–09) and the euro crisis (2010–). Such financial bubbles destabilize the real economy instead of serving it.

2. *A disconnect between the* infinite growth *imperative and the* finite resources *of Planet Earth.* The disconnect between the infinite growth that current economic logic demands and the finite resources of Planet Earth has produced a massive bubble: The overuse of scarce resources such as water and soil has led to the loss of a third of our agricultural land globally in roughly one generation's time.

3. *A disconnect between the* Haves *and the* Have Nots. This disconnect has given rise to an extreme inequity bubble in which the richest 1 percent of people in the world (adults with incomes over US$ 500,000) own 40 percent of the world's wealth while half of the world's population (50 percent) own just 1 percent of the world's household wealth.[4] The increasing polarization of wealth and income undermines equal access to opportunity and thus erodes basic human rights in society today.

4. *A disconnect between* institutional leadership *and* people. This disconnect results in a leadership void that shows up in the widely shared sense that we are collectively creating results that nobody wants. This collective condition of felt helplessness and disempowerment is a hallmark of our systemwide leadership void (or bubble) today.

5. *A disconnect between* gross domestic product (GDP) *and* well-being. This disconnect shows up as a bubble of material consumption that does not advance actual well-being. Research on developed countries shows that, contrary to popular belief, higher GDP and higher material consumption do not translate into more well-being, as we will discuss in more detail below.

6. *A disconnect between* governance *and the* voiceless *in our systems.* The disconnect between current governance mechanisms and the voices of the underserved is a governance failure in which people are affected by regimes that they are completely unable to influence or

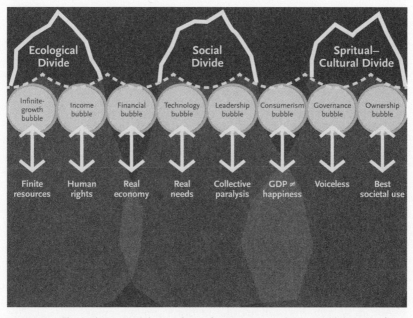

FIGURE 1. The iceberg model: a surface of symptoms and structural disconnects (bubbles) below it.

change. For example, many farmers in India have lost ownership of their seeds to Monsanto.

7. *A disconnect between* actual ownership forms *and* best societal use of property. The disconnect between actual ownership and best societal benefit results in a bubble in which state and private property, despite their merits, allow the overuse and mismanagement of the ecological and social commons in epic proportion.

8. *A disconnect between* technology *and* real societal needs. This disconnect generates technology bubbles that serve the well-being of a few in already overserved markets. For example, most R&D spending by the pharmaceutical industry caters to markets at the top while largely ignoring the needs at the base of the socioeconomic pyramid.

These bubbles and structural disconnects produce systems that are designed to *not* learn. The systems operate through *delayed* or *broken feedback loops* that prevent decision-makers from experiencing and personally feeling the impact of their decisions. In our current complex global systems, decision-makers often affect large groups of people with their actions but never see, feel, or become aware of their actions' consequences. Without feedback, or with delayed feedback, there is no learning. As a result, institutions tend to change too little and too late.[5]

POSITIVE EXTERNALITIES FLOW TO THE TOP, NEGATIVE EXTERNALITIES TO THE POOR

A second feature that the bubbles share concerns externalities. *Externality* is a term that is used in economics to designate unintended side effects on third parties or costs that are not accounted for in prices. Externalities can be positive (benefits) or negative (costs). For example, I may enjoy driving my car, but, unlike the cyclist behind me, I rarely notice the negative externality—air pollution—that I cause.

In today's society, positive externalities tend to flow to the top, while negative externalities tend to flow to the bottom of the socioeconomic pyramid. We see this both in organizations and in societies. Globally, for centuries, raw materials have flowed from the global South to the global North, from developing to developed countries, while toxic waste and toxic products have flowed the other way. All these flows are rationalized by economic theories such as comparative cost advantage. But these theories don't include the impact of externalities.

Whenever ecological issues and environmental disasters strike, the poor pay the highest price (e.g., after Hurricane Katrina in the United States and after the tsunamis of 2004 and 2011 in Indonesia and Japan). When food prices begin to soar as result of manmade environmental problems, the 2.5 billion people who live below the poverty line suffer the most.

In the United States, the 2008 economic meltdown brought the most suffering to low- and middle-income families. Today we know that toxic home mortgages were specifically targeted to the poor by the financial industry. While Wall Street profits have rebounded, the less-privileged have continued to lose: First they lost jobs; then they lost funding for teachers, school activities and meals, and libraries; then they lost heating assistance and medical services.

Yet those whose collective behavior created the crisis, the Wall Street bankers, are by and large back to enjoying their bonus packages. In fact, their leverage for extracting even more government subsidies in the future increased after 2008. In 1995, the six largest bank holding companies in the United States held combined assets valued at less than 17.1 percent of US GDP.[6] Thirteen years later, on the eve of the financial crisis in 2008, these organizations' assets were 55 percent of GDP. By 2010, it had only gotten worse, with their combined assets reaching 64 percent of GDP. That is, the ability of the six largest Wall Street banks to take excessive risk in order to privatize profits and socialize losses by forcing a taxpayer-funded bailout has gone up, not down.[7]

MONEY FLOWS THE WRONG WAY

A third feature concerns the flow of money. In order to achieve *economies of scale* and minimize lending risks, banks and financial institutions organize around financing large projects for well-known clients with sufficient security who use existing business models and known technologies in familiar markets.

Smaller projects that involve new entrepreneurs without track records or security require banks to make individualized loan decisions, which are riskier and more expensive. Decisions on whether to fund innovations in renewable energy, for example, require expertise that traditional loan officers usually do not have. As a result, entrepreneurs and companies that are small or new, or that are venturing into new sectors or sectors with traditionally small returns, have the most restricted access to capital and pay a higher price.

Thus, in an externality-unaware financial system like the one we have today, money flows the wrong way: Those who are innovative, step into new ideas, or even work intentionally with lower returns in order to create societal benefits pay the highest prices, while those who may already have more than they really need pay the lowest prices.

These are all examples of the same fundamental issue: The economic playing field is tilted to favor big players that privatize profits at the top and socialize losses. Which raises a question: Why is our economic playing field tilted in this way? This brings us to the fourth common feature: the role of special-interest groups.

GOVERNANCE IS DRIVEN BY SPECIAL-INTEREST GROUPS

Many organized interest groups, including the banking, agriculture, nuclear, oil, and pharmaceutical industries, command a disproportionate influence on the very regulatory bodies that were originally designed to supervise them. At issue is not only the vast amount of money and lobbying power that these groups command, but also the revolving-door practice that is pervasive in Washington, DC, and other capitals worldwide.

To give one of many possible examples, on November 5, 2008, the day after Barack Obama was elected president, Michael Froman of Citigroup, an influential Obama fundraiser during the election campaign, was appointed to assemble the Obama administration's economic team. While working in this role, Froman remained an employee of Citigroup for two more months, even as he helped appoint the very people who would shape the future of his own firm in the following weeks and months.[8] The result is history.

Likewise, many of the same people responsible for the deregulation of the financial industry during the Clinton administration returned to key government positions in the Obama administration, where they devised massive bailout programs for their former colleagues at their too-big-to-fail banks.

This pattern is repeated in the food industry. A revolving door between Monsanto, the agribusiness giant, and its two regulating government agencies, the Food and Drug Administration (FDA) and the Environmental Protection Agency (EPA), hinders effective oversight. The potential damage from this alliance is no less catastrophic than the alliances in the financial sector.

In all these cases, the problem arises when the political process is tilted by an uneven playing field and a lack of transparency. As we know from the economist Mancur Olson's work on collective action, groups with only a few members can organize themselves easily and speak with a common voice.[9] Obvious examples are the big players in finance, food, health, and energy. Larger and more diverse groups usually are not able to organize as easily and consequently have more difficulty making their members' interests heard. Ordinary taxpayers, who pay for the bailouts, and future generations are two good examples.

These structural issues matter a lot and need to be fixed. But they may not be the root cause of the landscape of pathologies discussed above. So, given all these bubbles and disconnects, what is the *force motrice* that keeps us reenacting these highly dysfunctional structures?

Mental Models That Give Rise to Systemic Bubbles and Disconnects

This force is called *thinking*. As Albert Einstein put it so eloquently: "We cannot solve problems with the same kind of thinking that created them."[10] Thinking creates the world. The structures of yesterday's economic thought manifest in the structures of today's institutions and actions. If we want to upgrade our global economic operating system, we need to *start* by updating the thinking that underlies it; we need to update the essence of *economic logic and thought*.

Using the iceberg model that guides the journey of this book, we refer to this deeper layer as "thinking," "mental models," or paradigms of economic thought.[11] Outmoded mental models have produced an *intellectual bankruptcy*: the bankruptcy of mainstream economic thought.

Ego-System Awareness versus Eco-System Reality

Today's thinking shapes how we enact tomorrow's reality. This link between thought and social reality creation is nowhere more visible than in our economy.

The eight disconnects that we listed above represent a decoupling of two worlds: a decoupling of the structure of *societal reality* from the structure of *economic thought*. We could also say that they're a decoupling of the structures of eco-system reality from the structures of ego-system awareness. Today's economic reality is embedded in a global eco-system of environmental, social, political, and cultural contexts that are highly intertwined and that evolve in uncertain, complex, and volatile ways. These conditions require a mindset on the part of decision-makers that is more open, attentive, adaptive, and tuned in to emerging changes.

Instead, what we often observe in current reality is a disconnect between reality and awareness; that is, between an eco-system-centric global economy and an ego-system-centric awareness of institutional decision-makers. The result is a war of the parts against the whole. We see the impact of this disconnect, for example, in the dramatic over-use of scarce resources, which is often spoken of as "the tragedy of the commons."[12]

Bridging the gap between eco-system reality and ego-system aware-ness is the main challenge of leadership today. Decision-makers across the institutions of a system have to go on a *joint journey* from seeing only their own viewpoint (ego-awareness) to experiencing the system from the perspective of the other players, particularly those who are most marginalized. The goal must be to co-sense, co-inspire, and co-create an emerging future for their system that values the well-being of all rather than just a few.

This is not just an ethical but an *economic* imperative. Let's consider the euro crisis, which emerged after the 2008 global financial crisis, as a case in point. The euro crisis is to no small degree a function of Ger-many and some other countries reverting to a nation-state-centered way of seeing reality. What made the EU such an unlikely success story after World War II? A Franco-German accord with other core EU countries in which all shared an intention to create a future that was different from the past. With the memories of the war still lingering, West Germany was willing to pay a bit more than a narrow state-centric interest would have required. The resulting EU process has largely been a success. The EU today has, contrary to conventional wisdom in the United States, the world's largest economy, with a GDP of US\$17.6 billion in 2011 (followed by the United States at US\$15.1 billion and China at US\$7.3 billion) that has benefited most of the 500 million citizens in its 27 member states.

The success of the EU suggests that good economics and good poli-tics require defining one's self-interest broadly (eco-centrically), not narrowly (ego-centrically), so that it is aligned with the well-being of others and the whole. Sadly, the emerging failures of the EU prove the same point. Bad economics and bad politics result from defining one's self-interest too narrowly. In the euro crisis, we can see in a nut-shell how a narrowly defined self-interest translates into poor economic and political decision-making. In September 2008, after the collapse of Lehman Brothers, the German finance minister claimed in front of the parliament that this was an American problem, not a European or

German problem.[13] The second and bigger error of judgment happened on October 12, 2008, when the German chancellor and finance minister met with their EU colleagues in Paris at the first crisis summit and decided that each country would develop its own rescue mechanism rather than a joint European mechanism that could have taken care of all of them.[14]

What is missing from how this story unfolded is a moment of *reflective disruption* in which all players would have come together, looked in the mirror, and realized what they were doing to themselves. They could have thrown out their nation-centric ego-view and replaced it with a mindset that could deal with the complex global eco-system realities they're up against now. This second view is what we call eco-system awareness, because it values and accounts for the well-being of others and the well-being of the whole.

A Journey from Ego-System to Eco-System Awareness

The surface landscape of symptoms and the eight underlying structural disconnects arise from the same deep source: a framework of economic thought that is stuck in the past. The framework we use today may have been appropriate in earlier times, but it is no longer in touch with the complex challenges and demands of our time.

How did we get here? What does the evolution of economic thought over time look like? What are the different frameworks of economic thought that are available to us now, and what might be next?

Figure 2 shows four stages, logics, and paradigms of economic thought, each of which devises a different solution to the principal problem facing each modern economy: How do you coordinate collaboration processes that are characterized by a division of labor? They are as follows:

1.0: The state-centric model, characterized by coordination through hierarchy and control in a single-sector society.

2.0: The free-market model, characterized by the rise of a second (private) sector and coordinated through the mechanisms of market and competition.

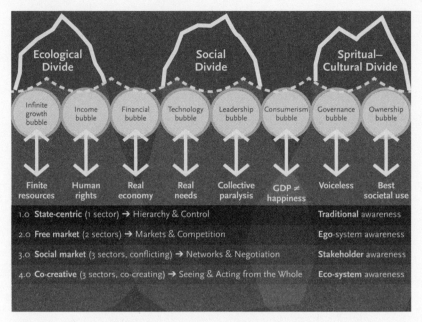

FIGURE 2. The iceberg model: symptoms, structures, thought, and sources.

3.0: The social-market model, characterized by the rise of a third
      (NGO) sector and by negotiated coordination among organized
      interest groups.

4.0: The co-creative eco-system model, characterized by the rise of a
      fourth sector that creates platforms and holds the space for cross-
      sector innovation that engages stakeholders from all sectors.

As in evolutionary stages, the earlier stages continue to exist at the later
stages: That is, all four coordination mechanisms are complementary;
they are not substitutes for one another.

Today, though, we are having the wrong conversation. Economic and
political discourse is often framed as a choice between more privatization, deregulation, and slashing of the welfare state and more regulation, government, and stimulus-based deficit spending. This debate
reflects the world of the twentieth century, not the world of the twenty-
first century.

To paraphrase the quote above attributed to Einstein, we cannot solve
the current 4.0 type of eco-system problems with the 2.0 and 3.0 ego-

system thinking that created them. What we need is to co-create a new economic framework that helps us to rethink and evolve all the core concepts of economics from an awareness-based view. We also need to link this framework to practical methods and tools for addressing challenges in our current reality.

Are you thinking now that this discussion of economic thought is getting a little boring? Well, it's exactly *that* pattern of thinking that keeps us from seeing past our blind spot. *The blind spot of our time is that we take mainstream economic thought for granted, as if it were a natural law.* But in reality, all so-called economic laws begin to melt and morph into something else the moment you begin to change the most important variable: the *quality of awareness* of the participants in a system. Who are these participants? They include leaders and change-makers in business, government, and civil society, as well as consumers, investors, and communities. They include you.

In chapter 3, we reconstruct the evolution of economic logic and thought as the deeper grammar that underlies the evolution of the economy. And we show that the essence of this developmental path can be traced as an evolution of human *consciousness*.

The frameworks of economic thought articulate four different economic logics or paradigms that give rise to four different operating systems. The 1.0 Economic Operating System is based on traditional awareness and hierarchical thinking. The 2.0 Economic Operating System is based on ego-system awareness and me-centric thinking (in neoclassical economics, this "me" is referred to as *homo oeconomicus,* an idea of a human being who acts only by maximizing self-interest). The 3.0 Economic Operating System is based on institutional stakeholder awareness and some negotiated coalitions that internalize concern for the well-being of key stakeholders. For example, corporations negotiate and partner with labor unions. The emerging 4.0 Economic Operating System (discussed in detail later) is based on eco-system awareness— that is, an awareness that values the well-being of all others and serves the well-being of the whole.

As the *laws* of economics morph along with the level of *awareness* that the agents in a system are operating from, we need to create a new economic science that accounts for the entire matrix (1.0 to 4.0) rather than limiting the inquiry to just one of its rows or paradigms (chapter 3 provides a detailed discussion). What we need today, to paraphrase the psychologist Eleanor Rosch, is an economic science that is performed with the mind of wisdom.[15] We need an economic science that describes and follows the journey from 1.0 to 4.0 on all levels, for individuals and teams as well as for institutions and systems.

Sources That Give Rise to Mental Models, Structures, and Symptoms

The journey from ego-system to eco-system awareness, or from "me" to "we," has three dimensions: (1) better relating to *others;* (2) better relating to the *whole* system; and (3) better relating to *oneself.* These three dimensions require participants to explore the edges of the system and the self.

Exploring the edges of the system means going to the place of most potential: for example, walking in the shoes of some of the most marginalized people, such as residents of remote villages in Africa or immigrants in a developed country (see chapter 7). It is our experience that the new in any system shows up first at the periphery. That's where you see the problems and the opportunities as if through a magnifying glass. Diverse stakeholder groups can use their shared experiences to become aware, to make sense of what is actually going on.

Exploring the edges of the self means shifting the inner place from which one operates. It means opening the mind, the heart, and the will. It means suspending old habits of judgment. It means empathizing. And it means letting go of what wants to die in oneself and letting come what is waiting to be born.

Over the past eighteen years, we have been working on creating environments for these types of outward and inward journeys across organizations, systems, sectors, and cultures. What is so surprising is how reliably this journey to the periphery of a system works. It's not easy. It's hard work. And you cannot engineer it in the old way, which is by controlling it. But you can create conditions that allow a deeper alchemy to work—that is, conditions that help leaders in a system to broaden and deepen their view of the system from ego to eco, from "me" to "we."

A new type of awareness-based collective action is emerging from this line of experimentation and work. It doesn't use the old collectivization model in which the common DNA is imposed from above, the old top-down pyramid that we all know only too well. In this more horizontal model, each individual node is mindful of the well-being of others. It is this shared awareness that allows for fast, flexible, and fluid coordination and decision-making that are far more adaptive and co-creative than any other organizational model currently being used in major societal institutions.

The Journey to U

We arrived in the United States in 1995 to work with the MIT Center for Organizational Learning, which had been founded by Peter Senge and his colleagues, together with a group of global companies, in the early 1990s. Upon arrival, we learned that Senge and his organization were part of the same MIT System Dynamics group that had produced the influential *Limits to Growth* study, which shaped our thinking earlier and helped to spark the worldwide environmental movement in the 1970s.[16]

In his work, Senge kept noticing how well developed the skills of the system dynamics PhD students were in analyzing the broken systems of our current society. But their practical impact on changing any of these systems was almost zero. Based on that puzzling observation, Senge became interested in the behavioral dimension of change.

Senge's book *The Fifth Discipline* is based on blending (1) system dynamics, (2) organizational change, and (3) the creative processes. This synthesis resulted in the concept for the MIT Center for Organizational Learning and in an initial set of methods and tools developed by this small group of action researchers at MIT.

After a few years, Senge and his colleagues noticed that the tools worked very well in the hands of some practitioners, but that in other cases the application of the same tools resulted in no significant change. Why are the same tools effective in the hands of some and ineffective in the hands of others? We have investigated this question in our research, which has included 150 interviews with leaders, entrepreneurs, and innovators (many of which were conducted by Otto and our colleague

Joseph Jaworski), as well as active participation in change processes in companies, governments, and communities.[17] The result of this eighteen years of work is a 2.0 framework for learning, leading, innovating, and profound systemic renewal. We call this framework Theory U for the shape of the drawing used to depict it. It has been fully described in Otto's book *Theory U* and in the book *Presence,* which Otto co-authored with Senge, Jaworski, and Betty Sue Flowers.[18]

The gist of this framework is simple: *The quality of results produced by any system depends on the quality of awareness from which people in the system operate.* The formula for a successful change process is not "form follows function," but "form follows consciousness." The structure of awareness and attention determines the pathway along which a situation unfolds.

Shifting the Inner Place from Which We Operate

We stumbled onto this deep territory of leadership research when we interviewed Bill O'Brien, the late CEO of Hanover Insurance. Summarizing his most important insights from leading transformational change in his own company, O'Brien said: "The success of an intervention depends on the *interior condition* of the intervener."[19] We might say it this way: The success of our actions as change-makers does not depend on *what* we do or *how* we do it, but on the *inner place* from which we operate (see figure 3).

When I (Otto) first heard O'Brien say that, I thought, "Boy, what do I really know about this inner place? I know nothing! Do we have *one* or *several* or an *infinite number* of these places?" I didn't know, because that place is in the blind spot of our everyday experience. We can observe *what* we do and *how* we do it. But the quality of the source (or inner place) from which we operate in "the Now" tends to be outside the range of our normal observation, attention, and awareness.

This puzzling insight into the deeper *source* level of social reality creation set us on an intriguing path of inquiring about and integrating recent findings in leadership, management, economics, neuroscience, contemplative practice, and complexity research. The essence of our

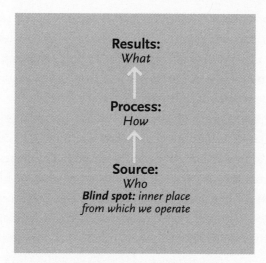

FIGURE 3. The blind spot of leadership.

view concerns the power of attention: We cannot transform the behavior of systems unless we transform the quality of attention that people apply to their actions within those systems, both individually and collectively.

Leading from the Emerging Future

In exploring this territory more deeply, we realized that most of the existing learning methodologies relied on learning from the past, while most of the real leadership challenges in organizations seemed to require something quite different: letting go of the past in order to connect with and learn from emerging future possibilities.

We realized that this second type of learning—learning from the emerging future—not only had no methodology, but also had no real name. And yet innovators, entrepreneurs, and highly creative people all express an intimate relationship with this deep source of knowing. Otto started referring to it as Theory U and presencing. *Presencing* is a blended word combining *sensing* (feeling the future possibility) and *presence* (the state of being in the present moment). It means sensing and actualizing one's highest future possibility—acting from the presence of what is wanting to emerge.

The proposition of Theory U, that the quality of the results in any kind of socioeconomic system is a function of the awareness that people in the system are operating from, leads to a differentiation among four levels of awareness. These four levels affect where actions originate relative to the boundaries of the system.

Consider the example of listening. We call the first level of listening *downloading.* It describes habitual behavior and thought and results in "same old, same old" behaviors and outcomes. This type of listening originates from the center of our habits, from what we already know from past experience. Here's an example: When President George W. Bush and Vice-President Dick Cheney received CIA briefings about an imminent attack on the United States prior to 9/11, they were so focused on getting the war against Saddam Hussein going that they were unable to hear and recognize the numerous strong warnings from the intelligence community. They were unable to hear anything that didn't agree with what they thought they already knew. That inability trapped the decision-makers inside the world of their preconceived notions and views.[20]

In contrast, level 4 listening, called *presencing,* represents a state of the social field in which the circle of attention widens and a new reality enters the horizon and comes into being. In this state, listening originates outside the world of our preconceived notions. We feel as if we are connected to and operating from a widening surrounding sphere. As the presence of this heightened state of attention deepens, time seems to slow down, space seems to open up, and the experience of the self morphs from a single point (ego) into a heightened presence and stronger connection to the surrounding sphere (eco). Examples of this shift are seen when a sports team raises its level of play to be *in the zone* or when a jazz ensemble *finds its groove.*

The two intervening levels are level 2 (factual listening) and 3 (empathic listening). We will discuss all four levels in more detail when we introduce the Matrix of Social Evolution in chapter 4.

What does it take for individuals, teams, institutions, and larger systems to shift their attentional logic and mode of operating from downloading to presencing?

Principles of Presencing

We will answer this question in much more detail throughout the book. But for now let us share a few key principles that reflect what we have learned over the past few years and which may resonate with some of your own experiences:

1. *Energy follows attention.* Wherever you place your attention, that is where the energy of the system will go. "Energy follows attention" means that we need to shift our attention from what we are trying to avoid to what we want to bring into reality.

2. *Follow the three movements of the U.* We refer to this as the U process because of the "shape" of the journey. In order to get to the deep point of transformation (at the bottom of the U), it is necessary first to go down the U (the left-hand side) by opening our minds, hearts, and wills, and then, after passing through the "eye of the needle" at the bottom, go up the U (the right-hand side) to bring the new into reality (see figure 4). In the words of our colleague, economist Brian Arthur, the three main movements of the U process are:

   a. Going down the U: *Observe, observe, observe.* Stop downloading and totally immerse yourself in the places of most potential, in the places that matter most to the situation you are dealing with.

   b. At the bottom of the U: *Retreat and reflect; allow the inner knowing to emerge.* Go to the places of stillness where knowing comes to the surface. Here you share and reflect on everything that you have learned from a deep place of listening, asking, "What wants to emerge here?," "How does that relate to the journey forward?," and "How can we become part of the story of the future rather than holding on to the story of the past?"

   c. Going up the U: *Act in an instant.* Explore the future by *doing.* Develop a prototype. A prototype explores the future by doing something small, speedy, and spontaneous; it quickly generates feedback from all the key stakeholders and allows you to evolve and iterate your idea.

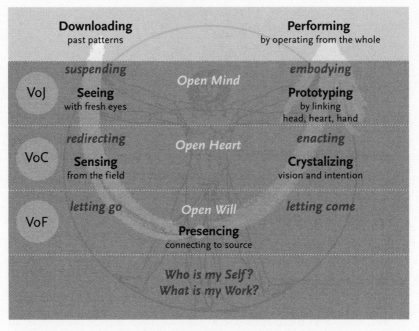

FIGURE 4. The U process of co-sensing and co-creating: presencing.

3. *Go to the edges of the self.* To apply this process in the context of institutions, we have to power it with a new leadership technology. The core of this technology focuses on tuning three instruments: the open mind, the open heart, and the open will. With an open mind, we can *suspend* old habits of thought. With an open heart, we can *empathize,* or see a situation through the eyes of someone else. With an open will, we can *let go* and *let the new come.*

4. *Pass through the eye of the needle.* At the deepest point of each U journey is a threshold. Crossing that threshold, passing through the eye of the needle, can feel like dying and being reborn. According to the Bible, "It is easier for a camel to go through the eye of a needle than for a rich man to enter the kingdom of God."[21] The phrase "eye of the needle" refers to a gate in ancient Jerusalem: For a man to fit his camel through Jerusalem's gate, he had to remove all the bags from the camel's back. Likewise, if we want to go through the eye of the needle at the bottom of the U, we have to let go of everything and offload all the baggage that isn't essential. Going through that gate

means encountering the two root questions of our journey: "Who is my Self?" and "What is my Work?" The capital-S *Self* is our highest future possibility. The capital-W *Work* is our sense of purpose or calling. It's what we are here on this earth to do.

5. *Transform the three enemies.* Why is the U journey the road less traveled? Why is it that a lot of people are aware of this deep process of knowing and yet it rarely happens in the context of our larger systems? Because the moment we commit ourselves to going on this journey, we start to encounter our three principal enemies: the *voice of doubt and judgment* (VoJ: shutting down the open mind), the *voice of cynicism* (VoC: shutting down the open heart), and the *voice of fear* (VoF: shutting down the open will).

6. *Always start by "attending to the crack."* Where do we meet the future first? "Seek it with your hands. Don't think about it, feel it" is the essential instruction that Bagger Vance gives to Junah in the Robert Redford movie *Bagger Vance*. The future shows up first in our feelings and through our hands, not in our abstract analysis. "Attending to the crack" means attending to the openings, the challenges, and the disruptions where we *feel* the past ending and the future wanting to begin.

7. *Hold the space for transforming the fields of conversation from debate to dialogue and collective creativity.* Each social field needs a container. Higher-level conversation like dialogue and collective creativity requires higher-quality containers and holding spaces. "Transforming the quality of conversation" in a system means transforming the quality of relationship and thought—that is, the quality of tomorrow's results.

8. *Strengthen the sources of presencing in order to avoid the destructive dynamics of absencing.* Modern society emerges from the interplay of two powerful social fields: presencing and absencing. The field of presencing works through the opening of the mind, the heart, and the will. We know that there are plenty of inspiring examples of this process across the planet. But everyone who works in institutions and systems also knows that there is another field out there. That field is characterized by getting stuck with the idea that there is only One

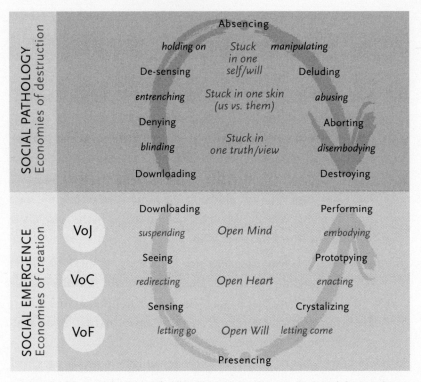

FIGURE 5. The social spaces of collective creation (presencing) and destruction (absencing).

Truth rather than operating with an open mind, by getting stuck in Us versus Them rather than operating with an open heart, and by being frozen inside one rigid identity rather than operating with an open will. What do we call social systems that have these three characteristics? Fundamentalist. Fundamentalism is the result of closing down and freezing our mind, heart, and will—as opposed to opening, warming, and illuminating them.

We live in the tension of these two fields. We are not one, but are often torn in two. Sometimes we operate from our highest future possibility (presencing). But every now and then we lose it and get stuck in old patterns of downloading (absencing). We experience this fragile nature of current reality not only in personal relationships, but also in the area of global development and change. We are torn between these two fields, and we need to learn how to strengthen our grounding in the field of presencing.

Social reality emerges continuously from the interplay of these two forces: the field of presencing that enables us to co-create from a deeper level of humanity and intention, and the field of absencing that, through our blind spot of not being aware, traps us in patterns of destruction and self-destruction (see figure 5).

The Journey of This Book

This book journeys through an emerging framework for transforming institutions, society, relationships, and self. The first four chapters invite you to travel down the left side of the U through four levels of the iceberg, from the visible top to the less visible underlying levels:

1. symptoms: disruption, death, and rebirth (chapter 1);
2. structure: systemic disconnects (chapter 2);
3. thinking: the Matrix of Economic Evolution (chapter 3); and
4. source: traveling through the eye of the needle (chapter 4).

The next four chapters take you up the right side of the U into envisioning, enacting, and embodying the new:

5. leading individual transformation (chapter 5);
6. leading relational transformation (chapter 6);
7. leading institutional transformation (chapter 7); and
8. leading from the emerging future (chapter 8).

Chapters 5 and 6 outline the personal and relational revolution that this book tries to illuminate. Chapter 7 focuses on what we call the Matrix of Institutional Transformation, a roadmap for the evolutionary path of key institutions and societal systems from 1.0 to 4.0. This map suggests that the transformational experiences necessary in education, health, finance, business, government, and civil society are not actually all that different. They all feature similar journeys of inverting and flipping pyramid-style systems to cultivate the soil of a co-creative field of shared intention, awareness, and action across institutional boundaries. Chapter 8 concludes with a specific view of what we, as the current generation of change-makers on this planet, are called to do over the next decade or two.

Each chapter ends with concluding remarks and practical questions for individual reflection and for group work. They are formulated to give you a practical tool to join the emerging global movement in seeing the ecological, social, and spiritual crises of our time as three aspects of a deeper issue that calls us to shift from egocentric to ecocentric as the gateway to transforming business, society, and self. The questions at the end of each chapter aid you in forming your own group. The website (www.presencing.com) and its global classroom sessions provide you ways to connect with others in order to co-sense and co-create our path forward.

1

On the Surface: Symptoms of Death and Rebirth

This chapter explores the symptoms at the tip of the iceberg of our current reality. We move from the toppling of tyrants to an exploration of the deeper fault lines that keep generating the disruptive changes of our time. We also look at these disruptive events from the viewpoint of change-makers: In the face of disruption, what determines whether we end up in moments of madness or mindfulness?

The Toppling of Tyrants

In the fall of 1989, two weeks before the Berlin Wall crumbled, we took an international student group to East Berlin, where we met with civil rights activists in the basement of a church. At one point, the professor who was with us, peace researcher Johan Galtung, put a prediction on the table: "The Berlin Wall will come down before the end of the year." Everybody doubted that, including the people who were organizing the resistance against the East German regime. And we were all wrong. The Wall came down and the Cold War came to an end just months after that meeting.

Nearly two decades later, in the fall of 2008, the bankruptcy of Lehman Brothers, a global financial services firm, sent shock waves around the globe and within hours brought the financial systems of the United States and Europe to the brink of collapse. Today the remaining Wall Street megabanks and their European counterparts have survived because of massive taxpayer-financed bailouts from their governments. On October 11 of that year, the head of the International Monetary Fund (IMF) warned that the world financial system was teetering on the "brink of systemic meltdown."[1]

In December 2010, Mohamed Bouazizi, a young fruit and vegetable seller in Tunisia, set himself on fire in protest of his treatment by police, who wanted to extract bribes from him and, when he refused, took away his merchandise and beat him. In January 2011, a twenty-six-year-old Egyptian activist, Asmaa Mahfouz, posted a video online urging people to protest the "corrupt government" of Egypt's president, Hosni Mubarak, by rallying in Cairo's Tahrir Square.[2] With that video she sparked and inspired an uprising among the Egyptian population. A week later, on January 25, thousands joined her in Tahrir Square. Within days, the movement counted millions. At first the Egyptian police responded with brutality. But less than four weeks after Mahfouz had posted her initial video, President Mubarak resigned.

A month later, a 9.0 earthquake struck off the coast of Japan, generating a massive tsunami that killed more than twenty thousand people. The Fukushima Daiichi nuclear power plant was protected by a seawall designed to withstand a tsunami of 19 feet (5.7 meters). Minutes after the earthquake struck, a tsunami of 46 feet (14 meters) arrived, easily crossing the seawall and knocking out the plant's emergency power generators. As a consequence, the radioactive fuel began overheating and put the plant on a path toward catastrophic meltdown.

As the year went on, the Arab Spring spread across the globe. Muammar Gaddafi was toppled in Libya. The Occupy Wall Street movement, which took inspiration in part from the Arab Spring, staged actions in more than a thousand cities across the globe.[3]

The collapse of the Berlin Wall, the demise of the Mubarak and Gaddafi regimes, the meltdown of the Fukushima Daiichi nuclear power plant, and the near-meltdown of the western financial system all share some features:

1. the end of an inflexible, centralized control structure, one that previously had been considered indestructible

2. the beginning of a spontaneous, decentralized grassroots movement of people letting go of their fear and waking up to another level of awareness and interconnectedness

3. the opening of some small cracks in the old system, followed by its crumbling and eventual collapse

4. the rebound of the old forces as soon as the memory of the collapse began to fade away; the old forces tried to obscure the actual root causes of the breakdown in order to extend their privileged access to power and influence (an example is Wall Street's financial oligarchy)

We believe that these kinds of events will keep coming our way. These disruptive changes mark the beginning of a new era that we have entered as a global community, an era of increasing disruption. Sometimes such movements will give rise to movements that bring about profound change, and sometimes they will falter and fail. In many cases, as we discuss later in the book, these disruptions are already on their way. It is too late to prevent all of them. So where is our point of control? It is in how we respond to the impact that these disruptions have on how we work and live.

A disruptive change affects not only our outer world, but also our inner self. Such moments bring our world to a sudden stop. They may be terrifying, but they also constitute a great blank space that can be filled in one of two ways: by *freezing* and reverting to the patterns of the past, or by opening us up to the *highest future possibilities*. The second response—leaning into, sensing, and actualizing one's emerging future—is what this book is about.

Presencing

At the moment when we reach the point of meltdown, we have a choice: We can freeze and revert to our deeply ingrained habits of the past, or we can stop and lean into the space of the unknown, lean into that which wants to emerge.

This second possibility—to lean into and connect to our highest future potential—we refer to as presencing. As noted in the introduction, the word *presencing* merges the terms *presence* and *sensing*. It means to sense and operate from the presence of an emerging future field. As we connect with this field of heightened awareness, our attention morphs from *slowing down, opening up, redirecting,* and *letting go* to *letting come, crystallizing,* and *embodying* the new. Figure 4 (see the introduction) summarizes this process.

The process of connecting to our Self, our highest future possibility, and moving toward action can be a sequence that we go through in an instant or over a period of many years. It is an archetype of the human journey. It is a process of opening up, of allowing something new to land, to emerge, and to come into reality through us.

A real-life example of this process was sparked by the video that Asmaa Mahfouz posted on January 18, 2011, which inspired people around the world. In it, she speaks from a place that transcends the three primary obstacles—doubt, cynicism, and fear—that prevent us from connecting to our source of deep presence and authenticity.

Instead of expressing doubt, which government propaganda tried to perpetuate, she speaks with great clarity. Instead of expressing cynicism, she speaks from a state of deep connection and empathy. And instead of expressing fear, which would isolate her, she speaks from a place of vulnerability, commitment, and courage:

> Four Egyptians have set themselves on fire to protest humiliation and hunger and poverty and degradation they had to live with for 30 years. Four Egyptians have set themselves on fire thinking maybe we can have a revolution like Tunisia; maybe we can have freedom, justice, honor, and human dignity. Today, one of these four has died, and I saw people commenting and saying, "May God forgive him. He committed a sin and killed himself for nothing."
>
> People, have some shame.
>
> I posted that I, a girl, am going down to Tahrir Square, and I will stand alone. And I'll hold up a banner. Perhaps people will show some honor. I even wrote my number so maybe people will come down with me. No one came except three guys—three guys and three armored cars of riot police. And tens of hired thugs and officers came to terrorize us. They shoved us roughly away from the people. But as soon as we were alone with them, they started to talk to us. They said, "Enough! These guys who burned themselves were psychopaths." Of course, on all national media, whoever dies in protest is a psychopath. If they were psychopaths, why did they burn themselves at the parliament building?
>
> I'm making this video to give you one simple message: We want to go down to Tahrir Square on January 25th. If we still have honor and want to live in dignity on this land, we have to go down on Janu-

ary 25th. We'll go down and demand our rights, our fundamental
human rights.[4]

The first time Mahfouz went to Tahrir Square, she was, as she says,
joined by three young men. The next time, a week after posting the
video blog, she was joined by over fifty thousand protesters, and a week
later, on February 1, over one million people protested peacefully. On
February 11, the supposedly "unsinkable" regime was finished and
Mubarak resigned.

This process of co-creating disruptive change is not a singular, isolated case. It is part of a much bigger picture that is starting to become
visible now. We have seen similar efforts in several other sectors, systems, and cultures. The change-makers embarking on these journeys
venture away from well-known paths and put themselves at the edges of
the unknown. They are connecting to deep sources of knowing, sensing
the future that wants to emerge. But more often than not, change leaders don't talk about this deep personal zone of change because there is
no widely understood or accepted language for doing so.

Mahfouz is a very visible figure at the tip of an iceberg that may represent, in the words of the author and activist Paul Hawken, "the largest
movement in all of social history."[5] It includes grassroots civil society
movements that have brought down the tyrant-led regimes in Egypt and
Tunisia, the Communist-led regimes in Eastern Europe, and the apartheid regime in South Africa. The movement also includes a new breed
of business entrepreneurs who create "hybrid" business enterprises that
aim for a triple bottom line, combining profitability with a social mission and environmental objectives.

This new global movement has no name, no leader, no ideology, no
single program, no single center. Instead people are sharing a new interior field, an emerging field of connection and consciousness, a collective
concern about the well-being of all living beings, including our planet.

Absencing

Of course, presencing doesn't happen if we are on autopilot. When confronting a moment of meltdown, instead of leaning into the future, we

can also choose to revert to habitual patterns of the past. Mubarak did that on February 10, 2011, when he initially refused to step down. Erich Honecker and the East German Politburo did it in the early fall of 1989, trying to hold on to their crumbling system. The Wall Street banks did it on the brink of collapse, when they still couldn't resist further expanding their power through, in the words of former IMF Chief Economist Simon Johnson, "a quiet coup."[6] The Catholic Church does it when, even in the face of the most heart-wrenching cases of child abuse, it holds on to its old institutional routines. But it's not just *them*. We all do this when we refuse to let go of what worked in the past but no longer does.

Whenever we respond to the inner space of emptiness by downloading the old rather than by leaning into the new, we are embarking on and co-enacting a journey of social pathology that looks roughly like this: downloading, denying, de-sensing, absencing, deluding, destroying, and (eventually) self-destroying.

As shown in figure 5 in the introduction, the absencing journey is the inversion of the presencing journey. Instead of opening the mind, heart, and will, the absencing cycle holds on tightly to the past. It does not dare to lean into the unknown, the emerging future. As a consequence, the space of absencing throws us into a trajectory of denial (not seeing what is going on), de-sensing (lacking empathy with the other), absencing (losing the connection to one's higher Self), delusion (being guided by illusions), and destruction (destroying others and ourselves).

A good illustration of absencing is what Hitler and the Nazis did to Central Europe and the rest of the world. Today, look at what we are doing collectively to our own planet. The fundamental pattern is the same.

Thus, being thrown into the space of absencing means getting stuck in the tyrannies of

1. One Truth (ideology)
2. One "Us" versus "Them" (rigid collectivism)
3. One Will (fanaticism)

The triple tyranny of "One Truth, One Us, One Will" is also referred to as fundamentalism. It's the structure that people rose up against in World War II. Whether we talk about the struggle for decolonization and independence in the global South, the struggles against the apartheid system in South Africa, or the struggle against tyrannical regimes in Eastern Europe, Latin America, and North Africa, the deeper struggle in all these places has always been the same: People keep rising and fighting against the same tyranny that emerges from the fundamentalism of One Truth (a closed mind), One Us (a closed heart), and One Will (a closed will). That rigid worldview has led to social structures defined by three key features:

1. unilateral, linear communication
2. low, exclusion-based transparency
3. an intention to serve the well-being of the few

The alternative is not well defined, but could be sketched as follows:

1. multilateral, cyclical communication
2. high, inclusion-based transparency
3. an intention to serve the well-being of all

How to achieve the second model is a central topic of this book. And what is striking today is that most people on the planet would probably reject the first model, which merely reproduces widespread structural and cultural violence.[7]

The battle over the fundamentalism we are referring to here will not be won by defeating Al Qaeda. It's a battle for the future of our planet. It will not be won by dropping bombs on other people. *The primary battlefield of this century is with our Selves.* It is a battle between the self and the Self: between our existing, habituated self and our emerging future Self, both individually and collectively. It is a battle between absencing and presencing that plays out across all sectors and systems of society today.

Moments of Madness and Mindfulness

What determines whether we as individuals, teams, institutions, and systems operate from the state of absencing or the state of presencing? What is the lever that allows us to shift from one state to the other? What can we do to move from madness to mindfulness?

Let us look at a concrete example. On April 26, 1986, an accident happened at reactor number four of the Chernobyl nuclear power plant in Ukraine. As the worst-case scenario started to unfold, the children and citizens of the city next door, Pripyat, received no warnings. Citizens of the region, Russian and European, were exposed to a cloud of nuclear radiation that first traveled north to Scandinavia and then covered almost all of Europe and its 500 million inhabitants.

Not only were Europe's citizens not warned about the potential threat, even the top Soviet leaders in the Kremlin were in the dark. Mikhail Gorbachev, who at the time was general secretary of the Communist Party, recounts: "I got a call around 5 A.M. I was told there was some accident at the Chernobyl nuclear plant. The first information consisted of 'accident' and 'fire.' The information report was that everything was sound including the reactor. . . . At first, I have been told there was no explosion. The consequences of this information were particularly dramatic. . . . What had happened? A nuclear explosion, a cloud, serious contamination? It was Sweden that alerted us!"[8]

Gorbachev was told that the accident posed no threat to the surrounding environment and was under control. No one, according to Gorbachev, told him in these early days that a series of explosions had occurred in the core of the reactor and had blown the twelve-thousand-ton cover of the reactor into the air, releasing a highly radioactive vapor into the environment. Later, high radiation levels set off alarms at the Forsmakr Nuclear Power Plant in Sweden, over a thousand kilometers away. The Swedish government alerted its population about radioactive dust.

Although radiation was still emanating unchecked from the Chernobyl plant, the evacuation of citizens living next to the plant did not begin until more than twenty-four hours after the accident. Only after Gorbachev formed a commission of nuclear experts and gave them access to unlimited resources, people, and technology did a full-blown crisis response begin.

At the same time that this crisis response was unfolding, many of the old patterns of downloading continued to play out—with disastrous consequences. The nuclear experts met in a hotel next to the damaged power plant in a city that had been fully evacuated, thereby exposing themselves to high levels of radiation that at least some of them must have been aware of. Even the traditional May First celebrations were held in Kiev, the capital of Ukraine, less than one hundred kilometers away from the disaster area. Local high officials attended.

In a later interview, Gorbachev reflected on the reaction of the nuclear experts: "These were outstanding people, specialists. I could not believe they would do something [so] irresponsible, suicidal. The experts underestimated the situation. The old criteria weren't any good anymore. There had been nuclear accidents before . . . [but] there had never been an accident of this scope. They [the nuclear experts] even thought the power plant would be back in service—by May or June."[9]

Then, finally, when the full gravity of the nuclear catastrophe had sunk in, the Soviet Union mobilized five hundred thousand people in the battle to prevent an even bigger catastrophe. The decontamination and cleanup efforts continue today, consuming 5 to 7 percent of annual government spending in Ukraine (2003–05 figures).[10]

Another example of responding to a challenge by downloading old patterns of behavior was provided by the French Minister for Public Health and Social Security, Pierre Pellerin, who claimed that the cloud of nuclear fallout, which had reached all of Northern, Central, and Western Europe, had never crossed the borders into France. (France still derives over 75 percent of its electricity from nuclear energy, the highest percentage in the world.)

The Chernobyl catastrophe is a stark example of how downloading old behavior in a context in which it no longer fits results in patterns of denial, data distortion, delusion, destruction, and self-destruction. But the story does not end here. Gorbachev realized that if the melted nuclear core had reached the groundwater beneath the reactor, Europe might have become an uninhabitable wasteland. He says, "Chernobyl showed us the true nature of nuclear energy in human hands. We calculated that our most powerful missiles, the SS-18s, were as powerful as 100 Chernobyls. . . . And we had 2,700 of them, and they were intended for the Americans. Imagine the destruction. . . . Chernobyl convinced everyone, Soviets and Americans alike, . . . [of] the magnitude of the nuclear volcano our countries are sitting on. Not just our two countries, but the entire world!"[11] A year and a half after Chernobyl, Gorbachev retired all of the Soviet Union's nuclear warheads with a range of five hundred to five thousand kilometers.

Watching the catastrophic events of Chernobyl unfold, Gorbachev allowed his thoughts to slow down and his mind to become aware, to let go of the old military logic of MAD—mutually assured destruction—and to let the seeds of disarmament germinate and grow. These seeds ended up changing the course of world history for the better.[12]

This story raises an obvious question: How should the course of disruptive events, those beginning to shake up our planet as we speak, affect *our* thoughts and awareness as a global community today? What is it that *we* need to let go of? And what seeds of the future do we need to let germinate and grow?

Fault Lines

Natural catastrophes like volcanic eruptions, earthquakes, and tsunamis tend to happen along the fault lines of tectonic plates—that is, in regions where the earth's tectonic plates meet and exert their massive force against each other. We can't fully predict where or when major ruptures and eruptions will happen. But knowing the geography of the fault lines means knowing the zones of potential impact.

Social and economic breakdowns and eruptions are very similar in this regard. They tend to show up along the fault lines that divide the collective social body of our communities and societies. Again, we cannot fully predict when or where a disaster will occur, but understanding the space of possibility allows us to be much more attentive to subtle signals that foreshadow bigger events like the collapse of the Berlin Wall, the meltdown of the financial system, and the toppling of authoritarian regimes.

What is the geography of the major fault lines that divide the collective socioeconomic body—the sum total of human relationships—today? We believe that there are three major fault lines, concerning three principal relationships that we engage in as human beings: (1) our relationship with nature and our planet; (2) our relationships with one another; and (3) our relationship with ourselves. When these relationships rupture, they create three divides: ecological, social, and spiritual-cultural.

THE ECOLOGICAL DIVIDE

The ecological divide is the fault line in the relationship between humans and nature. In spite of significant improvements in eco-efficient production methods, all advances in increased resource efficiency have been overshadowed by the so-called *rebound effect:* that is, by higher levels of total output (GDP) that lead to higher absolute numbers of resource use. Today we overuse the regeneration capacity of our planet by 50 percent. If current trends continue, our overuse will grow to an unimaginable three planets by 2050.[13] Of course, this is never going to happen, as severe ecological disruptions will set us on a different path. Nevertheless, it shows how irresponsible our current developmental path truly is. Here are some of the current and short-term symptoms:

Water. During the twentieth century, the global demand for fresh water increased sixfold, according to the United Nations Environment Programme (UNEP). This was accompanied by a reduced supply of fresh water. As a result, water is in short supply in countries where one-third of the world's population lives. Moreover, about one in every five people on earth lacks access to safe drinking water.[14]

Soil. The loss of topsoil is largely irreversible during the course of a human lifetime. Soil forms at a rate of approximately one centimeter every one hundred to four hundred years.[15] Yet, over the past forty years, soil erosion has caused nearly a third of the world's arable land to become unproductive.[16] This translates into two billion hectares of arable and grazing land worldwide, an area larger than the United States and Mexico combined.[17]

Climate. From 1995 to 2006, every year except one ranks among the twelve warmest years ever recorded.[18] Carbon dioxide is at record levels in the atmosphere. In November 2012, the World Bank released a report warning that the world is "barreling down a path to heat up by four degrees [Celsius] at the end of the century." The result would mean extreme heat waves, a likely sea level rise of 0.5 to 1 meter by the year 2100, with higher levels possible, and smaller island nations becoming unable to sustain their populations.[19]

Eco-systems. The Millennium Eco-System Assessment concludes that "over the past 50 years, humans have changed eco-systems more rapidly and extensively than in any comparable period of time in human history, largely to meet rapidly growing demands for food, fresh water, timber, fiber, and fuel. This has resulted in a substantial and largely irreversible loss in the diversity of life on earth."[20] About 60 percent of the eco-systems examined during this comprehensive four-year study were found to be degraded or were being used unsustainably.

According to the UNEP, which has made extensive efforts to put a price on the "services" humans derive from natural eco-systems, the ecological infrastructure of the planet is generating services to humanity worth over US$70 trillion a year, perhaps substantially more. "Mismanagement of natural and nature-based assets," says UNEP Executive Director Achim Steiner, "is undercutting development on a scale that dwarfs the recent economic crisis."[21]

THE SOCIOECONOMIC DIVIDE

With the financial crisis of the early twenty-first century, awareness of the socioeconomic divide within societies around the world has grown. The fault lines are increasingly visible. Globally, the richest 1 percent own 40 percent of the world's wealth, while half of the world's population own just 1 percent.[22] This disparity is one of many that reveal the rapidly deepening socioeconomic divide. On the income side, the numbers are similar: The top 10 percent receive one-half of the world's income.[23]

Although enormous progress has been made in lifting hundreds of millions of people out of poverty—particularly in Asia—the social divide has in fact deepened over the past thirty years, as evidenced by the following observations:

Hunger. One in eight people around the world go to bed hungry at night. Of those experiencing hunger, 98 percent live in developing countries.[24]

Poverty. Over 2.47 billion people live on less than US$2.50 a day; 1.3 billion people live in extreme poverty, meaning that they live on less than US$1.25 a day (in 2008 dollars).[25] Their most basic needs go unmet.

Inequality. Recent research points to issues related to income inequality, including civil unrest, immigration and refugee crises, recession, and slow economic growth.[26] In 2008, the International Labour Organization (ILO) conducted a global study of income inequality in more than seventy developed and developing countries.[27] Key findings include that, in 70 percent of countries surveyed, the income gap between the top and bottom 10 percent of the population increased over the preceding twenty years.[28]

THE SPIRITUAL-CULTURAL DIVIDE

While ecological and social divides concern the split between self and nature and between self and other, the spiritual-cultural divide concerns the split between self and Self. One symptom of this split is our level of happiness and well-being, and related issues of burnout, depression, and suicide. Burnout and depression have increased over the past fifty years, even in countries where material standards of living have been rising rapidly.[29]

In the past forty-five years, suicide rates have increased by 60 percent worldwide.[30] Suicide is the second leading cause of death (after accidents) among American high school and college students.[31] On a global scale, suicide is among the three leading causes of death in the fifteen to forty-four age group.[32] This shocking number is the tip of the iceberg of humans' violence against themselves.

In a 2011 lecture in Vienna, I (Otto) asked the audience members to turn to their neighbors and talk about where in their life and work they were experiencing something that was dying and where they saw something beginning or wanting to be born. One executive of a large international company put his experience like this: "I notice an incipient gap between what my organization makes me do, such as running cost-cutting and downsizing programs, and what I *really* want to do with my work and life going forward." He described his situation, saying that his organization required him to do things even when his personal feelings and thoughts would point in an opposite direction. But because those feelings and thoughts were not strong enough to convince him to change course, he kept going.

That incipient crack or gap is an important symptom of our current collective situation. Is this executive from Vienna a single case, or does he represent a much larger group? From our experience, we think it is the latter. For example, when I teach my class at MIT, roughly half the room is filled with midcareer executives from around the world. Early on in the class, I ask each participant to say what has brought him or her there. The comment I hear most often is something like this: "I am so *underinspired* by what my company asks me to do. The higher I climb on the corporate career ladder, the less inspired I get. I am here to learn how to reconnect with the sources of my energy and best work."

These cracks between exterior demands and interior aspirations and needs matter because, if not attended to, they can quickly morph into something larger, including burnout, depression, or worse. Think about the functional elites of the socialist regimes in Eastern Europe during the early 1980s. They knew that there was something deeply broken in the system. And yet almost no one dared to look carefully at the cracks on the surface and investigate their deeper systemic causes. What the business executives in Vienna and at MIT described is a subtle, early-stage crack that, if ignored, will only grow over time. It is no less serious than the cracks in the broken socialist regimes before their collapse. If you start paying attention to these initial cracks—the fault lines—you will begin to recognize them as voices telling you that *you need to change your life;* and, yes, that *all of us* need to change *our* lives!

Three Divides, One Stream

The three divides that compose the surface of symptoms are highly intertwined. For example, the loss of meaning in life and work (the inner void) is often filled with additional material consumption (consumerism), which deepens the ecological divide by further depleting resources. The intensification of the natural resource stream flowing from the developing to the developed countries, and the waste streams flowing the opposite way, leads in turn to a deepening of the social divide.[33] In short: inner void → consumerism → ecological divide → social divide.

While we spent most of the twentieth century addressing these problems one issue at a time, today we see that people are moving away from this approach. In particular, young people consider it common sense that these problems are not separate; they are three different aspects of one deeper issue. And they recognize that addressing the underlying issue will take a profound systems shift.

The process of becoming aware of this necessary system shift began in the last third of the twentieth century. During the late 1960s, '70s, and '80s, a new breed of civil society movements began to rise up. Vietnam War protests. Civil rights. Women's rights. Social justice. Fair trade. Environmental action. Antinuke. Antiwar. Antiapartheid. Anti–authoritarian regimes. These were followed by more recent movements: climate action. Arab Spring. Occupy. Local living economies. Slow food. Slow money. All these movements were harbingers and catalysts of a broadening and deepening of global awareness.

But the problem with the *first wave* of civil society movements was that they tended to focus on only one or two of the three divides. Environmental activists largely ignored the social and consciousness dimensions of change. The social justice movement paid little attention to the environment or to consciousness. And New Age consciousness movements got lost in personal liberation instead of using awareness as a gateway to social transformation.

Our colleague at MIT, Professor Phil Thompson, provides a vivid example of this from his experience as deputy general manager at the New York City Housing Authority (NYCHA) in the early 1990s. Years before he began working at NYCHA, the housing authority had been required by the federal Clean Air Act to stop incinerating garbage and to bag garbage in low-income housing projects for weekly pickup. This move was celebrated by many in the environmental movement. But in order to free up the resources necessary to bag garbage for more than five hundred thousand people, NYCHA had to cut a host of programs, including youth programs, maintenance, and other needed services. At the same time, NYCHA staff received little support from environmentalists to address the problems facing residents of public housing and therefore did little to promote recycling or other environmental initiatives there. The unintended result was a host of angry and disenfranchised citizens with no motivation to participate in the environmental program.

We will not see any significant progress unless *all three* of the deep divides are approached in an integrated way. This combined approach is what we believe we see in the currently emerging *second wave* of civic and social-entrepreneurial initiatives all over the world. The rise of this movement, in which people spontaneously act from an awareness of contributing to the well-being of the whole, is an enormous source of hope for the future of this planet.

Conclusion and Practices

This chapter described the symptoms of our current landscape. We believe that we have entered an age of disruption in which individuals, institutions, and societies face new types of challenges that require them to let go of habitual ways of responding. These moments of opportunity invite us to sense and actualize emerging future possibilities. But if we fail to lean into this deeper process of presencing, we will become stuck in the patterns of the past, frozen in a reaction that throws us into the cycle of absencing (denying, de-sensing, deluding, and destroying).

JOURNALING QUESTIONS

Take a journal (or blank piece of paper) and write your responses to the questions below. Spend no more than one to two minutes answering each question. Number your responses.

1. Where do you experience a world that is dying (in society, in your organization, in yourself)?
2. Where do you experience a world that is waiting to be born (in society, in your organization, in yourself)?
3. Where have you experienced moments of disruption? And what did you notice about your own process of presencing or absencing?
4. How do the ecological, socioeconomic, and spiritual-cultural divides show up in your personal experience of work and life?

CIRCLE CONVERSATION

Assemble a circle of five to seven individuals and hold a first meeting to share the context that each person brings to the circle. Respond to the following:

1. Introduce your personal story with one or two formative experiences that shaped the person you are.

2. Where do you experience a world that is ending/dying, and where do you experience a world that is beginning/wanting to be born?

3. What do you consider to be the root causes and issues of our current crisis and the three divides?

4. What do you personally feel is going to happen over the next ten to twenty years?

5. What would you like to do right now in order to make a difference going forward?

Structure: Systemic Disconnects

This chapter investigates the first level below the waterline of the "current reality iceberg." What are the structural issues that lead us to reenact patterns of the past and not connect to what is emerging? What is the underlying blind spot that, if illuminated, could help us to see the hidden structures below the waterline?

The Blind Spot I

The current system produces results that nobody wants. Below the surface of what we call the landscape of social pathology lies a structure that supports existing patterns. For example, in an organization, a departmental structure defines the division of labor and people's professional identities. In a modern society, the governmental, business, and nongovernmental sectors all develop their own ways of coordinating and self-organizing in a rapidly changing and highly intertwined world. A structure is a pattern of relationships. If we want to transform how our society responds to challenges, we need to understand the deeper structures that we continue to collectively reenact.

Eight Structural Disconnects

Here we lay out eight issue areas or visible symptoms of problems in the underlying structure. Table 1 lists each issue as follows. Column 1 describes the symptom broadly; column 2 explains the structural disconnect that gives rise to the issue in row 1; and column 3 spells out the limits that the whole system is hitting.

Addressing the root causes of these structural disconnects is like

TABLE 1 Structural Disconnects and System Limits

	Ecological issue	Income issue	Financial issue	Technology issue	Leadership issue	Consumerism issue	Governance issue	Ownership issue
Surface Symptom	1.5 planet footprint	Top 1 percent own more than bottom 90 percent	US$1.5 quadrillion speculation bubble	Quick technological fix syndrome	Collectively creating results that nobody wants	Burnout, depression, consumerism without well-being	Inability to face challenges at scale of whole system	Overuse of scarce resources; tragedy of the commons
Structural Disconnect	Decoupling of unlimited growth and finite resources	Decoupling of Haves and Have Nots, of wealth and basic need	Decoupling of financial economy and real economy	Decoupling of technological solutions and societal needs	Decoupling of old leadership tools and new challenges	Decoupling of GDP and well-being	Decoupling of parts and whole	Decoupling of current ownership forms and best societal use
Systemic Limit	Limits to growth → cultivating finite resources	Limits to inequality → embodying human rights	Limits to speculation → organizing around the real economy	Limits to symptom fixes → focusing on sustainable solutions	Limits to leadership → direct, distributed, dialogic self-governance	Limits to consumerism → attending to inner and relational sources of happiness and well-being	Limits to competition → redrawing boundaries of competition and cooperation	Limits to state and private property → property rights for the commons

touching eight acupuncture points of economic and social transformation. If addressed as a set, these acupuncture points hold the possibility for evolving our institutions in ways that bridge the three divides. Let's take a closer look at each one.

1. *The ecological disconnect.* We consume resources at 1.5 times the regeneration capacity of Planet Earth because of a mismatch between the unlimited growth imperative and the finite resources of the planet. As a consequence, we are hitting the limits to growth, as the title of the Club of Rome study famously put the matter, which calls for a better way to preserve increasingly scarce resources.

2. *The income and wealth disconnect.* The top 1 percent of the world's population own more than the bottom 90 percent, resulting in wealth concentration in one part of society and unmet basic needs in another. As a consequence, we are reaching dangerous levels of inequality, as we discuss in more detail below. This calls for a better realization of basic human rights through a rebalancing of the economic playing field.

3. *The financial disconnect.* Foreign exchange transactions of US$1.5 quadrillion (US$1,500 trillion) dwarf international trade of US$20 trillion (less than 1.4 percent of all foreign exchange transactions).[1] This disconnect is manifest in the decoupling of the financial economy from the real economy. As a consequence, we are increasingly hitting the limits to speculation.

4. *The technology disconnect.* We respond to societal issues with quick technical fixes that address symptoms rather than with systemic solutions. As a consequence, we are hitting the limits to symptom-focused fixes—that is, limits to solutions that respond to problems with more technological gadgets rather than by addressing the problems' root causes.[2]

5. *The leadership disconnect.* We collectively create results that nobody wants because decision-makers are increasingly disconnected from the people affected by their decisions. As a consequence, we are hitting the limits to leadership—that is, the limits to traditional top-down leadership that works through the mechanisms of institutional silos.

6. *The consumerism disconnect.* Greater material consumption does not lead to increased health and well-being. As a consequence, we are increasingly hitting the limits to consumerism, a problem that calls for reconnecting the economic process with the deep sources of happiness and well-being.

7. *The governance disconnect.* As a global community, we are unable to address the most pressing problems of our time because our coordination mechanisms are decoupled from the crisis of common goods. Markets are good for private goods, but are unable to fix the current tragedy of the commons. As a consequence, we are increasingly hitting the limits to competition. We need to redraw the boundary between cooperation and competition by introducing, for example, premarket areas of collaboration that enable innovation at the scale of the whole system.

8. *The ownership disconnect.* We face massive overuse of scarce resources, manifested in the decoupling of current ownership forms from the best societal use of scarce assets, such as our ecological commons. As a consequence, we are increasingly hitting the limits to traditional property rights. This calls for a possible third category of commons-based property rights that would better protect the interest of future generations and the planet.

As discussed in the introduction, these issue areas share common characteristics. Among them are that they (1) embody systemic structures that are designed *not* to learn; (2) are unaware of externalities; (3) facilitate money flowing the wrong way; and (4) allow special-interest groups to rig the system to the disadvantage of the whole.

These eight issues are symptoms of a disease that afflicts the collective social body. But what drives this pattern of organized irresponsibility? These symptoms are driven by structural disconnects that cause the system to hit a set of real-world limits. Each disconnect could be the topic of a book on its own—and in fact many books have been written about each one, such as *Limits to Growth,* which sparked a wave of global awareness in the 1970s. But that book, despite its significant impact, did not address other dimensions, such as financial bubbles, which are one of the key drivers of the unlimited growth imperative.

This book is an invitation to look at the entire set of disconnects as a *whole system*. What do we see when we contemplate them as a system? We see ourselves. The problem is *us*. It is we who burn resources beyond the capacity of our planet to regenerate them. It is we who participate in economic arrangements that replicate the income divide and the consumerism and burnout bubble that come with it. And it is we who use mostly traditional banks for our financial transactions in spite of our knowledge that these banks are a big part of the problem.

Each area is a part of the system that has lost its connection to the whole. Before we continue with our journey below the tip of the iceberg, let's take a moment to look at three interesting data points that tell us something about the current health of our society.

The Economic Condition of Society Today

Let us first consider the link between GDP and health or well-being. The relationship between GDP and average life expectancy is often used as an indicator of the quality of health in a country. There is in fact a close link between GDP and health up to a level of US$5,000 to US$8,000 annual income per capita (see figure 6). This link weakens significantly as GDP rises above that level. In other words, an increase in material output as measured by GDP in developed countries does *not* translate into better health or increased life expectancy.

If a GDP increase in developed countries does little to increase the well-being of its citizens, what does improve their welfare? Surprisingly, the leverage to increase well-being seems to be connected to reducing the size of one of the above-mentioned issue bubbles: *inequality.*[3]

Figure 7 shows that health and social problems are more common in countries with wider income inequalities, such as the United States. On the other end of the spectrum are countries with fewer health and social problems, such as Japan, Sweden, and Norway. These countries have the lowest income inequalities among the developed countries.

These two data points raise a question: To increase the health of citizens in developed countries, would we be better off focusing on reducing the income and inequality bubble instead of focusing on improving health-care delivery?

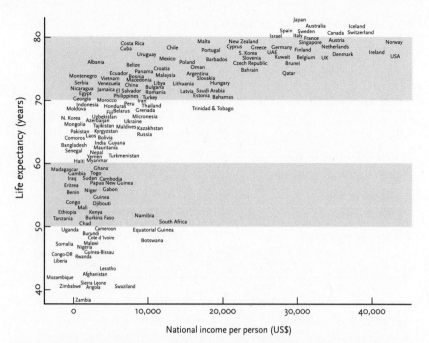

FIGURE 6. Only in its early stages does economic growth boost life expectancy. Source: United Nations Development Program, *Human Development Report* (New York: Oxford University Press, 2006).

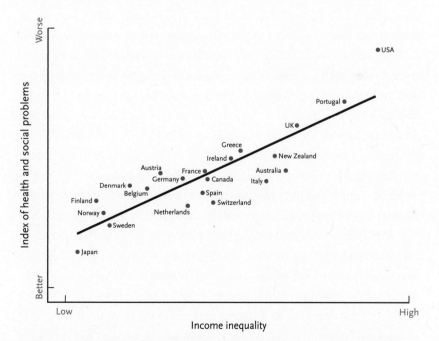

FIGURE 7. Health and social problems are closely related to inequality among rich countries. Source: Richard Wilkinson and Kate Pickett, *The Spirit Level: Why Equality Is Better for Everyone* (New York: Penguin, 2009), 20.

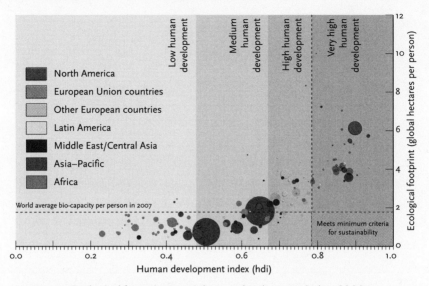

FIGURE 8. Ecological footprint versus human development index, 2008.
Source: Global Footprint Network and WWF, *Living Planet Report 2012* (Gland, Switzerland: WWF, 2012), 60.

Nobel Laureate Joseph Stiglitz argues in *The Price of Inequality* that even after the 2007–08 financial crisis, "the wealthiest 1 percent of households had 220 times the wealth of the typical American, almost double the ratio in 1962 or 1983."[4] Stiglitz emphasizes that inequality results from political failure and argues that inequality contributes not only to the social pathologies pointed out above, but also to economic instability in the form of a "vicious downward spiral." The results are daunting: almost a quarter of all children in the United States live in poverty.[5]

The third data point connects this conversation to the ecological disconnect. Figure 8 depicts the sustainable development challenge to our current economy. This challenge is visualized through two thresholds. The first is the average available biocapacity per person. The second is the threshold of high human development. What would sustainable development look like? All countries would need to be in the sustainable development quadrant at the bottom right of the figure. The distance between most countries and that quadrant shows the magnitude of our challenge.

The Evolution of Capitalism as an Evolution of Consciousness

The disconnects discussed above, and the distance of most countries from the sustainable development quadrant in figure 8, are not the only daunting challenges that our societies face. According to the British historian Arnold Toynbee, societal progress happens as an interplay of challenge and response: Structural change happens when a society's elite can no longer respond creatively to major social challenges, and old social formations are therefore replaced by new ones. Applying Toynbee's framework of challenge and response to the socioeconomic development of our societal structures today, we briefly review capitalism's evolution (see also table 2).[6]

SOCIETY 1.0: ORGANIZING AROUND HIERARCHY

Think of Europe at the end of the Thirty Years' War in 1648, of Russia after the October Revolution in 1918, of China after the Chinese Civil War in 1949, or of Indonesia at about the time when Sukarno became its first president. Recent turmoil had created the felt need for stability—that is, for a strong visible hand, sometimes in the form of an iron fist—to provide security along with the vital allocation of scarce resources in line with much-needed public infrastructure investment. In that regard, we can view twentieth-century socialism in the Soviet Union not as (according to Marxist theory) a postcapitalist stage of economic development, but as a precapitalist (quasi-mercantilist) stage.[7] The core characteristic of this stage of societal development is a strong central actor that holds the decision-making power of the whole. This could be an emperor, a czar, a dictator, or a party. Examples are manifold and include eighteenth-century European monarchs, as well as Stalin, Mao, Mubarak, and Sukarno, all of whom led coercive states whose appetite for lengthy democratic processes and discussions was, shall we say, limited. In a recent visit to the *favelas* of São Paulo, I (Otto) learned about the "pacification" strategy of the Brazilian police, who went into the *favelas* and drove out the drug lords. The young people in the *favelas* argued that the police presence was a good thing for two reasons. It reduced

TABLE 2 The Challenge-Response Model of Economic Evolution

	Primary societal challenge	Response: coordination mechanism	Primary sector/ players	Primary source of power	Dominant ideology	Primary state of consciousness
Society 1.0: *State*-Driven, Mercantilism, Socialism	Stability	Commanding: hierarchy	State/ government	Coercive (sticks)	Mercantilism; socialism (state-centric thought)	Traditional awareness
Society 2.0: *Free-Market*-Driven, Laissez-Faire	Growth	Competing: markets	Capital/business; state/government	Remunerative (carrots)	Neoliberal and neoclassic (market-centric) thought	Ego-system awareness
Society 3.0: *Stakeholder*-Driven, Social-Market Economy	Negative domestic externalities	Negotiating: stakeholder dialogue	Civil society/ NGOs; capital/ business; state/ government	Normative (values)	Social democratic or progressive thought	Stakeholder awareness
Society 4.0: *Eco-System* Driven, Co-Creative Economy	Global disruptive externalities, resilience	Presencing: awareness-based collective action (ABC)	Cross-sector co-creation: civil society/NGOs; capital/business; state/government	Awareness: actions that arise from seeing the emerging whole	Eco-system-centric thought	Eco-system awareness

the level of random violence and allowed the community to get access to vital social services. So, in their eyes, the so-called 1.0 police structure was actually a step in the right direction.

The positive accomplishment of a state-driven society, which we call Society 1.0, is its stability. The central power creates structure and order and calms the random violence that preceded it. The downsides of Society 1.0 are its lack of dynamism and, in most cases, its lack of nurturing individual initiative and freedom.

SOCIETY 2.0: ORGANIZING AROUND COMPETITION

Historically, the more successfully a society meets the stability challenge, the more likely it is that this stage will be followed by a shift of focus from stability to growth and greater individual initiative and freedom. This shift gives rise to markets and a dynamic entrepreneurial sector that fuels economic growth.

At this juncture, we see a whole set of institutional innovations, including the introduction of markets, property rights, and a banking system that provides access to capital. These changes facilitated the unprecedented explosion of economic growth and massive industrialization that we saw in Europe in the nineteenth century, and that we are seeing in China, India, and other emerging economies today. *New York Times* journalist and bestselling author Thomas Friedman links the rise of the emerging economies with the rise of a global virtual middle class that includes not only today's actual middle class, but also the global community of Web and cellphone users who physically still live in poverty but who mentally already share an aspirational space with the current global middle class. Says Khalid Malik, the director of the UN's Human Development Report Office: "This is a tectonic shift. The Industrial Revolution was a 10-million-person story. This is a couple-of-billion-person story."[8]

Awareness during this stage of development—Society 2.0—can be described as an awakening ego-system awareness in which the self-interest of economic players acts as the animating or driving force. The bright side of this stage is the burst in entrepreneurial initiative. The dark side of this stage includes negative externalities such as unbounded commodification and its unintended side effects, including child labor, human trafficking, environmental destruction, and increased socioeconomic inequality.

The two main sources of power at this stage are state-based coercive legal and military power (sticks) and market-based remunerative power (carrots). The great positive accomplishments of the laissez-faire free-market 2.0 economy and society are rapid growth and dynamism; the downside is that it has no means of dealing with the negative externalities that it produces. Examples include poor working conditions, prices of farm products that fall below the threshold of sustainability, and highly volatile currency exchange rates and stock market bubbles that destroy precious production capital.[9]

SOCIETY 3.0: ORGANIZING AROUND INTEREST GROUPS

Measures to correct the problems of Society 2.0 include the introduction of labor rights, social security legislation, environmental protection, protectionist measures for farmers, and federal reserve banks that protect the national currency, all of which are designed to do the same thing: limit the unfettered market mechanism in areas where the negative externalities are dysfunctional and unacceptable. The resulting regulations, products of negotiated agreements among organized interest groups, serve to complement the existing market mechanism.

As society evolves, sectors become differentiated: first the public or governmental sector, then the private or entrepreneurial sector, and finally the civic or NGO sector. Each sector is differentiated by its own set of enabling institutions. Each sector also evolves its own forms of power (sticks, carrots, and norms) and expresses a different stage in the evolution of human consciousness, from traditional (1.0) and ego-system awareness (2.0) to an extended stakeholder awareness that facilitates partnerships with other key stakeholders (3.0). (See table 2.)

Stakeholder capitalism, or Society 3.0, as practiced in many countries, deals relatively well with the classical externalities through wealth redistribution, social security, environmental regulation, farm subsidies, and development aid. However, it fails to react in a timely manner to global challenges such as peak oil, climate change, resource scarcity, and changing demographics. Over time, response mechanisms such as farm subsidies or subsidies for ethanol-based biofuel become part of the problem rather than the solution.[10] There are three essential limitations of Society 3.0: It is biased in favor of special-interest groups, it reacts mostly to negative externalities, and it has only a limited capacity for intentionally creating positive externalities. Table 2 summarizes these stages of societal evolution.

Moreover, global externalities such as climate change, environmental destruction, and extreme poverty are not being addressed effectively by domestic mechanisms, as the breakdown of international climate talks has put on display. Since the governance mechanisms of a 3.0 society give power to organized interest groups, they systematically disadvantage all groups that cannot organize as easily because they are too large (e.g., consumers, taxpayers, citizens) or because they do not yet have a voice (future generations).

Summing up, twenty-first-century problems cannot be addressed with the twentieth-century vocabulary of welfare-state problem solving. The challenge that most societies face is how to respond to externalities in a way that strengthens individual and communal entrepreneurship, self-reliance, and cross-sector creativity rather than subsidizing their absence.

SOCIETY 4.0: ORGANIZING AROUND THE EMERGING WHOLE

As we move to deal with the complexity of the twenty-first century's landscape of challenges, we face some contradictory trends: (1) a further differentiation of societal subsystems that have their own ways of self-organizing; (2) a business subsystem that in many countries dominates and interferes with other sectors (government, civil society, media); and (3) a lack of effective platforms that engage all stakeholders in a focused effort to innovate at the scale of the whole system.

The most significant change at the beginning of this century has been the creation of platforms for *cross-sector cooperation* that enable change-makers to gather, become aware of, and understand the evolution of the whole system, and consequently to act from impulses that originate from that shared awareness.

Each stage discussed above is defined by a primary *challenge*. Society 1.0 deals with the challenge of stability. The next challenge is growth

(2.0), followed by externalities (3.0). Each challenge requires society to respond by creating a new *coordination mechanism.* The response to the lack of stability was the creation of a centralized set of institutions around state power. Markets were the response to the growth challenge, and NGO-led stakeholder negotiations attempted to address negative externalities. Each phase led to the rise of a new societal *sector:* The stability challenge created a central power or government; the growth challenge created the rise of businesses; and the attempt to address the negative externalities created different NGOs that supported stakeholder groups such as labor activists, environmentalists, and human rights activists. And again, each area has its own source of *power:* sticks, carrots, and norms.

Each configuration also comes with a specific set of core beliefs, which we discuss in more detail in chapter 3. Society 1.0 has an ideology of state-centric core beliefs (state planning). Society 2.0 adopts a market-centered set of core beliefs (market competition). Society 3.0 operates according to a communication- or discourse-centric set of beliefs that typically integrates both markets and government (examples: twentieth-century Keynesianism or the European-style social-market economy). The last column in table 2 anticipates an emerging stage that we refer to as Society 4.0 or, to use another placeholder term, the co-creative eco-system economy, which innovates at the scale of the whole system. In this developmental framework, each system's players operate with a different state of awareness. The 1.0 economies operate according to the primacy of traditional awareness: complying with existing mindsets and rules. The 2.0 economies awaken to the ego-system awareness that Adam Smith famously captured when he wrote: "It is not from the benevolence of the butcher, the brewer, or the baker that we expect our dinner, but from their regard to their own interest. We address ourselves, not to their humanity but to their self-love, and never talk to them of our own necessities but of their advantages."[11] In 3.0 economies, this self-interest is widened and mitigated by the self-interest of other stakeholders who organize collectively to bring their interests to the table through labor unions, government, NGOs, and other entities.

In the emerging 4.0 stage of our economy, the natural self-interest of the players extends to a shared awareness of the eco-system. Eco-system awareness is an internalization of the views and concerns of other stake-holders in one's system. It requires people to develop the capacity to perceive problems from the perspective of others. The result is decisions and outcomes that benefit the whole system, not just a part of it.

A close look at today's economies and societies reveals an awakening of eco-system awareness in numerous arenas. For example, the move-ments for Slow Food, conscious consuming, fair trade, LOHAS (Life-styles of Health and Sustainability), socially responsible investing, and collaborative consumption are all extending their reach to include the concerns of others in the economic process. They can be seen as fore-runners of the 4.0 state of the economy.

One Map, Many Journeys

The previous section introduced the developmental map. But the map is not the journey or the territory. The journey differs according to the historical context for each country and civilization. A quick tour through some of the main regions of our global economy illustrates various jour-neys and their different territories from 1.0 to 4.0. At this point, we are looking at the evolution of society from 1.0 to its current, modern form—that is, a form that is characterized by the *division of labor* and the *differentiation* of multiple subsystems.

EUROPE

At the end of the devastating Thirty Years' War (1618–48), Europe was ready to move to Society 1.0. In 1648 the territory that today is referred to as Germany had eighteen hundred kingdoms. Over time, territorial integration increased, and the French Revolution greatly accelerated societal innovation across Europe, giving birth to Society 2.0. Start-ing in the early to mid-nineteenth century, negative externalities such as poverty, exploitation of low-income workers, and child labor led to a variety of societal responses and eventually to Society 3.0. Features of Society 3.0 include social security legislation, environmental laws, and consumer protection regulations. The postwar twentieth century was, from a European point of view, a significant success story for Society 3.0.

But toward the end of the century some of those achievements began to crumble when unemployment, environmental issues, and financial bubbles created problems that European governments were unable to address with a 3.0 mindset, as the euro crisis after 2008 well demonstrates.

THE UNITED STATES

Society 2.0 was born with the American Revolution. The state-centered 1.0 version of society never had a strong home base in the United States. In fact, 1.0 institutions, seen from a US perspective, might resemble more what people did not like about Europe—what made them leave the Old World for the New World. Early Society 2.0 in America was not formed to limit an oppressive US state, but to limit the oppressive European colonial states. As a consequence, even today, mistrust of government or anything that looks like a 1.0 structure runs deep in many parts of US culture. The 2.0 version of a market economy, however, was firmly grounded at home.

Throughout the twentieth century, particularly during the Great Depression of the 1930s, negative externalities in the form of mass unemployment and poverty moved the United States toward Society 3.0. Major milestones on that journey were a series of financial bubbles that sparked the creation of the Federal Reserve System in 1913 and the New Deal, which President Franklin D. Roosevelt introduced in 1933–36 (and which included white industrial workers in the North but not black farmworkers in the South). A period of relative economic stability followed, until 1980.

In the 1980s the neoliberal Reagan-Thatcher revolution began to move the country backward from 3.0 to 2.5, so to speak, by reshaping the institutional design in favor of deregulation, privatization, and tax reduction, particularly for the rich and super-rich. The deregulation of the financial system continued through several Republican and Democratic administrations. The disastrous end of the Glass-Steagall Act in 1999 happened on the watch of Democrats (under President Clinton), not Republicans, permitting commercial banks to engage in securities activities and effectively setting the stage for the near-total collapse of the global financial system less than a decade later.

President Obama's health care reform legislation (the Affordable Care Act) completes the 3.0-related innovations that started in the early twentieth century. For the time being, as we write this in early 2013, the country remains politically paralyzed and deeply divided between 2.0 fundamentalists (on the far Right), 3.0 believers (on the traditional Left), and people who think that neither one nor the other will do the trick and that something entirely different is needed today.

AFRICA

Research suggests that the human species originated in Africa. When the nineteenth-century colonialist Europeans and other Westerners imposed a ruthless regime of exploiting the soil and the people of Africa, millions of slaves were sold to the Americas and elsewhere. Thus, the introduction of the modern state came with an iron (and malevolent) fist. The governments that were put in place by European colonial powers first and foremost served those powers' interests.

The Arab revolution of 2011 that was ignited in Tunisia and Egypt is directed against the last strongholds of those cynical and corrupt 1.0 regimes that have continued to exist in North Africa, where Western powers have repeatedly turned a blind eye to civil rights violations in exchange for cheap oil.

Throughout the late twentieth century, the World Bank (among others) facilitated a push toward Economy 2.0 institutional innovations. The so-called Washington consensus called for market-oriented changes (deregulation, privatization, less government, and less government spending) that guided World Bank policies from 1979 to 2009. As various countries within Africa now move from 1.0 and 2.0 to 3.0 on a variety of paths, questions remain: how to help fragile states whose core societal functions and institutions have been deeply disrupted? How can a 4.0 approach that incorporates all stakeholders and all sectors strengthen the resilience and innovation capacity of the whole system?

JAPAN

When European powers colonized Asia, only two or three countries escaped that fate. Japan was one of them, Thailand and Bhutan the others. Having imported Buddhism, Confucianism, and elements of Chinese culture in the first centuries A.D., Japan developed its own version of Society 1.0 over many centuries, notably through the Tokugawa shogunate. The forced opening of Japan by Commodore Perry in 1854, followed by the Meiji Revolution in 1868, brought to Japan a second major wave of foreign culture and technology, this time from the West. It set the country on a path toward Society 2.0 and 3.0. Losing the Pacific War reimposed core elements of Society 2.0, though many cultural elements of Society 3.0 remained (e.g., *keiretsus*—informal sets of interrelated companies).

CHINA

With five thousand-plus years of history, China is one of the world's oldest civilizations and home to more than 1.3 billion people. It was among the most advanced societies and economies for much of its history, but missed the Industrial Revolution in the nineteenth century and saw its decline accelerate through invasions by colonial powers from Europe. After a period of civil war in the first part of the twentieth century, China moved into the 1.0 stage under the leadership of Mao (1949), and thirty years later into stages 2.0 and 3.0 under the leadership of Deng Xiaoping and his successors.

In the Organisation for Economic Co-operation and Development (OECD) countries, stages 1.0 to 3.0 tend to blend together as a single economic system ("many countries, one system"). In contrast, in China there are highly developed market economies in one part of the country and largely traditional state-led economies in other parts of the country, making China a new type of model that can best be described as "one country, many systems." China's success story of the past thirty years has no parallel anywhere in the world—not in the industrialization of the United Kingdom or the United States, not after the Meiji Revolution in Japan, and not in the German *Wirtschaftswunder* after World War II.

Yet, like everyone else, the Chinese today face massive challenges, including environmental issues, rising inequality, rising expectations from its emerging middle class, slowing growth, and increasingly disruptive and depressed global business environments. In its twelfth Five-Year Plan (2011–15), China focuses both on economic growth and on innovations to make progress on its path toward a harmonious society. While the Western media focus on China's environmental issues and civil rights violations, Chinese industry has emerged as a leader in core technologies for renewable energy. What would a stage 4.0 Chinese economy and society look like? How can China prototype and scale an eco-system economy that has the capacity to navigate and innovate at the scale of the whole?

INDONESIA

With 17,000 islands, Indonesia is the world's largest archipelagic state and home to 240 million people, making it the fourth most populous country and the third most populous democracy. It is also home to the world's largest Muslim population. The nation is blessed with vast natural resources—it is the region with the second highest biodiversity on the planet. Located between China and India, Indonesia has always been a crossroads of international trade. Along with trade came the cultural influences of Hinduism and Buddhism (starting in the seventh century B.C.E.), Islam (starting in the thirteenth century), and Europe, with three and a half centuries of colonization by the Dutch (starting in the sixteenth century). The highly diverse Indonesian people united across all their divisions in a fight for independence from the Dutch and the Japanese, leading to a unified country and independent state in 1945–49.

During the era of founding president Sukarno, from 1945 to 1967, the country was run by an authoritarian, centralized government. During the following Suharto era, from 1968 to 1998, the country moved from an authoritarian 1.0 system to a 2.0 structure that blended authoritarian government with the market and foreign direct investment. After the revolution in 1998, the country moved into the 3.0 stage of its economic development, featuring its first direct presidential election (2004), the decentralization of government (2005), and the rise of civil society participation in multisector dialogue on the complex issues of economic, political, and social development. Indonesia is a founding member of the Association of Southeast Asian Nations (ASEAN) and has been one of the fastest-growing G20 members since the economic crisis in 2008.

INDIA

India's ancient history dates back to the Indus Valley civilization in South Asia around 2500–1900 B.C.E. Different kingdoms and sultanates stabilized the country from the Middle Ages until the eighteenth century, when European outposts began to create their own economic dominance. They brought technology and infrastructure into the country and began an alliance with the Indian elite class. The result was a shift in India's economy. It no longer exported goods, but raw materials. India was a British colony from 1858 until the end of World War II. After its independence, when Gandhi's notion of self-reliance was an important economic concept, India's economic system stayed closed to external economies or economic partners. In the late 1980s, India held only 0.5 percent of the global market. This changed after a financial crisis in 1989–91. The IMF pushed for a liberalization of India's economy and opened the door for international investors. As a result, the Indian economy exploded with a growth rate between 7 and 9 percent. The result of this development was a dual economy with a 2.0 economy dominated by large corporations that took over the role of the government and created an infrastructure in the areas where they needed it. And it left a 1.0 economy without an infrastructure outside of these corporate-regulated areas. As current growth rates start to slow down, the next steps will have to deal with the larger eco-system conditions. Current levels of corruption and the growing tensions in the overall system create new challenges for which 1.0, 2.0, and even 3.0 economies can offer no satisfying answers.

BRAZIL

With more than 200 million inhabitants, Brazil is the world's fifth most populous country. Recognized as having the greatest biodiversity on the planet, Brazil has an economy that has grown swiftly in the twenty-first century, and it has pioneered conditional cash transfer programs that have lifted millions of people out of poverty. After three centuries of Portuguese colonial rule, Brazil declared its independence in 1822, abolished slavery in 1888, and became a presidential republic in 1889. For much of the twentieth century, until 1985, it was shaped by authoritarian military regimes that guided the country through various more or less 1.0 (state-centric) stages of economic development. With Fernando Henrique Cardoso as minister of finance (1992–94) and then as president (1994–2002), the country created a solid 2.0 economic foundation, which President Luiz Inácio Lula da Silva was able to leverage while taking the economy to 3.0—that is, to a social-market economy that creates growth by putting money into the hands of the most marginalized citizens (through conditional cash transfers). Today, under President Dilma Rousseff, Brazil is facing heightened expectations, slower growth, and a new set of infrastructure challenges that will require the country to go beyond "more of the same."

RUSSIA

In 1917, two revolutions ended the reign of the Russian czar and marked the beginning of the Russian Civil War. In 1921, at the end of this civil war, the Russian economy and living conditions were devastated. In 1922 the Russian Communist Party established the Soviet Union and a centralized economic system, a 1.0 economy. Collective agricultural production and restricted production of consumer goods were primary features of this centralization. In 1929, Stalin introduced the so-called Five-Year Plans that became the central planning tool for communist countries. The Soviet Union quickly increased its industrial production in the years prior to World War II and then again in the 1960s under Brezhnev, when it also became one of the world's largest exporters of natural gas and oil. But the 1965 "economic reform" that aimed at introducing entrepreneurial management ideas reflected the limitation of the centralized 1.0 economy.

The war in Afghanistan, economic problems, and then the political changes that led to the revolutions in Eastern Europe ended the Soviet Union. In 1990, Mikhail Gorbachev introduced perestroika and glasnost, which marked the transition from a centralized 1.0 to a 2.0 society. After his removal from power and with guidance from Harvard advisers, this transition took full effect in the form of "shock therapy."

The result was nothing short of catastrophic, with a rapid increase in poverty and even worse living conditions. At the same time, a small group of well-connected individuals managed to seize ownership of formerly state-owned enterprises. The poor and the less privileged suffered under a system with little regulation. These negative externalities of the 2.0 market economy were accompanied by several political and economic crises, including hyperinflation and the financial crisis of 1998. A year later, the new president, Vladimir Putin, brought back some of the centralized power structure, better balancing the dynamics of 1.0 and 2.0. Fueled by high energy prices, Russia has seen much higher and more consistent growth rates since that time.

The often harsh criticism in the Western media of Russia usually misses two points. One, it took the West an awfully long time to move from 1.0 (during the Thirty Years' War) to 2.0 (with the Industrial Revolution). Why not give Russia at least a few years to sort these things out? And, two, in a world of ever-increasing resource scarcity, Russia is sitting on a gold mine of resources. As time goes on, the value of these resources will rise and turn Russia into a sought-after partner of both the EU and the emerging East Asian economic zone.

Globalization 1.0, 2.0, 3.0—and 4.0?

What this mini-tour demonstrates is that every country and world region takes its own developmental path. Still, the pathways of social and economic evolution across cultures do have some commonalities. We can track them as an evolution from low to high complexity, or, in terms of consciousness, from traditional and ego-system awareness to eco-system awareness.

Yet there are also recent examples of countries that have moved backward, from 3.0 structures toward 2.0. The neoliberal Thatcher-Reagan revolution, for example, spurred many countries to scale back their domestic 3.0 accomplishments, such as social security, in order to be "competitive" in the global 2.0 competition and global capital markets.

So what is going on? One way to read the current flow of events is that waves of globalization replicate on an international level the same stages that we saw previously in individual countries:

a journey from globalization 1.0 (the United Nations system, founded in 1945 after World War II) to

2.0 (globalization of markets and capital markets, particularly after the end of the Cold War system and the collapse of the Berlin Wall in 1989), to

3.0 (globalization of civil society, particularly after the World Trade Organization–related "battle of Seattle" in 1999), and perhaps to

4.0, an emerging future state of global cross-sector co-creation for protecting the commons

Conclusion and Practices

This chapter investigated the first dimension of our blind spot: structural disconnects. As a set, these systemic disconnects could spur the next wave of institutional renewal, just as a hundred years ago the crisis of the 2.0 laissez-faire market economy catalyzed a whole new wave of institutional innovations that today we associate with the 3.0 social-market economy.

JOURNALING QUESTIONS

Take a journal (or blank piece of paper) and reflect on how the systemic disconnects show up in your world by writing your responses to the questions below.

1. Where does your food come from?

2. What roles does material consumption play in your life?

3. What makes you happy?

4. What is your relationship to money?

5. Given the four stages of economic development discussed in this chapter, how do you see the past, present, and future of your own community and country?

CIRCLE CONVERSATION

Form a circle of five to seven individuals and discuss the organizational or professional context that each person brings to the circle. Ask the following questions (or some variation):

1. Introduce your own organization by relating one or two formative experiences that shaped its culture as it is today.

2. Where does your organization experience a world that is ending/ dying, and where does it experience a world that is beginning/wanting to be born?

3. What do you consider to be the root causes of the problems that you face in your institutional and professional work today?

4. What do you personally feel is going to happen in and to your organization over the next ten to twenty years?

5. What would you like to do right now in order to make a difference for your organization going forward?

3

Transforming Thought:
The Matrix of Economic Evolution

We are torn between two worlds: the world of new leadership challenges on the
one hand, and the world of old economic and management tools on the other.
Between these two lies a yawning abyss. In this chapter, we explore this gap
by continuing to explore the iceberg: from symptoms (level 1) and structural
disconnects (level 2) to underlying paradigms of thought (level 3).

The Blind Spot II: Consciousness

In order to meet the challenges of our time, we need to shift our thinking as individuals and as a society. The profound changes that are necessary today require a shift in our paradigm of thought and a shift in
consciousness from an ego-system to an eco-system awareness. The
deeper we move into the complex, volatile, and disruptive challenges of
the twenty-first century, the more this hidden dimension of leadership
moves to center stage. The blind spot in the twentieth-century toolkit
of economics and management can be summarized in a single word:
consciousness.

Today's economy works as a set of locally embedded and globally
interlinked eco-systems. The word *ecology* was coined in 1866 by the
German biologist Ernst Haeckel to mean the study of a living organism
and its surroundings. As noted in the introduction, its Greek root is
oikos, which means "the whole house" or "the place to live."[1] The word
system denotes a set of interdependent components forming an integrated whole. Thus an *eco-system* is a system whose elements interact
with their surroundings, the ecological, social, intellectual, and spiritual
context as a unit—the whole house.

Today's real economy is a set of highly interdependent eco-systems, but the consciousness of the players within them is fragmented into a set of ego-systems. Instead of encompassing the whole, the awareness of the players in the larger system is bounded by its smaller subparts. The gap between eco-system reality and ego-system consciousness may well be the most important leadership challenge today—in business, in government, and in civil society.

Wherever you go, leaders and change-makers are working to bridge that gap. When the leader of a company works with departments that need to improve their collaboration around a common core process, that person is trying to move the departments from ego-system awareness (of their own departmental needs) to an extended stakeholder awareness (of their shared process needs across the firm). When a group of leaders convenes the key players in the value chain in order to facilitate cross-institutional collaboration and innovation, they are doing the same thing: extending the ego-system awareness in their institutions to an eco-system awareness of the entire extended enterprise. When an NGO such as Oxfam or the World Wildlife Fund (WWF) campaigns against child labor or environmental destruction, it tries to extend the awareness of everyone in the system (including consumers) to include the well-being of others, particularly the most marginalized groups.

Facilitating this sort of shift is not an esoteric or peripheral endeavor by people on the fringes. It's a mission-critical process for millions of institutions and enterprises that is being facilitated by leaders, change-makers, coaches, and consultants. Despite their practical relevance, consciousness and awareness are not variables in the framework of mainstream economics and management. They are a blind spot. With the notable exception of some recent work in behavioral economics, economic theory has built models of competition and transactions based on assumptions about *given preferences*. Little knowledge is being developed or attention being paid to the conditions that allow a system to shift from one *state* of operating to another—for example, from ego-system awareness to eco-system awareness.

Mainstream economic theory and the traditional management tool-kit assume a two-dimensional "flat" space for economic action that is limited to a single state of operational awareness. But there are multiple states of awareness and consciousness that economic and managerial actors can operate from. If these different states of awareness were incorporated into economic theory, and if policymakers paid attention to their impact on what outcomes we create, a whole new dimension of policy, innovation, and collective action would emerge.

Social Fields

In physics, we know that matter behaves differently in different states. For example, water, H_2O, freezes at 32 degrees Fahrenheit. Above that temperature, ice melts. At 212 degrees Fahrenheit, water boils and evaporates, and so on. In each case the H_2O molecules are the same, but they behave quite differently.

In the case of social fields, we see the same phenomenon. Depending on the state of consciousness of a social field or the quality of people's awareness, social systems enact completely different structures and behaviors. Just like water in the physical system, the makeup of people in a social system stays the same under a given set of conditions. The difference between natural laws and the social field is that the actors in social systems are able to initiate change. In other words, they are sitting in the water while the temperature changes—and they potentially can get their hands on the temperature control. When their field state of awareness or conversation changes, the actors relate to one another in different ways, and end up co-creating very different results.

Oikos: The Origins of Economic Thought

For Aristotle, economy was an integral part of his practical philosophy, along with ethics and politics. In its original meaning, the managing of "the house" related to the *whole house* and was not yet separated from the *polis*—that is, the association and community of free citizens. And until the seventeenth or eighteenth century, the term *economy* related to the management of the whole house, and not to activities that serve the purpose of making money, which was described as *commerce*.

Modern-day economics has developed in ways that separate the economy from the *polis*. Economics has become a narrow set of propositions that deal only with the so-called economic subsystem of society. Economics no longer deals with the whole house—that is, with the economic subsystem's impact on society as a whole and its social-ecological-cultural context. Instead economics refers to those as externalities.

Given this background, it is even more remarkable that in the early years of the twenty-first century, we are seeing a return to the original meaning of *oikos*. The social and ecological challenges for today's institutional leaders are starting to redirect the course of economic inquiry toward its *oikos*-related origins by forcing us, once again, to broaden our perspective. What "the whole house" refers to has changed. It is no longer just our "small" individual house, our local micro-conditions; it also refers to the regional and global house we live in, and thus to the macro- and mundo-conditions on our planet and to the sum total of our social, ecological, and spiritual-cultural relationships.

To sum this up, the way we think about the relationship between society and economy is changing. While the first economic concepts saw the economy as being firmly integrated in the larger societal whole, modern economics conceive of the economy as an autonomous subsystem in the larger societal whole. The challenges we are dealing with as a society force us to rethink this mental model, and to include the impact of our actions on the environmental, social, and cultural context in which we are operating.

The Death of Economic Monotheism

Another important building block of contemporary economic thought concerns the bias toward an *economic monotheism* that puts the primacy of one coordination mechanism atop all economic activities: the *invisible hand* of the market.[2] This mechanism is *omnipotent* in the sense that it isn't limited by other coordination mechanisms, as we saw in the deregulated financial markets before the 2008 crisis. It is *omnipresent* through its ever-increasing penetration of all sectors and systems of society. And it is *omniscient* in its assumed access to all information.

As the economic monotheisms of the past have resulted in a long list of catastrophic failures—including the state-fundamentalist monotheism that led the Soviet Union into a collapse in 1991 and the market-fundamentalist neoliberal model that put the world financial system at the brink of collapse in 2008—an increasing number of leading economists, including Nobel laureates Joseph Stiglitz and Paul Krugman, have pointed to various structural flaws in mainstream (neoclassical and neoliberal) economic thought. Economic thought systems matter because they are at the heart of an intellectual battle over the future direction of our society. Simon Johnson, an MIT professor and former IMF chief economist, argues that a power struggle between Wall Street and government lies at the heart of our current crisis.[3] In a primitive political system, according to Johnson, power is transmitted through violence (carried out by military coups and militias, for example; see the coercive power discussed in table 2 in chapter 2). In a more developed society, power is transmitted through money (in the form of bribes, kickbacks, campaign contributions; see the remunerative power discussed in table 2). But in the most advanced societies, power is transmitted through cultural capital, such as belief systems (see the normative power discussed in table 2).

Says Johnson, "By 1998, it was part of the worldview of the Washington elite that what was good for Wall Street was good for America."[4] That belief system has given Wall Street a de facto veto over public policymaking that no other group or industry enjoys. Since the beginning of the financial crisis in 2008, this unparalleled influence of Wall Street on Washington has only increased. As a result, the financial crisis has not led to an independent review of the financial sector or to possible new regulations to prevent future meltdowns. Instead, the six largest banks in the United States became even larger, and society as a whole is even more dependent on them.[5]

Sadly, in this critical clash of economic ideas, one dogma-based system is fighting another one: Left versus Right; twentieth-century thought versus eighteenth- and nineteenth-century thought; or, in the language introduced above, 3.0 versus 2.0. We need to articulate a different view of economic, political, and spiritual affairs—a view that is not primarily Left or Right, that is not wrapped around the primacy of this mechanism or that one, that doesn't believe that the solution to our problems lies with Big Government, Big Corporations, Big Money, or Big Ideology.

Today's change efforts need to be in touch with the *emerging realities* of our century; we need to harness the power of individual and collective entrepreneurship in order to co-create new solutions across sector boundaries. This requires strengthening collective attention in order to source innovation from the field of future possibility.

We need a new culture of communication and a framework of economic thought that does not simply put another single dogma at the center of the intellectual universe, but that puts our shared reality at the center of our attention. What is needed is the ability to *hold and evolve our collective attention* at the same rate at which the reality around us keeps changing. Contrary to conventional wisdom on the progressive Left and the neoconservative Right, we do not need to impose another ideology or set of beliefs onto reality. Instead, we need to hold the space for opening and heightening our attention collectively in such ways that our old economic ideas become subject to change. Only when we allow our shared economic reality to change us—and our thinking—will we start to develop economic ideas that can be helpful, healing, and transformative.

The Matrix of Economic Evolution

Our economies evolved around challenges and responses. Societies responded to the challenges of instability, growth, and domestic externalities by updating their economic logic, and by innovating new coordination mechanisms (hierarchy, markets, networks, eco-system awareness). Each new stage came with an evolutionary change in consciousness, from traditional to ego-centric to stakeholder-centric and, maybe, in the emerging next stage, to eco-centric.

The structural disconnects discussed in the previous chapter are social pathologies that affect our lives today and that originate in the underlying architecture of economic thought. All economic systems deal with the production, distribution, and consumption of goods and services. Societies in different regions, times, and cultures have developed different ways of structuring these processes. In this book, we have identified five approaches to managing them:

1. Organizing around place-based communities (premodern)

2. Organizing around centralized power: the state (one sector; centralized state)

3. Organizing around competition: state plus market (two sectors; decentralized markets)

4. Organizing around special-interest groups: state plus market plus NGOs (three sectors; conflicting relationships)

5. Organizing around the commons (three sectors; co-creative relationships)

We have also noted that the economic logic of each earlier stage continues to exist in the later stages—but is mitigated by a new meta-context that is defined by 2.0, 3.0, or 4.0 practices, respectively.

Following Thomas Kuhn's work on scientific revolutions and Arnold Toynbee's work on the rise and fall of civilizations, we can state that whenever an economic paradigm is unable to provide useful answers to a period's biggest challenges, society will enter a transitional period in which, sooner or later, it replaces the existing logic and operating system with an updated and better one. What, then, is the driving force for moving an economy or a society from one operating system to another? We believe that there are two primary ones: exterior challenges (the push factor) and the development of consciousness (the pull factor).

Societal evolution happens when the forces of push and pull meet and align: the external challenge that can no longer be ignored and the internal resonance with an awakening human consciousness and will. Wherever these two forces align, we see mountains move, as they did in 1989 with the collapse of the Berlin Wall; in 1991 with the collapse of the Soviet Union; in 1994 with the collapse of the apartheid system in South Africa; and in 2011 with the collapse of the Mubarak regime in Egypt and the Gaddafi regime in Libya.

We have seen numerous 1.0 tyrants tumble. And we believe that in this decade we will see many more walls go down. And yet the eight structural disconnects remind us that there are still major structures that need to be rethought, reinvented, and transformed. Just as a hundred years ago the Western economies moved from 2.0 to 3.0 by invent-

TABLE 3 The Matrix of Economic Evolution

Stage	Nature	Labor	Capital	Technology	Leadership	Consumption	Coordination	Ownership
0.0: Communal; *Premodern Awareness*	Mother Nature	Self-sufficiency	Natural capital	Indigenous wisdom	Community	Survival	Community	Communal
1.0: State-Centric: Mercantilism; State Capitalism; *Traditional Awareness*	Resource	Serfdom, slavery	Human capital	Tools: Agricultural Revolution	Authoritarian (sticks)	Traditional (needs-driven)	Hierarchy and control	State
2.0: Free Market: Laissez-Faire; *Ego-Centric Awareness*	Commodity (land, raw materials)	Labor (commodity)	Industrial capital	Machines: first Industrial Revolution (coal, steam, railway)	Incentives (carrots)	Consumerism: mass consumption	Markets and competition	Private: exchange of private ownership in markets
3.0: Social Market: Regulated; *Stakeholder-Centric Awareness*	Regulated commodity	Labor (regulated commodity)	Financial capital (externality-blind)	System-centric automation: second Industrial Revolution (oil, combustion engine, chemicals)	Participative (norms)	Selectively conscious consumption	Networks and negotiation	Mixed (public-private)
4.0: Co-Creative: Distributed; Direct; Dialogic; *Eco-Centric Awareness*	Eco-system and commons	Social and business entrepreneurship	Cultural creative capital (externality-aware)	Human-centric technologies: third Industrial Revolution (renewable energy and information technologies)	Co-creative (collective presence)	CCC: collaborative conscious consumption	ABC: awareness-based collective action	Shared access to services and common resources

ing mechanisms to mitigate negative domestic externalities, we are again facing a new set of issues: global externalities and an age of disruption that will keep generating systemic breakdowns. It's not a matter of dealing with one more financial crisis and then we're done. It's a matter of addressing the systemic limits at their root.

Table 3 looks at the eight elements that together make an economy work and describes their development through the stages of our economic evolution worldwide.

Reading the Matrix

The Matrix of Economic Evolution maps both the journey of our economic development and the possible development space going forward.

Here is how we suggest that you read the matrix. Note the shaded cells in each column of the matrix, indicating the critical factor in each developmental stage. In the 0.0 stage, "Mother Nature" is shaded, indicating that nature is the critical factor for the production function. Then, at stage 1.0, dependent labor (serfdom and slavery) became the critical developmental factor. The production function changes from one factor (nature) to two (nature, labor). In stage 2.0, when economies move from state-centered societies to market economies, industrial capital becomes the critical developmental factor. Capital allows the new players in the market economy to be productive, and as a result the production function of the economic system now has three factors (nature, labor, capital).

In stage 3.0, technology emerges as a critical factor, and with that the factors of production evolve to four (nature, labor, capital, technology). And finally, in the currently emerging stage 4.0, all of the factors may turn out to be bottlenecks, or critical factors, in the economy:

Nature—resource scarcity and reducing our ecological footprint

Labor—unleashing the power of entrepreneurship

Capital—redirecting the flows of global capital to serving the commons

Technology—building core technologies for the third Industrial Revolution

Leadership—co-creating the capacity to sense and realize an emerging future

Consumption—empowering CCC (collaborative conscious consumption)

Coordination—coordinating by ABC (awareness-based collective action)

Ownership—innovating by commons-based property rights

A word about stage 0.0: Western civilization has colonized and destroyed most of these early cultures.[6] Picturing the evolution from 0.0 to 4.0 as a linear process is somewhat misleading. Instead, we suggest seeing the evolution as a more circular process, with 0.0 at the top; it moves counterclockwise to 1.0 and 2.0, continues around to 3.0, and finally ends up at 4.0, near the starting point. Western thought tends to conceive of history as a linear process, while the Eastern view is more cyclical. Both meta-views have their strengths and their blind spots. If we combine them, we end up with something like a spiral, or a U. The U is an evolutionary form that combines both cyclical and linear elements. But a journey on the U ends at a place that is different from the starting point, because something is born in the process and unfolds on the journey.

Some economies, such as those of Europe, go through these stages over several hundred years. Other countries, such as China, take much of this journey in thirty to sixty years. In both cases, it is unclear what a future 4.0 logic and stage of the economy would look like. We have occasionally seen the world move backward, as it did during the neoliberal revolution from 1980 to 2008 in the West. Thus it is possible for countries to make choices and to move in both directions.

We believe that there is no more important research challenge today than to invent and prototype the *institutional innovations* that will power, scale, and sustain Economy 4.0. In other words, we need to upgrade the economic operating system from ego-system to eco-system logic and awareness.

Questions

While the public conversation in the twentieth century tended to be fixated on just *two* alternatives, market-centric versus government-centric, the matrix in table 3 makes it possible to imagine 390,623 *additional* ways to address current challenges. The remainder of this chapter will focus on broadening economic discourse beyond its old 2.0 versus 3.0 format.

Framing this century's challenges through the lens of 2.0 and 3.0 thought is like driving a vehicle while looking in the rear-view mirror. If you do that, you'll miss seeing what is right in front of you—in this case, an oncoming tsunami of disruptive change. Here are some questions that will guide our inquiry into the eight acupuncture points of deep systemic change throughout this chapter:

1. *Nature:* How can we rethink the economy and nature from "take, make, and throw away" to an integrated closed-loop design, in which everything that we take from the earth is returned at the same or a higher level of quality?

2. *Labor:* How can we relink work—the profession we choose to pursue—with Work—what we really love doing?

3. *Capital:* How can we relink the financial economy and the real economy by recycling financial capital into the service and cultivation of ecological, social, and cultural commons?

4. *Technology:* How can we create broad access to the core technologies of the third Industrial Revolution, blending information technology, regenerative energy, and social technologies in order to unleash individual and collective creativity?

5. *Leadership:* How can we build a collective leadership capacity to innovate at the scale of the whole system?

6. *Consumption:* How can we rebalance the economic playing field so that consumers can engage in collaborative, conscious consumption and become equal partners in an economy that creates well-being for all?

7. *Coordination:* How can we end the war of the parts against the whole by shifting the mode of consciousness from ego-system to eco-system awareness?

8. *Ownership:* What innovations in property rights would give voice to future generations and facilitate the best societal uses of scarce resources and commons?

These eight elements, from nature to ownership, define the core of any economic system. Our notions about each element change profoundly in the journey from 0.0 to 4.0. Understanding these changes and shifts allows us not only to understand our current reality, but also to identify the potential of the future.

The next pages follow the journey of each of the eight key factors, or acupuncture points, from 0.0 to 4.0. If you are not particularly interested in all the details of the evolution of economic thought, you can jump to the concluding remarks at the end of each section, or you can skim the rest of the chapter and read the sections that interest you most.

1. Nature: Relinking Economy with Nature

All economic activity arises from nature—and returns to it. Nature in economic thought and action has been transformed from its original function as *mother* (0.0) to a *resource* (1.0) to a *commodity* (2.0) to a *regulated commodity* (3.0). In the emerging next stage of economic thought, we might reframe the role of nature in terms of *eco-system* and *commons,* which we collectively cultivate and steward for the well-being of future generations and the whole (4.0).

THE JOURNEY FROM 0.0 TO 3.0

The transition from 0.0 to 1.0 was marked by an agricultural revolution. As long as humans limited their economic activities to harvesting and hunting in order to feed and clothe themselves, their impact on nature was limited. But when people started to settle in one place and to cultivate the land, they began to interfere more deeply with the natural ecosystem. They began to use tools to cut trees and plow the land.

Over thousands of years, humans focused their economic activities on advancing agricultural production, and through these efforts developed a complex system of seeds, tools, livestock, and cultivation practices. The eighteenth century brought the next profound economic revolution—the Industrial Revolution—which first took shape in England and eventually moved the entire economic system from 1.0 to 2.0. This process continued throughout the nineteenth century and into the twentieth.

With simultaneous inventions in cotton spinning, steam power, and iron making, as well as in ownership structures, the Industrial Revolution took human intervention to a different level. What had started with picking fruits morphed into blasting holes in the ground to extract metals and fossil fuels to feed the global industrial machine. As the sociologist Max Weber famously put it: "This order [i.e., capitalism] is now bound to the technical and economic conditions of machine production which today determine the lives of all the individuals who are born into this mechanism, . . . with irresistible force. Perhaps it will so determine them until the last ton of fossilized coal is burnt."[7]

As this journey of burning fossil fuel is now closing in on its last ton with irresistible force, we are confronted with negative externalities that have prompted the system to move to the next evolutionary stage. The introduction of standards and regulations helped the industrial economy to evolve from 2.0 to 3.0 throughout the twentieth century. These institutional innovations protect the regeneration of nature, labor, and capital and also help to stabilize incomes on the consumer side, which fuel the mass consumption that keeps the industrial machine running and growing.

The flip side of this story of material growth and success is the rapid depletion of our common resource pool. Although the introduction of new technologies has reduced the material footprint of economic value creation to some degree, the dematerialization of industrial production has been surpassed by the total growth rate of the overall economy. The net result is that our extractions from the earth have continued to grow until the present day. In 2005, for example, 58 billion metric tons of materials entered the economy to keep our global industrial production running (one metric ton equals 2,204.6 pounds). On a global per-person basis, according to Juliet Schor in her book *Plenitude,* the average material use has been 8.8 metric tons, or just under 50 pounds per day. The US consumer used more than 2.5 times that amount (23 metric tons per person per year, or 139 pounds per person per day).[8]

IN SEARCH OF 4.0

How can we rethink and redesign our economic processes in ways that will reintegrate economic cycles with nature?

The structure of economic thought is disconnected from the ecosystem realities of our planet. The 0.0 unity with our planet is gone. We have—through our economic thought—turned our planet into a commodity. We have created an economic machine that requires the resources of 1.5 planets.

How can we reconcile this contradiction? Here are four propositions and principles as a conversation starter.

1. *All economic activity arises from and returns to nature.* What started as an obvious and natural connection between economic activity and the natural world during the early stages of economic development faded in the later stages. Yet the actual role of nature in the economic process has increased steadily.

   The current global GDP of US$60 trillion would drop to zero in an instant without nature. Our entire economy and society rely on the eco-system services of nature. According to a 2010 UNEP study, the total value of all eco-system services (which accounts for only part of nature's contribution) amounts to at least US$70 trillion a year.[9] In other words, the unassessed value that nature creates for our economic process and well-being is higher than the value of all produced goods and services (global GDP). Yet nature has disappeared almost completely from the categories of modern economic thought into what can only be called a massive institutionalized blind spot.[10]

2. *Commodity fiction.* We run a 1.5 planet–footprint economy in a one-planet ecological reality. Why? Because of commodity fiction. In all modern economic theory, nature is thought of as a commodity. This is, as we learned from reading Karl Polanyi's book *The Great Transformation,* a fiction. A commodity is a product that we produce for the market with the purpose of consumption. But Planet Earth is not produced by us, nor is its purpose to be consumed by us. If anything, the planet is a gift that has been handed to us. This deep sense of responsibility can still be found today among farmers when they talk about their land, and also among entrepreneurs when they talk about their enterprise. None of them considers the earth or the essence of their enterprise to be a commodity. Yet this deep human understanding is not reflected in modern economic thought.

   The intellectual root cause of the 1.5 planet–footprint problem originates from economic frameworks that conceive of nature as a commodity—in other words, just about every mainstream economic framework today.[11]

3. *Biomimicry.* How would nature design the economic processes that we cultivate and manage? Janine Benyus, author of *Biomimicry* and cofounder of the global network Biomimicry 3.8, asks this critical question. Reflecting on the key principles of nature and its eco-systems, here are a few that stand out:[12]

   a. *Zero waste.* Nature is designed as a zero-waste system. Every output is someone else's input. There is no such thing as waste in nature. By contrast, the human economy is full of waste: waste that is produced while sourcing from nature. Only tiny fractions of our waste are being cycled back into a closed-loop system of reuse.

   b. *Solar energy.* Nature operates on 100 percent renewable energy. Cells, like the human economy, need an external source of energy. But unlike the human economy, which has located those sources predominantly in fossil fuels, cells turn to sunlight as their sustainable source of energy.

   c. *Diversity and symbiosis.* All eco-systems are based on the principles of diversity and symbiosis: different species working together in symbiotic and harmonious ways. By contrast, industrial production promotes monocultures and single-variable maximization that reduce resilience and make the system vulnerable to disruption.

4. *Closed-Loop Designs.* In order to create well-being for all without destroying the planet, we would have to increase resource productivity by a factor of five—or we would have to reduce resource use by 80 percent (at current rates of consumption). Ernst Ulrich von Weizsäcker, coauthor of the book *Factor Five,* thinks this is quite possible if all the key players started to move in this direction.[13] It would mean replacing the current industrial paradigm (take, make, and throw away) with one that manages closed-loop cycles of materials and energy. The approach of William McDonough and Michael Braungart around rethinking the economic process as an

earth-to-earth closed loop that integrates economics, eco-system science, chemistry, design, and systems thinking is another pioneering example for this line of work.[14]

The practical challenge in implementing these approaches lies in bringing together interests and players from the entire business eco-system in order to make them see, think, talk, and work together—a challenge that we will inquire into more later, when we talk about the issue of leadership.

SEEING OUR FUTURE: CULTIVATING OUR COMMONS

There is a whole landscape of emerging examples that embody these principles: the Slow Food movement; community-supported agriculture (CSA); local food; local living economies; and sustainable sourcing practices.[15]

Biodynamic (organic) farming is one of these examples and close to our hearts because Otto grew up on a biodynamic farm in Germany.[16] A biodynamic farm is based on the principles of zero importing (a closed-loop cycle), zero waste (every output of one sector is an input for another), diversity (crop rotation and diverse eco-systems instead of monoculture), and a symbiotic relationship among all these elements of the larger living system (the idea that each farm has a unique *living individuality*).

On a very small scale, a biodynamic farm embodies many of the principles identified above. But how can we scale up these practices to the level of the whole food system, and eventually the whole economy? We will return to this question when we share the stories of BALLE (the Business Alliance for Local Living Economies) and the Sustainable Food Lab later in this chapter and in chapter 7.

2. Labor: Relinking Work (Jobs) with *Work* (Purpose)

All economic value creation starts with applying work to nature. That was true in the days of hunting and gathering, and it is true today. In both cases we apply creativity to nature. The result of that co-creative activity emerges in the form of some "added value." In the case of, say, an apple, we know that almost all of the value comes from Mother Nature.

Nature takes care of the "production" process, and we just do the harvesting, sorting, packaging, and distributing.

But an Apple computer is quite different. It is produced by a global web of collaborative value creation, including people with design ideas in Cupertino, California, and tens of thousands of others throughout the value chain processing the raw materials from around the world, manufacturing the core components and building blocks in Asia, assembling the components in China, and shipping and distributing the products through Apple stores in consumer markets. The ratio of work to nature is much higher than in the case of the apple that we harvest in our backyard.

What gets lost in translation throughout this journey to a global division of labor is meaning. Meaning emerges from seeing one's own connection and contribution to the whole. But being underpaid in Asia as I assemble a product for the global supply chain of, say, the iPad—what meaning and purpose can I derive from that? Very little. Today's challenge of reinventing labor does not concern only the issues of jobs and living wages. It also concerns the issue of meaning, that is, of relinking work (jobs) with Work (passion and purpose).

THE JOURNEY FROM 0.0 TO 3.0
As depicted in table 3, the role of work and labor has changed profoundly throughout history. In the 0.0 stage, work was still embedded in communal practices for the purposes of subsistence. In the 1.0 stage, most labor was performed by slaves or indentured servants. Labor was an embodiment of dependency, and in many places it still is. When Aristotle wrote about the *oikos* in his practical philosophy, he referred to households that were operated mainly by slave labor.

Then came the Industrial Revolution and with it what Karl Polanyi called the commodity fiction of labor (2.0)—that is, the idea that labor is a commodity.[17] In the 2.0 economic world, most people are no longer slaves or bondsmen, but instead of selling their bodies they sell their *time*. An employer pays them, and that gives him the right to tell his employees what to do. Compared with the 1.0 world (slavery), this is major progress. But the 2.0 world does not feature anything like entrepreneurial freedom for employees. It is more an evolved form of dependency. Moving from a hard 1.0 type of dependency (bondage) to a soft

2.0 type of dependency (labor as a commodity) has often, but not always, improved the lives of workers, which is why, in the shift from 2.0 to 3.0, unions, social security, and other worker protections emerge.

The evolution to a 3.0 economy has been another big leap forward. But then, particularly toward the end of the twentieth and the beginning of the twenty-first centuries, 3.0 solutions began hitting the wall in the form of (1) jobless growth that increased mass unemployment in developed countries; (2) awareness that continued exponential growth would ruin the planet rather than solve the employment issue; and (3) an acknowledgment that the 3.0 solution to the labor problem was more fragile than we thought: It worked only in some parts of the world, and it worked only for a limited time, when growth was supercharged by cheap fossil fuels. Put bluntly: It worked because we paid for it with our children's future.

IN SEARCH OF 4.0

With these funds gone, what do we do now? Let's consider three views. The first view says that we should muddle through and continue operating as a 3.0 economy. The second suggests that we should go back to 2.0 (which includes dismantling unions, social security, and regulations on the financial sector and to protect the environment). A third group of voices, less prominent, suggests returning to a 1.0 or 0.0 state of the economy (possibly, but not necessarily, in the form of totalitarian fascism).

We believe that none of these options is viable today. What we need today is a different conversation focused on how we can move *forward*—instead of backward—by creating a path to 4.0. That conversation should start with the honest acknowledgment, especially by politicians and economists, that more of the same will never solve the unemployment issue. The 1.0, 2.0, and 3.0 toolkits of the past are out of date and will never be sufficient to take on the huge challenges we are facing now.

Instead, we need to collectively examine the root causes of our current predicament. Consider the following four concepts as input for such a 4.0 conversation.

1. *The discourse of denial.* The public debate over deficit reduction and the promise of future growth that would bring back the industrial

jobs that went to China and India all argue that we are just in another cyclical downturn that will be solved as soon as the recession ends. This argument ignores demographic trends, ecological breakdown, and the current level of economic distress. According to the World Bank in 2012, "Some 200 million people—including 75 million under the age of 25—are unemployed. Over the next 15 years an additional 600 million new jobs will be needed."[18]

So what are we offering to the 600 million young people still looking for work? The current debate is not addressing the scope of this challenge. The debate moves back and forth between the 2.0 and 3.0 perspectives, but does not step out and take a serious look at current reality. Two myths in particular keep us locked into the old patterns of thinking: the myth of growth and the myth of money.

2. *The myth of growth.* One argument that has caused the debate to stagnate is the assumption that we will solve our economic woes over the next two or three decades through accelerated growth. *Nothing* could be further from the truth. This is a delusional myth for at least three reasons:

   a. *Ecological limits.* If we solve the employment problem by doing more of what we've been doing for the past decade, we will produce severe ecological breakdowns in less than a generation.

   b. *Social limits.* If we add to the unemployed the working poor in the United States and the welfare-dependent in Europe, the result is a more accurate number of people for whom the current system doesn't produce sufficient work. The size of this group is probably 20 or 30 percent of the adult population. In other countries, particularly in the global South, this number exceeds 60 or 70 percent. What do we do with that largely excluded group?

   c. *Jobless growth.* Even though the economy continues to grow in many parts of the world, it is not producing the quantity of jobs that will be needed.

While the growth myth has been attacked for the past forty years by the global environmental movement, this next myth has largely been ignored.

3. *The myth of money.* What is it that drives teachers, entrepreneurs, engineers, and others to do their best work? It's the connection to their inner source of inspired creative energy. Connecting with that source is what drives profound innovation and renewal for people of all ages across all cultures. The problem is that we have organized our economy and our economic thinking around a really bad idea: that we should work for money. That idea is one of the biggest creativity killers. Sadly, this mindset is instilled when parents try to motivate their children with rewards: "If you do this, we will give you that." This is the first attack on any child's inner creativity. The second one comes in school, where old-style teaching does the same thing: "If you do *A*, that will get you *B*, and with that you will be admitted to *C* [college]." The third attack happens in the workplace in the form of management incentives, tying bonus payments to targets, and other best practices that are taught in business schools and that, as research tell us, kill creativity in the organization.[19]

These practices poison all real creativity because they disconnect what we do for a living (our work) from what we really care about (our Work or passion). All great inventors, creators, and entrepreneurs, all great social activists, share the same inner journey and source of satisfaction: *loving what you do and doing what you love.* That, according to the late Steve Jobs, arguably a good example of a Working entrepreneur, "is the *only* way to do great work."[20] It is recognizing the connection to this deep source of knowing that can help us in moments when all other navigation instruments fail.

4. *Relinking work and entrepreneurship.* The essence of 4.0 is to provide an institutional context that allows us to relink work (jobs) with Work (purpose). The evolution of work from 1.0 (slavery) to 4.0 (Work) is a journey that has been gradually shifting the locus of control from outside (dependence) to inside the networked individual (networked independence). That journey started with gradual emancipation from 0.0 structures (traditions), 1.0 structures (bondage), 2.0 structures (labor-market dependencies), and finally 3.0 structures (welfare-state dependencies), and has led us to a point where we can strengthen the conditions for individual and communal entrepreneurship.

In order to step into this emerging 4.0 space, we need more enabling infrastructures that invite more people into the generative space of co-sensing and co-creating the future that they care about. Today there are not just thousands or millions of people who are trying to enter such a space, but hundreds of millions, even billions. We need to take a fresh look at the bigger picture. None of the current issues, from poverty to unemployment to environmental destruction to the global economic crisis, can be solved in isolation. We need an integral approach to tackling them. We need to create new types of enabling infrastructures that help people to co-sense, co-develop, and co-create their entrepreneurial capacities by serving the real needs in their communities.

These infrastructures combine the following elements and provide access to:

1. enabling spaces: innovation happens in nurturing places
2. key challenges: challenges are the raw material for all learning
3. sensing mechanisms that allow people to see themselves as part of a bigger picture
4. capacity-building mechanisms
5. capital
6. technology
7. community: a global web of mentors, partners, and entrepreneurs who collectively create prototypes for Society 4.0

As a global community, we must ask ourselves whether we are willing to accept that we are not separate from one another, but are ecologically, economically, socially, and spiritually highly interdependent and connected. And if we agree that we are, are we willing to lend a hand to one another?[21]

If the answer is yes, then a high-leverage economic intervention point would be to simply create an *economic human right* to basic income for every human being on the planet. If this basic need were combined with free or inexpensive access to health care and education, we would create a much more equal and level playing field. It would be a world in which everyone had a fair chance to pursue their entrepreneurial aspirations and dreams. In other words, we could put our creativity into the service of the larger community.

This idea may sound radical, but it really isn't. It is just naming what some parts of our global society are already doing. But since our thinking is still stuck in 2.0 types of transactional frameworks, we tend to be blind to the co-creative elements of an emerging 4.0 economy, which operates through the *economies of presencing* rather than through the *economies of transactional benefits*.

A case in point: Otjivero-Omitara is a small village in Namibia. From January 2008 to December 2009, this village became the first place to experiment with unconditional cash transfers, in the form of a basic income grant (BIG). The idea of BIG is that basic income is a universal human right. During the two-year experiment, each person, regardless of income, received a monthly grant of 100 Namibian dollars (US$13). After only one year, child malnutrition had declined from 42 percent to 10 percent, household poverty had dropped from 76 percent to 37 percent, school dropout rates had declined from 40 percent to 0 percent, and crime went down by 42 percent. Over the same period, entrepreneurial activity and self-employment went up by 300 percent.[22]

The ideas behind cash transfers are simple: Basic income is a human right, and if you give it to people without conditions, you reduce government bureaucracy and create demand on a local level that in turn fuels micro-entrepreneurial opportunities and new ventures. In this instance, cash transfers to the poor kickstarted and strengthened the economy at the level of the micro-entrepreneur. The cost of creating such a cash transfer for the entire population in Namibia would be 2.2 to 3 percent of the country's GDP.[23]

Is this amazing example spreading like wildfire and sparking other, similar efforts around the world? No, at least not at the speed and scale necessary. Why not? Because it contradicts the current habits of economic thought that believe in extrinsic rather than intrinsic motivation of human behavior. People do not believe the results of the Namibian experiment because they contradict their 2.0 economic belief structures, which see human behavior as driven by rewards and punishment rather than by passion and purpose. That being said, we have seen very significant efforts in Brazil and Latin America that have pulled tens of millions of people out of poverty by offering conditional cash transfers.

SEEING OUR FUTURE: IGNITING GLOBAL FIELDS OF SOCIAL ENTREPRENEURSHIP

The seeds of the future are already planted. This future is visible in the first wave of current social entrepreneurship, which we discussed earlier. And in our work we also see a whole second wave of emerging future social entrepreneurship, a wave composed of millions of individuals—many of them feeling a bit stuck in traditional big institutions—who would love to become involved in this emerging global movement. How can these two waves of entrepreneurship and socially responsible awareness meet and connect? Let's look at one example.

The Business Alliance for Local Living Economies (BALLE)

BALLE's founding executive director, Michelle Long, grew up in the Midwest in a fairly traditional, conservative environment. As an undergraduate, she pursued a degree in business and upon graduation was offered a position with a large pharmaceutical company—at the time a coveted first job for career-oriented students such as her. But she soon became disillusioned; while she was working hard, she saw no larger purpose to her work other than making more money for the corporation. Then one day she was asked to perform a task she felt was unethical. Choosing to decline, she realized that she was not on the journey she wanted to be on. In spite of her family's disapproval, she decided to quit her job and embark on a journey around the world to seek a more compelling path.

Over the next two years, her travels took her many places, including India. There she realized that many of the practices and customs that she had thought of as "the way things are" were not the way things were at all in this new context. Rather, much of what was natural for her was strange to the people she met in India, and vice versa. Realizing there was no single, natural way to do things, she had a revelation: Perhaps it is possible to create an entirely *new way* of doing things that is not business as usual in India or the United States, but is instead a way that works better for everyone.

With this new impulse, Michelle returned to the United States and enrolled in business school, where she entered an entrepreneurship competition with what at the time was a novel idea: to create an online marketplace connecting artisans and farmers in developing countries with consumers in the West who wanted to buy products in line with their community and environmental values. Michelle won the competition and, with backing from venture capitalists and other traditional stakeholders such as the World Bank, left business school to pursue this idea.

However, as her business took off, something started to bother her. She felt removed from what was going on in the communities she was trying to serve and began to sense that it was not really her place to be solving problems in distant lands she knew little about when there were so many problems in her own backyard. It was then that she discovered an important truth for her: She wanted to be taking direct action in the places she loved and felt connected to.

So she took the next big leap. She paid off all fair trade suppliers, closed down her company, and set up all the vendors—the fair trade artisans—with a brand-new initiative through Overstock.com, which later became WorldStock.com. Michelle went on to follow her passion and joined an initiative that would link place-based efforts to regenerate local economies. The result is a vibrant national network, BALLE, which is now North America's fastest-growing network of socially responsible businesses, and Michelle serves as its executive director. (For more details on BALLE, see chapter 7.)

The story of Michelle and of BALLE is a good example of what may well be the greatest dormant superpower on this planet: the power of the untapped potential of entrepreneurial creativity to build up social mission–driven enterprises—hybrid enterprises that combine personal initiative with a social mission and with business.

3. Capital: Relinking Financial with Real Capital

Capital is the quintessential concept of economics, as is reflected in the term *capitalism*. At the same time, there are probably few notions today that are more misunderstood. Most people think of capital as money.

However, capital has different forms: It can be physical, human, industrial, financial, social, or spiritual. One characteristic that all these forms of capital have in common is that we expect capital to generate a profit. The term *profit* comes from Latin, meaning "to make progress."

Capital is a young word, originating in the Latin *caput*, the "head." As indicated in table 3, earlier in this chapter, the concept of capital has changed significantly over the course of human and economic history.[24]

THE JOURNEY FROM 0.0 TO 3.0: NATURAL, HUMAN, INDUSTRIAL, AND FINANCIAL CAPITAL

Capital was not in the vocabularies of 0.0 societies. From today's view, 0.0 economies used capital in the form of physical tools and indigenous wisdom to relate to the natural cycles of Mother Nature. Nor was the word used during the Agricultural Revolution, in what we're calling 1.0. Instead, advanced forms of physical equipment, craftsmanship, and knowledge of how to use tools were examples of capital.

In the Middle Ages, capital meant financial assets that people invested in businesses. What we know as capital began in the British colonial empire as merchant capital and later morphed into industrial capital. Without the accumulation of physical, human, and financial capital, the growth miracle of the Industrial Revolution would not have been possible. Both the quantity and the quality of capital changed. Physical capital took the form of heavy machinery. Combined with industrial organization and the contemporary type of schooling, new forms of production initiated unprecedented growth and shifted the center of gravity from individual human skills to industrial organization and mass production. In order to make this shift possible, a new dimension of financial investments was required to facilitate the blending of all these components.

Thus the Industrial Revolution actually gave *capital* a new meaning—the meaning that we associate with it today. Adam Smith was one of the first to emphasize the profit expectation. Karl Marx used the term *capital* to describe the central category of his economic analysis. He described the movement of capital from money (M) to real capital and finally back to money (M'). The difference between M and M' was profit, which was the progress achieved throughout this cycle. Marx saw the inherent contradictions between the *forces of production* (such as progress in productivity) and *relations of production* (such as ownership) as key drivers of societal transformation and change.

The actual evolution of society, however, turned out to be somewhat different than Marxist theory anticipated. Capitalism 2.0, rather than collapsing because of its inherent contradictions, turned out to be remarkably flexible and resilient, reinventing itself in the form of capitalism 3.0. It took on the form of a stakeholder-driven social-market economy that promised to take better care of its regulatory frameworks for the environment, labor, and finance. Starting with Bismarck's social security legislation in the 1870s in Germany and continuing with the Federal Reserve Act in December 1913 and the US New Deal in the 1930s, a whole string of regulatory innovations in many places around the world helped the economy to move from 2.0 to 3.0. While this process took more than half a century in the West, in China it took only a decade to move the (rudimentary) social safety net coverage for 15 percent of the population in 2000 to 95 percent in 2010 (adding more than a billion people within a single decade).

The Industrial Revolution in the 2.0 economies was driven primarily by the growth of physical and human capital. In contrast, the rise of the 3.0 economies came with unprecedented growth and accumulation of financial capital, which fueled an ever-increasing decoupling of the financial and real economy over the course of the twentieth century.[25]

THE GROWING GAP BETWEEN THE FINANCIAL AND THE REAL ECONOMY

One reason for the widening gap between the financial and the real economy is the advantage that financial capital has over nonfinancial capital. Physical and human capital are confined to specific locations and contexts, while financial capital can travel the globe. As Joseph Stiglitz wrote in *The Price of Inequality:*

> Imagine, for a moment, what the world would be like if there was free mobility of labor, but no mobility of capital. . . . In its early history, the United States had such conditions, and indeed a very different process played out. Territories and the new western states of the Union competed for settlers with the older states on the Eastern Seaboard. This led across the nation to the expansion of voting rights, in

the right to run for political office, and in public education, which in turn contributed to the vast expansion of literacy in the United States (relative to what it had been before, and what it was in Europe).[26]

Today, financial capital tends to be global, while labor and physical capital tend to be local. Financial capital can change owners and places in seconds. Labor and physical capital cannot. Moreover, the value of physical capital often decreases with use, while the value of financial capital (apart from inflation) does not diminish through use. On the contrary, through the mechanism of interest and compound interest, financial capital tends to grow exponentially over time, while physical capital tends to be limited and finite.

These structural differences translate into a structural advantage of financial over physical capital that keeps driving the deepening disconnect between finance and the real economy. The results of this disconnect were on display during the financial crisis of 2007–08. Enabled and fueled by the deregulation of the financial industry during the Reagan and Clinton administrations in the 1980s and 1990s, the gap between the financial economy and the real economy widened dramatically, as exemplified by the following data points:

1. *The financial bubble.* In 2006, the McKinsey Global Institute (MGI) calculated that the world's financial markets were struggling to find investment opportunities for US$167 trillion in global "liquidity."[27] That sum was unprecedented, roughly 3.5 times the aggregate global GDP of US$52 trillion at the time. The deputy secretary of the US Treasury during this time, Robert Kimmitt, estimated the figure at US$190 trillion.[28]

2. *The profit bubble.* There is a growing gap between the profits of the financial sector and those of the rest of the economy. The profits of the former jumped from less than 16 percent of domestic corporate profits (1973–85) to 41 percent by the first decade of this century.[29] This change reflects the advantages the financial sector has over the real economy, but a highly profitable financial sector in a real economy with a shrinking profit base is not sustainable. The return on capital must be earned in the real economy. Consequently, when the financial sector is that much more profitable, this profit is created

by a bubble that at some point will burst and make the real economy
pay the price.[30]

3. *The compensation bubble.* "From 1948 until 1979," say Simon Johnson and James Kwak, "average compensation in the banking sector
was essentially the same as in the private sector, . . . until 2007 the
average bank employee earned twice as much as the average private sector worker."[31] But what creates a huge public outcry are the
bonuses paid to investment bankers. Wall Street paid US$18 billion
in year-end bonuses to its New York City employees in 2008, the year
when it received a government bailout of US$243 billion.[32]

The gap between financial capital of US$190 trillion looking for
highly profitable investment opportunities and a real economy and
social sector without access to the financial capital needed to operate
and grow is at the heart of the worldwide economic crisis.[33] It's related
to the problem we discussed earlier, that foreign exchange transactions
of US$1.5 quadrillion dwarf international trade by a factor of 75.[34] The
consequences of this problem are evident in all dimensions of the three
divides. Moreover, the real economy struggles more and more to compete
with profit expectations that an artificially inflated financial economy
imposes on the rest of the economic actors. Small and medium-sized
companies struggle to gain access to cost-effective loans, although it is
they that create most of the new jobs that are desperately needed today.

The result? This situation is comparable to a circulatory system that
pumps all the blood into the head, leaving the other organs to starve.
Something in this system is broken and needs to be fixed. Money does
for the economy what blood does for the human body: It keeps the system moving, connected, and alive. If that circulatory system is broken,
it means that the health of the whole economy is at risk.

The 3.0 response to these crises is more and better regulation,
including (1) limiting the size of banks so that they are no longer capable
of taking a country hostage (by being "too big to fail"); (2) regulating
financial products (limiting derivatives); (3) taxing speculative financial
transactions; and (4) separating the core banking business from the
investment business so that risky investments no longer put core banking services, especially loans to small and medium-sized companies and
innovators, at risk.

But these regulations barely scratch the surface of the deep underlying problem and the myths that keep us from seeing the new reality of capital and money.

IN SEARCH OF 4.0

We need a serious conversation about the role of capital and money in a twenty-first-century economy. To start this conversation, here are four propositions that challenge some of the conventional wisdom that keeps our thinking boxed into an old frame.

1. *The financial system is too efficient.* The main problem with our current financial system, according to Bernard Lietaer, author of *The Future of Money,* is that it is too efficient.[35] It focuses too narrowly on short-term financial profitability, with no awareness of its negative side effects on people and the planet. The result of this system is an economy that turns our companies into machines that are designed to generate financial profit and negative externalities at an unprecedented level, compromising the longer-term health, resilience, and survival capacity of the system. In contrast to markets in the real economy, the financial sector trades a good that is merely a legal construct, and consequently follows different rules from those that apply to other goods and services in the economy. The guideline "what's good for the financial sector is good for the whole country and economy" or, in the case of the United States, "what's good for Wall Street is good for America," does not apply, as became painfully visible when the financial meltdowns destroyed roughly US$50 trillion of capital[36] and worldwide about 30 million jobs between 2007 and the end of 2009.[37] Rather than improving the efficiency of a financial services industry that extracts profits by generating one bubble after another, what we need is a more effective financial market that *serves* the needs of the real economy.

2. *Money is not capital.* Capital is an entrepreneurial capacity that propels the economy and drives the transformative process of value creation. Financial capital allows entrepreneurs to take an idea and move it toward action: to hire people, build a product that they envision, and create the infrastructure required to sustain a business. As described by the economist Joseph Schumpeter, this process is

"creative destruction."[38] What drives it? In Schumpeter's view, it is the entrepreneur. Schumpeter thought that capitalism would eventually destroy itself by crowding out entrepreneurs from increasingly bigger and more bureaucratic companies.[39] While his view on entrepreneurs rings true to many, there is an even deeper force at work that drives entrepreneurial activity and value creation across all sectors of society. It is the force of *creativity*: individual and collective creativity, which we believe is the ultimate source of all capital and value creation.

Redesigning a postbubble financial economy requires us to redesign the flow of money so that it *serves* the actualizing of our creative resources across all sectors of society. We need to redesign our money and capital flows from operating externality-blind to operating externality-aware. In other words, the economy needs to move from 3.0 to 4.0.

3. *Money is not a commodity.* A 2010 survey in the United Kingdom found that 66 percent of the surveyed individuals did not know what portion of their checking account was used in various ways by their bank.[40] Despite the importance of London as a global financial hub, for most people, how the monetary system works is something of a black box. Much of our current banking system is based on the belief that money is a commodity. To debunk that belief, let us take a quick tour through the history of money as a drama in four acts, following the economic paradigms from 1.0 to 4.0.

   The prologue (0.0): physical. Initially "money" had different physical forms, such as grain, silver, gold, or salt—material objects that had value in themselves.

   Act 1.0: representational. Money moves from the physical value of gold or silver to a representational value as a legal or social construct based on trust that economic actors will accept the representation as an agreed-upon form of payment.

   Act 2.0: commodity. Money becomes a market commodity. That happens when private banks begin to create money with the primary purpose of making a profit. While at first this injects much more money into the economy and thereby fuels growth and development, sooner or later the financial and the real economy begin gradually to decouple.

Act 3.0: regulated commodity. As a commodity, money turns into a vehicle for creating financial bubbles. The moment the bubble bursts, the real economy falters and everyone pays the price. The response to these crises are regulations such as the Glass-Steagall Act of 1933, which followed the stock market crash of 1929, and Basel III, which followed the market crash of 2007–08. The market deals with money as a regulated commodity. Regulations aim to ensure that the mistakes of the past don't repeat themselves. In that regard, they are effective. The shortcoming of most regulations is that they only look one way: into the past. They fix the problem of yesterday's bubble but are usually unable to anticipate the next bubble.

Act 4.0: intentional money for the realization of creativity. This act is still being written in the emerging history of money. It concerns the use of money to achieve *intentional collective creativity.* The history of money is a history of consciousness; that is, it's a story of increasing degrees of awareness and intention. Physical money (0.0) has its own intrinsic value. Representational money (1.0) receives its value through a social construct agreed to by the economic players. Money as a commodity (2.0) is even more intentionally used by some (the bankers) but unfortunately not by other participants in the economic process. Regulation (3.0) increases the number of stakeholders that intentionally co-shape the systemic use of money. The rise of the whole demand-side or Keynesian economy is a good example of this school of thought: making the systemic features of money work for the benefit of the whole. But still many players remain excluded from the process. Money 4.0, which does not yet exist, would maximize the capacity of all economic actors to shape the systemic use of money in a more intentional, collective, and creative way.

The main purpose of money 4.0 and capital 4.0 is to *relink the creation of money with entrepreneurial intention in our communities.* The function of all money and financial mechanisms is to serve the real economy—that is, to serve the well-being of all by opening a field of individual and collective creativity. Money and capital are enabling conditions in our economy for the creation of products and services that meet the needs of the community. But they are not products (or commodities) themselves. This means that we need to link their governance more intentionally to the evolution of our needs and systems. What types of money and financing do business and social entrepreneurs need? And how can we provide access to capital to all groups and creative people in society—particularly to the next generation of entrepreneurs?

The problem with Wall Street is not just that it requires more regulation, but that our banking institutions operate in an emerging 4.0 world with a 2.0 mindset and toolkit. The main problem is not the greed of some individual bankers but the design of the system. A twenty-first-century finance system needs to be designed according to principles of fairness, inclusiveness, transparency, and effectiveness for the real economy—none of which are part of the design of our financial systems today.

A 4.0 system would put these principles to work. The flows of money and capital would be redirected from the US$190 trillion bubble of profit-seeking capital into those sectors of society that today are underfunded—basically, the whole *regenerative* side of the economy: innovation, education, health, sustainability, and the environmental, social, and cultural commons.

Money 4.0 requires not just regulation, but an awareness of and connection to the evolving whole of a given economic system. Some first examples of a new breed of banks are Triodos Bank and GLS Bank, both in Europe, and BRAC Bank, in Bangladesh. Triodos and GLS Bank guarantee their customers that their deposits will be invested in ecological and social enterprises. One hundred percent of their loans are made public, for example on an interactive Google map, to create transparency. BRAC Bank, the third-largest bank in Bangladesh, was founded in 2001 with the purpose of serving the "missing middle," medium-sized enterprises that create desperately needed employment opportunities. These banks develop financial products that address key challenges of their society: financial tools for regenerative energy; loans for entrepreneurs who still operate primarily with cash; and phone banking systems that allow families in remote rural areas to efficiently receive cash transfers from relatives abroad. All of these innovations are examples of a financial sector in service of the real economy.

4. *Money does not equal money.* Any transfer of money is not only a technical act, but is also mirrored in the real economy through one of four actions:[41]

a. *Making a speculative transaction.* Speculative transactions keep money in the financial sector without moving it back into renewal of the ecological, social, or cultural commons. Speculation results in the creation of financial bubbles that, once they burst, hurt rather than help the real economy.

b. *Making a purchase.* Buying a good or service is an economic transaction that is clearly defined by time and location. When both sides agree to a transfer, the transaction is completed.

c. *Making a loan.* Using money to provide a loan has a different quality than a purchase. Will the borrower be able to repay the loan? What is the purpose of the loan? Has the borrower been successful in the past? Is there a market and need for the borrower's entrepreneurial idea? How long will it take? A loan (1) lengthens the time horizon of the transaction; (2) deepens the investigation into the person and how the money will be used; and (3) requires an assessment of the borrower's future capacity to repay the loan. This also indicates that a loan just for consumption makes only limited sense because the investment does not create any surplus.

d. *Making a gift.* Gifts of money are often overlooked in economic discourse. We give money to our kids by paying for their education, or to a charity. We do not expect a monetary return, but the gift enables others to actualize their potential. Gift money plays an important regenerative role in an economic system that is still not well understood.

From the viewpoint of the recipients, these four types of financial transactions create very different footprints in the real economy: (a) A speculative transaction tends to harm agents in the real economy in the long run once they end up paying the price of irrational volatility and depression after the bust. (b) In a purchase, the seller must deliver exactly what the customer wants, which gives the recipient a limited degree of freedom. (c) In a loan, the borrower is free to use the money to realize his or her entrepreneurial idea. (d) A gift enables the recipient to invest in the future without being limited by short-term profitability, the greatest degree of freedom. Contrary to conventional wisdom, gift money often generates the highest productivity over the long term because it allows recipients to radically sense and actualize the emerging future, rather than satisfying the expectations of funders or other stakeholders who tend to driven by viewpoints and indicators of the past.

The deeper structural problem of our financial crisis today falls into two categories. One, there is too much activity on level 1 money: the speculative sphere of *fictitious* value creation. And, two, there is too little activity on level 4 money: in the gift economy that could enable a new breed of entrepreneurs and social entrepreneurs to regenerate an economy with a social mission that works for all. In short: We need to move money from level 1 (the ego-sphere of speculation) to level 4 (the eco-sphere of societal renewal).

Economic theory rightly emphasizes the importance of investments and the structural importance of loans for innovation and entrepreneurship. But what is less well understood by economists today is the even higher productivity of the gift economy, as well as the toxic impact of an oversized casino economy that is driven by speculation instead of serving the development of the real economy. Remarkable exceptions, like Amartya Sen, Joseph Stiglitz, Juliet Schor, Paul Krugman, Raghuram Rajan, Riane Eisler, and Simon Johnson, confirm the rule.

This is what we call the co-creative eco-system economy; it includes continuous reinvestment of money from the financial sector into nonfinancial forms of capital formation, that is, natural, human, social, and cultural-creative capital. A better balance among these spheres of monetary activity lies at the heart of the 4.0 financial system.

SEEING OUR FUTURE: COLLECTIVELY CREATIVE CAPITAL

The ideas we have discussed here are not abstract ideals possible only in a distant future. They are already being practiced and experimented with in many places around the globe. Here are a few examples.

GLS Bank and Triodos Bank

Two European banks, as noted earlier, provide glimpses of an emerging 4.0 model of financial institutions: GLS Bank in Germany and the Dutch Triodos Bank, with branches in six European countries. Both banks provide financing to leading innovators in ecological and social businesses. Their innovative financial products serve entrepreneurs who are addressing urgent societal and economic challenges. These banks operate according to principles of the triple bottom line and transparency. Their depositor clients know what their money is used for and know that 100 percent of their deposits flow into ecological and social investments.

BRAC Bank

The development NGO BRAC is known by almost every Bangladeshi. Founded in 1974, it currently operates in ten countries globally. In Bangladesh, 5 million children have graduated from BRAC's 32,000 schools; its health program reaches 92 million people there; and since 1974 BRAC has built up a microfinance sector that serves all of Bangladesh as well as eight other countries. But it has realized that microfinance is not sufficient. For entrepreneurs to be successful and grow, they need loans that go beyond microfinancing. The founders of the NGO decided to establish BRAC Bank to serve this market segment not served by conventional banks, focusing primarily on making cost-effective larger loans that can be delivered in a standardized loan application process. This required BRAC Bank to invent a new business model that allows them to reach out to unbanked small businesses and entrepreneurs. It is these businesses that create new jobs, and with that address poverty at its root.[42]

Complementary Currencies

There is a largely ignored global movement around creating complementary currencies. Complementary currencies are local and regional currencies that complement a national (or regional) currency. One example is the Chiemgauer, a local currency started in 2003 in southern Germany to promote local commerce; it has 2,700 participants, including 750 businesses. Another is the local exchange trading (LET) system founded in the 1980s in Canada. There are similar systems in over fifteen countries. In Japan, a local currency called the *kurin* has about 570 participants.[43]

The main purpose of all these initiatives is to strengthen the local economy by creating a system that supports local and regional economic transactions. Only local businesses accept the currency; participants can barter their services in exchange for the currency; and because the currency is not accepted outside its region, there is an incentive to spend it faster than the national currency. The result is an increase in local transactions.

In 1932 a small town in Austria, Worgl, conducted a well-known experiment with complementary currencies. Confronted with hyper-inflation and high unemployment, the town's mayor, Michael Unterguggenberger, issued a local currency that citizens could use to pay for infrastructure projects and was accepted by local businesses. As a result, employment rose and the local economy stabilized. As this model started to be replicated in other towns, the central government intervened and banned the local currencies, claiming that only national governments could issue money.

Examples of complementary currencies that have been experimented with suggest that they work better the more they are embedded in a functioning local structure and the more the overall economy is in a state of crisis (as in 1932). Thus complementary currencies can be seen as an investment in the resilience of a system.

CONCLUSION: RECLAIMING OUR OWNERSHIP OF CAPITAL

The core economic challenge today lies in the gaping disconnect between the real and the financial economy. That disconnect originates in how we think about money and capital. The conventional wisdom conceives of money and capital in terms of four myths: (1) efficient financial markets are good for the economy; (2) capital is money; (3) money is a commodity; (4) money equals money. On the surface, each statement seems to make sense. And yet on consideration, each of them is dead wrong. What we need instead are:

1. new tools to monitor and measure a comprehensive economic and social impact across all four levels of money and its uses (speculat-

ing, purchasing, lending, and gifting) to increase transparency and
awareness on impact;

2. a concept of capital that relinks the actual creation of capital with
   its source: the collective creativity of all actors in an economic
   community;

3. a concept of money that debunks the commodity fiction and makes
   the creation of money transparent and aligned with the entrepreneurial intention in a community; and

4. a healthier balance among the four spheres of money-related actions,
   achieved by eliminating level 1 (the casino economy) and strengthening level 4 (the gift economy) in order to allow more people to tap and
   realize their full entrepreneurial potential.

A 4.0 economy would also relink the individual intentions of all actors
with a shared intention. Individual examples of financial institutions
that have begun to operate in this way do exist, but in the larger scheme
of things, they affect only a very small fraction of the total deployed
capital today. The Global Alliance for Banking on Values, a network
of twenty financial institutions that focus on relinking finance with a
shared intention for positive social change, sets a positive example.

4. Technology: Relinking Technology with Collective Creativity

All economic value creation involves the use of knowledge and technology. This is true for farming as well as for industrial and postin-
dustrial production. While technological tools have greatly improved
people's lives, in recent decades technological systems have also created
challenges.

THE JOURNEY FROM 1.0 TO 3.0: TOOLS, MACHINES, AND SYSTEMS

Technology evolves in waves (see table 3). The first wave came in the form
of tools (1.0). Humans developed tools that allowed them to improve on
what they could do physically with their own bodies. Simple examples
include the ax, shovel, plow, and knife.

The second wave of technology came in the form of machines (2.0). The steam engine, railways, and inventions in the textile and steel industries gave rise to a whole set of interrelated machines that fueled the first Industrial Revolution and replaced physical labor with coal-powered machines. These machines allowed levels of productivity to skyrocket.

The next wave came in the form of the second Industrial Revolution (oil-based energy, the combustion engine, the petrochemical industry) and changed manufacturing from individual machines to system-centric automated production. While individual machines still needed human operators, in the 3.0 world many operators were replaced by automation in the form of a mathematical algorithm. Today's automated production lines in car manufacturing plants are an impressive and intriguing example of this 3.0 wave of advanced manufacturing technology.

The imperatives of the industrial systems world, in the words of German sociologist Jürgen Habermas, started to "colonize the lifeworld," that is, people's *experience* of life and work.[44] The main thrust of 3.0 technologies is a system-centric view in which functional specialists control the key algorithms of the whole, and masses of users in these systems often feel disempowered and unable to change the basic specifications of the design. Think about the automated "customer service" systems of major companies that make you provide the same information four times before you're connected to a real person—*that's* how system-centric feels. Mass production and mass consumption penetrate all aspects of society.

Finally, the fourth wave of technological innovation is about to give rise to another Industrial Revolution that blends ICT (information communication technologies) with renewable energy, the smart grid, and awareness-based social technologies: a more human-centric turn in production and use. Just as 2.0 machines changed the dominance of 1.0 tools by being powered through energy, and 3.0 automated systems changed the dominance of 2.0 machines through the application of mathematical algorithms, we now see 4.0 technologies beginning to change the dominance of the old system-centric technologies.

We call this incipient fourth wave *human-* or *life-centric* technology because it is organized around empowering individual and collective human experiences: that is, around the core process of becoming aware and the actions that arise from it. Applied to technology, it means shifting the locus of technology invention from optimizing abstract systems to co-shaping a creative human process that leads to changing the experiences that people have with the system, with one another, and with themselves.

The real disruptive change has little to do with cloud computing or faster data processing, but is the shift from optimizing abstract systemic functions or "systemic imperatives," in the words of Habermas, to creating a *shared field of human awareness* that facilitates a new quality of entrepreneurship that *sources action from the emerging whole.*[45] We refer to this transformative journey as the U process.

Jeremy Rifkin refers to the convergence of ICT, biotech, nanotech, renewable energy, and the smart grid as the third Industrial Revolution.[46] Just as the earlier waves of technology created an economic sphere that mirrors and amplifies the mechanical (1.0), motoric (2.0), and systemic (3.0) functions of the human being, the focus of our current technological innovations seems to duplicate and amplify the cognitive and communicative functions (4.0). As we see connections strengthen between humans and machines and between machines and machines, a question arises: Where is this journey taking us?

WHY THE FUTURE DOESN'T NEED US

One scenario that has been discussed in this context is the one that the movie *The Matrix* popularized: a future ruled by machines. A few years after the *Matrix* trilogy came out, Bill Joy, then chief scientist at Sun Microsystems, reminded us in his brilliant article "Why the Future Doesn't Need Us" that rule by machines isn't just a movie fiction: "Our most powerful twenty-first-century technologies are threatening to make humans an endangered species." He continued: "The experiences of the atomic scientists clearly show the need to take personal responsibility, the danger that things will move too fast, and the way in which a process can take on a life of its own. We can, as they did, create insurmountable problems in almost no time flat. We must do more thinking up front if we are not to be similarly surprised and shocked by the consequences of our inventions."[47]

IN SEARCH OF 4.0

What would it take to move from technology 3.0 (system-centric) to 4.0 (human- and life-centric)? Here are four propositions as conversation starters.

1. *Debunk the liberation myth.* Not too long ago we were having serious conversations about what to do with all the free time given to us by new technologies in communication, production, and the household. If we had maintained the material consumption level of the 1950s, it would have taken only an eleven-hour workweek per person or employee to produce the output needed.[48] But our present reality is obviously quite different. Today our lives are more hectic than ever. Not only do we work more hours, but we have more trouble controlling our time. Every moment of the day is subject to interruption by several communication devices. Technology, it seems clear, doesn't just liberate. Consider the following thought, displayed on a poster that a friend from Indonesia shared with us: LIFE WAS MUCH EASIER WHEN APPLE AND BLACKBERRY WERE JUST FRUITS.

   Think of our attention and our ability to pay attention as the sacred space that we want to savor, protect, and cultivate because it is our well of strength and well-being. We know how much attention matters, given our earlier discussions in this book. So what is the current state of our sacred space? *Under attack!*

   We know that multitasking is a myth. When we multitask, we just shorten the amount of time we give to each task. Technology doesn't liberate. People do. We have to first change the mindset and awareness with which we put our technologies to work. If we use technology in a 4.0 environment but we operate with a 3.0, 2.0, or 1.0 mindset, then we simply continue to create a mess around us, and also within ourselves.

   Developing and using advanced technologies means that we need also to advance the inner awareness with which we deploy these technologies. If we can do that, then technology becomes a force of liberation. If we can't, we create a set of systemic imperatives and dependencies that create a system around us that eventually "doesn't need us," as Bill Joy put it succinctly.[49] Summing up: Whether technology is a force of liberation or a force of dependency depends on the inner place—the quality of awareness—from which we operate.

2. *Debunk the technology-fix myth.* Regardless of the societal challenge being discussed, one usually hears two responses or suggestions for dealing with it. One group suggests that throwing new technology at the problem will solve it. This is the "technology fix." The other group believes that technology may be necessary but is not sufficient and that deeper change is necessary. This deeper change includes transforming our thinking and awareness.

   Despite technology's many failures, the belief that it can magically solve our global and local crises around water, food, energy, health, and sustainability is as strong as ever. The wonderful appeal of the proposition that technology will fix the problem is that it sounds easy. The fix does not require that we address underlying issues or engage in a profound change process. Climate change? No problem! Let's just throw some geoengineering at it, like a global shield around the planet that will deflect the sun's rays away from the earth.[50]

3. *Relink R&D investments with pressing societal needs.* Today's global investments in research and development (R&D) are around US$1.2 trillion. The Gross Domestic Expenditures on R&D (GERD) indicator summarizes the R&D expenditures of business, government, universities, and nonprofit organizations. As might be expected, over 70 percent of GERD takes place in industrialized countries.[51] This has implications for the kinds of technologies and innovations that result from these investments. Urgently needed innovations that improve life in nonindustrialized countries are underresearched. Investments in R&D are driven by profitability expectations and/or by political decisions—military research, for example. Relatively little research is done on neglected diseases. Ninety percent of industrial production in the health sector concentrates on noncommunicable diseases, which are predominant in developed countries, rather than on tropical infections, for instance, in low-income populations living in nonindustrialized countries. This inequity creates the so-called 90/10 gap.[52] Neglected diseases are shunned by the pharmaceutical industry because the return on investment is so low.

4. *Lead the third Industrial Revolution.* Technology is one of the most powerful forces today. But what is the deeper nature of that force?

The twentieth-century German philosopher Martin Heidegger followed this question in his work. He noted that the root of *technology* goes back to the Greek word *techne,* meaning "art." Art is a realization of the creative process. Thus the source of technology leads us to the source of creativity. From that angle we can differentiate between two types of technology: technologies that are (from the viewpoint of the user) creativity-*appreciating* and technologies that are creativity-*depreciating.*

Following that distinction, the fundamental criterion for future public policy and public investment in technology could be this: Does the use of a specific technology *improve* or *stifle* our creativity? Are we, for example, turning users of technology into passive recipients of content that others produce, or are we empowering users of technology to co-create their own content and share it?

Does that distinction matter? Think about it. It puts into focus whether technology is appreciating or depreciating our reservoir of collective human and life creativity—which at the end of the day is the ultimate source of all forms of economic capital.

SEEING OUR FUTURE: UNLEASHING DISTRIBUTED COLLECTIVE INTELLIGENCE

Where do we see the seeds of the future? Here are a few examples.

Wikipedia

Wikipedia, which invites anyone to collectively co-create the encyclopedia, was launched in January 2001. During its first year, 20,000 entries were posted; three years later, the pool of articles exceeded 1 million in 100 different languages. Ten years after its founding, Wikipedia posted 19.7 million articles, and it has become the world's seventh most popular website.[53] Wikipedia decided in 2002 not to accept commercial advertisements; it chose a foundation as its legal form and relies on donations to maintain its operations. In one of its first fundraisers, in 2005, it raised US$94,000; in its 2011 fundraiser, it raised US$16 million.

Linux

On August 25, 1991, in Helsinki, Linus Torvalds was so frustrated with existing operating systems that he began to develop his own and announced this system with the following email and invitation:

> Hello everybody out there using minix—
>
> I'm doing a (free) operating system (just a hobby, won't be big and professional like gnu) for 386(486) AT clones. This has been brewing since april, and is starting to get ready. I'd like any feedback on things people like/dislike. . . . This implies that I'll get something practical within a few months, and I'd like to know what features most people would want. Any suggestions are welcome, but I won't promise I'll implement them :-)
>
> Linus (torvalds@kruuna.helsinki.fi)[54]

Twenty-two years on, the project he announced in his email has morphed into one of the most successful operating systems in the world and has revolutionized a billion-dollar industry. How did that happen? Linus's early decision to develop the whole process in an open-source format allowed all developers to use the code for all purposes (commercial and noncommercial), to adapt it to the users' specific needs, and to share their modified versions with the whole community. This approach allowed him to move from an email in 1991 to a collaborative global community of developers from most of the world's countries and cultures; a foundation orchestrates the evolution and cultivation of that global community.

What do these examples have in common? They no longer design and deliver products to users. Instead they create a platform in which a distributed community of users and developers co-create the content or products (apps) themselves. Users move from being recipients of products and services to becoming their co-creators, co-authors, and also co-users.

CONCLUSION: RECLAIMING OUR ACCESS
TO ENABLING TECHNOLOGIES

Throughout history, technology has morphed from a tool to a machine and from there to an automated system. Today we stand at the edge of the next jump in technological innovation, which may take us from system-centric technologies to human- or life-centric technologies that we can shape and give meaning to. If we succeed in making this leap, we will strengthen the use of creativity-enhancing technologies that facilitate co-sensing, co-creating, and co-using.

What does it take? It takes the formation of some intentional communities of creation, like the one that Torvald started with a simple email. To create these communities more often, more intentionally, and also more inclusively, we need supportive holding spaces and people. These communities of creation, once formed, might have a huge impact on this century's journey.

5. Leadership: Relinking Leadership with the Emerging Future

We all know what the absence of leadership looks like: We collectively create results that nobody wants. Unless we radically regenerate our leadership capacity today, none of the other topics discussed in this book will have any chance of being implemented.

THE JOURNEY FROM 1.0 TO 3.0: STICKS, CARROTS, AND NORMS

The essence of leadership has always been about sensing and actualizing the future. It is about crossing the threshold and stepping into a new territory, into a future that is different from the past. The Indo-European root of the English word *leadership, leith,* means "to go forth," "to cross a threshold," or "to die."[55] Letting go often feels like dying. This deep process of leadership, of letting go and letting the new and unknown come, of dying and being reborn, probably has not changed much over the course of human history. The German poet Johann Wolfgang von Goethe knew it well when he wrote, "And if you don't know this dying and birth, you are merely a dreary guest on Earth."[56]

But what *has* changed is the structure of the collective social body in which this process is enacted. As indicated in table 3, that social body has changed from a single-pyramid-type structure in which leadership is centralized and hierarchical (1.0), to a more decentralized multi-pyramid structure in which leadership happens through delegation and competition (2.0), and from there to a more participatory, relational, and networked structure in which multiple stakeholder and interest groups negotiate and engage in dialogue with one another (3.0). These are the three main vocabularies of leading and organizing today: centralization and hierarchy; decentralization and competition; and participatory-relational forms of networked stakeholder dialogue.

The problem is that none of these mechanisms is adequate for solving today's problems. The helplessness that many people feel is a symptom of this deeper issue: Our inherited leadership vocabulary is no longer fit to meet the challenges of our time. Climate chaos, food shortage, financial oligarchies, poverty—how do we respond to issues like these with the old organizational vocabulary?

Here is the hard truth: *We can't.* We need a new vocabulary to deal with the mess we are in today, and a new collective leadership mechanism that allows a diverse constellation of players to connect, co-sense, and co-create.

IN SEARCH OF 4.0

What would it take to develop a 4.0 leadership mechanism that could respond to the key challenges of our time at the "source" level?

There Is Only One Real Leadership Issue in the World

The primary leadership challenge today is the fact that our economic reality is shaped by globally interdependent eco-systems, while institutional leaders, by and large, operate with an organizational ego-system awareness. Most leadership issues can be boiled down to this one primary contradiction: We have an objective economic reality that works as a global eco-system, and then we have individuals and institutional leaders focused according to their institutional ego-system awareness. Consequently they consider the concerns of others to be externalities. The same problem is replicated inside institutions: Individual leaders attend to their individual targets (usually tied to bonuses) and ignore the well-being of the whole.

But what happens when the global eco-system reality meets a leadership that operates with an ego-system awareness? Pressing issues around the commons are not addressed. The results are summarized in the discussion of the three divides in the previous chapter.

How can we reconcile a reality that already operates in a 4.0 world (eco-) with a leadership awareness that is largely stuck in a 2.0 universe of thought (ego-)? That reconciliation is the essence of leaders' new work, which is to help our organizations and stakeholders to move from ego- to eco-system awareness in order to catch up with the reality of our globally networked world.

For companies, it is often NGOs that facilitate the process of extending awareness from the boundaries of the organization to the well-being of suppliers, partners, customers, and communities. Consider the case of Nike. When NGOs hit Nike with a public campaign against child labor in Asia during the 1990s, the company first reacted by telling the public that they weren't at fault; it was just an issue with their suppliers overseas and whether or not they met Nike's standards. Soon Nike management realized that a "not our job" response was not good enough to protect its main asset as a company—the Nike brand.

Nike had no choice but to treat its suppliers' problem as if it were their own. Nike managers had to extend their awareness and their management processes from the boundaries of their own organization (ego-system) to the extended global enterprise (eco-system).

Three Leadership Myths

Three pervasive leadership myths reinforce the mind-matter split that cements the status quo that we observe all around us. All of them sound like sensible propositions, but all of them send us in the wrong direction.

Myth 1: *The leader is the guy at the top.* Leadership challenges that institutions are facing today cannot be solved with this old understanding of leadership. In order to face today's leadership challenges, many, *many* people in the organization—sometimes *everyone*—need to be involved.

Myth 2: *Leadership is about individuals.* In fact, leadership is a *distributed* or collective capacity in a system, not just something that individuals do. Leadership is about the capacity of the whole system to sense and actualize the future that wants to emerge.

Myth 3: *Leadership is about creating and communicating a vision.* The problem with this myth is that it focuses primarily on broadcasting a message rather than on something much more important: *listening.* Listening is the most important gateway to co-sensing and co-creating the emerging future. The world is full of grandiose leadership visions that were beautifully communicated—before they crashed and burned. Think Enron, Lehman Brothers, GM, AIG, Goldman Sachs, and the Bush-Cheney-Rumsfeld vision leading up to the Iraq War. The problem was not a lack of vision. The problem was that the vision was completely out of touch with reality. The problem was a lack of listening.

All great leadership starts with listening. That means listening with a wide-open mind, heart, and will. It means listening to what is being said as well as to what isn't being said. It means listening to the latent needs and aspirations of all people.

The Missing Mechanism: Collective Sensing and Prototyping

To learn to listen collectively, we need co-sensing mechanisms that help leaders and users in a system across institutional boundaries to listen, see, and make sense of the current situation together. One way to engage in co-sensing is to go on learning or sensing journeys together. Another approach to collective sensing is to invite a representative group of stakeholders in the larger eco-system (the "extended enterprise") to engage in a collective process of sharing and dialogue.

The problem is not that people do not think about the larger eco-system or extended enterprise, but that we think about them in separate institutionalized silos. Most of us don't have a place that allows us to sense and think about the evolution of the larger eco-system *together.* It's these activities of co-sensing that activate the senses of the collective system. Without this collective activation through sensing, it is very rare that a shift to the deeper levels of the U will happen without an external shock.

What's also missing is a place to engage in practical prototyping experiments around exploring the future. Prototyping explores and evolves an idea by *doing.* The key mantra of prototyping can be found in the words of Dave Kelly, co-founder of the design company IDEO: "Fail early to learn quickly." You prototype an idea before you have fleshed it out completely. Prototyping is an experimental way of exploring and getting feedback from stakeholders in order to move forward.

The feedback continues the process of co-sensing and co-creating. A 4.0 stage of leadership requires a new set of enabling infrastructures that can support an eco-system to engage in co-sensing (sense-making), co-inspiring (connecting to source), and co-creating (prototyping) new possibilities together.

THE ESSENCE OF LEADERSHIP IS PRESENCING

The essence of leadership is about connecting, stepping into, and acting from the field of the future that wants to emerge. The question is, how do we do it? Where can we get guidance when we need to take a step forward? In 2005, Steve Jobs told the Stanford University graduating class how he dealt with this question: "You can connect the dots only by looking back. Not by looking forward." OK, you can't connect the dots by looking forward. But then where does your guidance come from? Jobs continued: "You've got to find what you love. . . . Your work is going to fill a large part of your life, and the only way to be truly satisfied is to do what you believe is great work. *And the only way to do great work is to love what you do.* If you haven't found it yet, keep looking. Don't settle."[57]

The *only* way to do great work is to love what you do, and to do what you love. Countless other entrepreneurs and innovators have confirmed this deep truth with their own life stories. But how we can create an institutional infrastructure that would allow us to operate from the same deep source on a collective systems level?

What we have learned is that the *inner* principle "do what you love and love what you do" needs to be complemented by an *outer* principle of deep immersion in the world, particularly a deep immersion in the marginalized edges of our world, with the practice of "always being in dialogue with the universe," as Alan Webber, the founder of the journal *Fast Company,* puts it. "The universe," says Webber, "actually is a helpful place. That means: Whatever the response you are getting, you look at it from the assumption that it wants to help you in some way." In explaining this important principle of all social entrepreneurship, Webber continues, "If you're open in relation to your idea, the universe will help you. It wants to suggest ways for you to improve your idea."[58]

What's necessary today is to lift up this deep entrepreneurial core process that Jobs and Webber talk about to the level of collective entrepreneurship, where the same process could happen on the scale of the whole system or eco-system. Jobs, for example, was a genius at inventing products and services that are in sync with our generation's aspirations and lifestyle. But he was not particularly empathic or innovative in improving the lifestyle or pay of the workers in China who produce the iPad and iPhone under harsh conditions and with minimal compensation. True 4.0 or eco-system leadership would focus on the well-being of all participants in an eco-system, not just a few of them.

SEEING OUR FUTURE

Working with people in different systems over the past eighteen years, we have learned that this process of helping diverse stakeholder groups in eco-systems to sense and actualize future possibilities requires new infrastructures or holding spaces for five critical process steps: (1) *co-initiating*, i.e., helping stakeholders in fragmented systems to connect and discover common ground; (2) *co-sensing*, i.e., helping people to walk in each other's shoes, to see the system from the edges, and to develop capacities for collective sensing; (3) *co-inspiring* through deep reflection practices and intentional moments of stillness that help us to connect to our deeper sources of knowing; (4) *co-creating*, or exploring the future through hands-on prototyping; and (5) *co-evolving*, or scaling and sustaining the new. There are many different methods and tools for providing these different holding spaces—but without these enabling conditions, very few useful things tend to happen on the level of fragmented larger systems.

6. Consumption: Relinking the Economy with Well-Being

Every economy has two main sources of value creation: the production and the consumption sides. All economic value creation *originates* in the quality of experience that we have as users, consumers, and citizens. Just as it is true to say that without nature there would be no economy, it is equally valid to say that without consumption all economic value creation would be worth nothing. The ultimate purpose of an economy is to meet the needs of its members.

This proposed primacy of the user/consumer experience in all matters of economic value creation contrasts sharply with the actual *asymmetry* of power that tilts the economic playing field heavily to the disadvantage of users, consumers, and citizens.

THE JOURNEY FROM 0.0 TO 3.0: FROM CONSUMERISM TO CONSCIOUS CONSUMPTION

Viewed from this angle, what does the journey of the economy look like? As we have already discussed, this journey has evolved through stages. In the 0.0 stage, economic activities were subsistence driven—that is, driven by the immediate needs of a local community. In 1.0, the production function began to differentiate through the Agricultural Revolution as production became more methodical and intentional.

In the 2.0 economy, the differentiation of the production function continued, resulting in the first Industrial Revolution. Mass production led to mass consumption. Professional advertising, sales strategies, and product design slowly became part of the industrial management process. In the 3.0 economy, we see the second Industrial Revolution, as well as marketing and branding moving into the mainstream of management, thereby giving rise to a global culture of consumerism that took material consumption to previously unknown levels of scale. At the same time, consumer rights movements grew and resulted in various regulations to protect consumers and their interests.

The journey from 1.0 to 3.0 created a civilizational model of mass consumption that currently uses 50 percent more resources than the planet can regenerate each year. Addressing this problem requires rethinking the roots of consumerism. In the words of the Uruguayan writer Jorge Majfud, "Trying to reduce environmental pollution without reducing consumerism is like combating drug trafficking without reducing drug addiction."[59] Which is, needless to say, a precise description of the US "war on drugs."

IN SEARCH OF 4.0

What would a 4.0 postconsumerism economy, one that would respond to our global challenges at the level of their source, look like? And how could we get from here to there, from 3.0 to 4.0?

Step 1 on such a journey is to debunk three more myths:

Myth 1: *Production and consumption are separate.* In this thinking, the economy is conceived of as a *value chain* that starts with product design and raw materials and ends with consumers. In between, a sequence of processes apply labor, machinery, and organization to raw materials and assemble an amazing array of products that are packaged and then shipped to distributors and customers. What is wrong with this picture? Isn't this what we see going on in factories?

Nothing is wrong. Except that the customer stands at the end of the process, and his or her needs don't mark the beginning of the production sequence. The difference between consumer needs being at the source or at the end of this whole sequence is the difference between 4.0 and 3.0. As long as the customer stands at the end of this process, the old industrial management thinking dominates, in which fixed capital investments such as machinery need to be kept operating in order to reap economies of scale. A steady flow of products is thus pushed into the market and down the throats of customers by billion-dollar marketing budgets that manipulate consumer attention with ever-increasing firepower (3.0). The consumer is a *target* of economic activity rather than a *partner* whose evolving needs are being identified and served.

If the customer is positioned at the end of the pipeline, and if the purpose of commercials and marketing that bombard her is to create wants rather than meet needs, these commercials are part of a materialistic onslaught that only increases production's ecological footprint without increasing true value for the customer and user base. However, if customers were positioned at the source of the pipeline, a shared assessment of their real needs, including the needs of the underserved, would mark the beginning of the entire process of value creation. The result would be a more level playing field between producers and consumers/users, and with that the opportunity for both groups to have an open, transparent, and inclusive dialogue—a common starting point for innovation and business development.

Myth 2: *Consumers are separate from one another.* Consumers, so the myth goes, are boxed into a rationality that maximizes individual gains without any regard for the interests of the larger community. To some degree, this myth describes societal reality. The ideology of consumerism that every citizen is exposed to by advertising has had an impact and reflects existing communication patterns. Consumerism has become part of the global mainstream culture of materialism today. But there is another emerging narrative that is worth noting, one that has not been scripted by the marketing industry.

This other story is about customers who are starting to co-create the economy in a more conscious, collective, and intentional way. This movement has deep roots that go back to the "taxation without representation" boycott of British trade goods in 1769 in Philadelphia, which started the American Revolution. Its roots also include Gandhi's boycott of British goods and his advocacy of homespun cloth, and the boycott, starting in the 1970s, of corporations that did business with the apartheid system in South Africa—a boycott that de facto launched the birth of the socially responsible investment movement. And they include the Fair Trade Movement, which was started in the early 1980s by conscious consumers around the world concerned about the well-being of people and the planet. That movement has changed business practices in many industries and continues today in various forms of conscious, collaborative consumption that we will discuss in more detail below.

In all these examples, we see a similar theme: Consumers have begun to extend their awareness of the ego-system (the well-being of oneself) to the eco-system (the well-being of all). Individuals are aware of the impact that their purchasing decisions have on producer communities that may be thousands of miles away. When the Fair Trade Movement began to eliminate the intermediaries between coffee producers in South America and coffee consumers in Europe, fair trade activists started to consciously redesign an economic system based on principles of transparency, inclusiveness, and fairness.

Today examples of a 4.0 consumer movement are emerging every-where: farmers' markets, slow or local organic food, community-supported agriculture (CSA), organic-fabric clothing, eco-tourism, urban agriculture, car sharing, zero-emission cars, and renewable energy. Instead of just boycotting a product, the 4.0 consumer makes informed and intentional choices to support and co-create economic processes that are more inclusive, sustainable, transparent, and collaborative.

Myth 3: *Material consumption creates well-being.* This statement sounds logical but is empirically questionable, as we know from our discussions in chapter 2. An increase in material consumption in developed countries does not translate into more well-being. Well-being originates with our experiences as users, consumers, and citizens. That experience is shaped by factors that are exterior (e.g., the products) and ones that are interior (the process of becoming aware). The interior process of becoming aware is what the late cognition scientist Francisco Varela focused on in his research when he described the processes of *suspending, redirecting,* and *letting go.* In the context of Theory U and presencing, we refer to this interior experience as the U process of opening the mind, the heart, and the will.

Thus, the strategy for enhancing our well-being without destroying the planet builds on reducing the flood of useless widgets and mindless commercials and increasing the capacity of the system to redirect resources to people's real needs, while strengthening their capacity to access their inner sources of well-being and happiness.

CLOSING THE FEEDBACK LOOP THROUGH ECONOMIC DIALOGUES

An economy that no longer separates (1) consumers from production, (2) consumers from one another (ego-system awareness), and (3) consumers from themselves (their sources of happiness) closes the feedback loop between consumers and producers (exploding myth 1), consumers and communities (exploding myth 2), and consumers and themselves (exploding myth 3). What would begin to emerge from this is an economy that is more transparent (by providing access to information), inclusive (by including all key players), and reflective (because the system can see itself).

For this shift to happen, the economy needs different patterns of communication, particularly between consumers and producers. The current communication model is unilateral, nontransparent, and linear. It is unilateral in that information flows only one way, as in the case of commercials. It is nontransparent in that access to information is restricted. It is linear because there is no feedback loop built into the system; the system cannot see itself.

But what is needed is a model of communication that creates missing links between the different actors in an economy. This model would be multilateral, which means that many parties could join the conversation. It would also be transparent by providing open access to information, and cyclical by allowing the group or the system to reflect on and see itself.

SEEING OUR FUTURE: THE POWER OF COLLABORATIVE CONSCIOUS CONSUMPTION

How do we see the 4.0 future of empowered, conscious, collaborative consumers emerging? There are four driving forces.

The first is *technology*. The World Wide Web continues to revolutionize the economy by providing easy access to information and thereby to a more level playing field. A combination of life-cycle analysis and digitized information will soon allow our cell phones to display the environmental footprint of products on supermarket shelves. This development will continue the megatrend toward transparency and could create easy-to-use metrics that help consumers make more informed and sustainable choices and connections. For example, www.renttherunway.com and www.couchsurfing.org are websites that connect unused resources in a community (clothing and accommodation, respectively) to unmet needs that other consumers have; they are places to make peer-to-peer exchanges.

A second driving force is *awareness:* More and more people have a desire to participate in lifestyles that are healthy, mindful, and sustainable. For example, in the United States this movement is referred to as LOHAS (Lifestyles of Health and Sustainability) and includes roughly one in four adult Americans—nearly 41 million people. That represents a US$290 billion market opportunity for goods and services focused on health, the environment, social justice, personal development, and sustainable living.[60]

A third driving force is the *increasing intensity of disruption and breakdown*. The more the old formal system is disrupted and moves toward collapse, the more we will see new patterns of connection and self-organized collaboration emerge. For example, in Indonesia after the financial crisis in 1997, numerous informal, local economy networks started to emerge.

A fourth driving force has to do with economic *human rights*. More and more people around the world find it unacceptable that we operate a US$60 trillion economy and yet are unable to reduce the number of people who live in poverty. The use of conditional cash transfers in South America is one step in a long journey toward economic human rights as the foundation of a future "global domestic policy," or *Weltinnenpolitik*.[61]

7. Coordination: Relinking the Parts with the Whole

Modern economies are based on a local, regional, and global division of labor. Over the past few hundred years, the division of labor has led to amazing productivity worldwide. But how do we coordinate and link all these individual activities in the context of an ever-changing whole?

As indicated in table 3, throughout economic history societies have coordinated their economic activities differently: (1) through centralized planning, (2) through markets, and (3) through negotiation/dialogue. These mechanisms gave rise to three stages of economic development:

1.0: Hierarchy and planning → rise of centralized economies
   (one societal sector)

2.0: Market and competition → rise of liberal market economies
   (two societal sectors)

3.0: Negotiation and dialogue → rise of social-market economies
   (three conflicting societal sectors)

Today we may be at the cusp of generating a fourth answer to the coordination problem, 4.0: awareness-based collective action (ABC), giving rise to an intentional market economy.

THE JOURNEY FROM 0.0 TO 3.0:
DEGREES OF SEPARATION

These four coordination mechanisms differ in how they connect to the economic actors that they coordinate. The structure of this relationship has been evolving, by and large, from exterior to interior, and from unaware to aware. Here is how:

1. In a centrally controlled economy, economic behavior is navigated through exterior mechanisms such as targets and plans (sticks).

2. In a market economy, economic behavior is navigated through the largely exterior mechanisms of price and competition (carrots).

3. In a social-market economy, the market is embedded in and navigated through negotiation, networks, and dialogue (norms), i.e., through mechanisms that are partly exterior and partly interior to economic actors and their awareness.

4. In a co-creative eco-system economy, the market is embedded in and navigated through the mostly interior mechanism of common awareness (ABC: action that arises from seeing the whole).

Thus the journey from stage 1 (central planning) to stage 4 (ABC) is a journey of increasing our degree of consciousness and interiorizing the whole. In stages 1 and 2, the well-being of the whole is mainly outside the consciousness of the individual actors, while in stage 4, the well-being of the whole is almost entirely interiorized in the consciousness of individual actors. Referring to our earlier discussions, we could also say: The journey from stage 1 to 4 is a journey of increased interiorization of externalities in the awareness of economic decision-makers.

Table 4 offers two dimensions for defining how a society coordinates itself: according to a primacy of the whole or a primacy of the parts. The evolution of economic coordination mechanisms began with 1.0, central planning (in the lower left quadrant). It moved from there to 2.0, markets and competition (in the lower right). Both the *visible hand* of central planning and the *invisible hand* of decentralized markets have one thing in common: They do not require the individual decision-maker to consider the well-being of the whole. If the individual or the organization meets the targets (of central planning) or pursues their own self-interest (in the market), then the visible or invisible hand will magically take care of the whole.

TABLE 4 Four Economic Coordination Mechanisms:
A Journey of Interiorizing the Whole

System Integration/ Degree of Interiorizing the Whole	Primacy of the Whole	Primacy of the Parts
High	4.0: ABC*: *head, heart, and hand (intentional)*	3.0: Negotiation and dialogue: *head, heart, and hand (ad hoc)*
Low	1.0: Central planning: *visible hand*	2.0: Markets and competition: *invisible hand*

* Awareness-based collective action.

That's what the theory said! In reality, the story unfolded somewhat differently—namely, with overwhelming externality problems. These circumstances prompted economic systems to evolve into the upper two quadrants, in order to operate from all three or four of them. Prompted by the global rise of the NGO sector, most economies have moved to include negotiation and dialogue among stakeholders as part of their de facto coordination mechanisms today.

The shift to the upper quadrants reflects a much higher degree of awareness of externalities on the part of individual decision-makers. It means creating holding spaces in which actors and decision-makers can *internalize* the impact that their decisions have on others and the state of the whole (externalities). In the case of negotiation and dialogue, the interiorizing of externalities is usually limited to some subset of the system, such as one's own network or interest group. Coordinating via ABC internalizes the externalities of the whole eco-system. For ABC to work, groups must open up and link their common interests (head), their collective action (hand), and their shared solidarity and empathy (heart). Negotiation and dialogue require essentially the same process but tend to be limited to parts of the system.

The struggles of Northern Europeans (especially Germans) to interiorize the externalities of their Southern European neighbors in the current euro crisis and vice versa, and the struggle of the white American middle class to extend the Social Security system to people of color and those without jobs (many of whom were left out of the New Deal of the 1930s) in the early twentieth century, are vivid examples. At the core of these struggles is the need to rethink our definitions of "we" and "them."

So which of these mechanisms represents good governance? None of them individually. Good governance would be the ability to activate and operate all four of these mechanisms as needed.

PASSING LIKE MESSI

Consider a seemingly simple example: a soccer team. How do you make eleven guys (or girls) play together as a team?

The 1.0 approach is to strictly follow the plan that the coach lays out before the match. But such an inflexible team would likely perform poorly against a good opponent. Switching to the 2.0 solution would give individual players more freedom to act on their own.

Let us take this idea to the extreme. Say that you assemble eleven of the best players in the world and hope that somehow their individual brilliance will add up to make them a fabulous team. We can all think of many instances in which that did not happen, such as the collapse of the Miami Heat in 2011 in the finals against Dallas (for the basketball fans among us). Or (no offense intended) the failures of the French and British teams in the 2010 World Cup tournament (for the soccer fans among us). All three teams had absolutely brilliant individual players. But they didn't succeed as teams.

When one realizes that brilliant individuals do not necessarily make a brilliant whole, the next step is to move to a different coordination mechanism, which we call 3.0. Here you allow for more creativity in your team; you allow parts of the team to form subgroups that pass the ball better and faster. But you also retain the team's standard positions and roles: defense, midfield, strikers.

Making 4.0 happen requires "blowing up" these traditional roles and ways of thinking. The 4.0 philosophy goes back to the concept of *total football,* which Rinus Michels developed when he coached for Ajax Amsterdam and the Dutch national team in the early 1970s. Both teams were powered by the same core group of players. The best and most famous player in that group, Johan Cruyff, moved on and signed with CF Barcelona in 1973. It was Cruyff who brought the philosophy of total football from Holland to Spain, from Ajax to CF Barcelona. Later, when he became the manager of CF Barcelona (1988–96), he evolved the philosophy of total football into what today is called tiki-taka soccer, which is the philosophy of the two current best teams in the world, CF Barcelona (which won foureen titles with its coach "Pep Guardiola" in four years, 2008–12), and the Spanish national team, which was the 2012 UEFA Euro and 2010 FIFA World Champion. Again, both teams are organized around the same core group of players and developed around the same core philosophy.

What sets CF Barcelona and the Spanish national team apart? It is a soccer philosophy that (1) uses a very methodical system that focuses on controlling the ball through a lot of one-touch or two-touch short-distance passing; (2) requires players to think in terms of the whole, not the parts (while focusing on the *uninterrupted movement* of the ball as the central coordinate of attention); (3) punctuates that one-touch passing with sudden bursts of creativity that open up deep spaces on the other side; and (4) operates as one team in which all players play (or can play) *all* the roles and positions (defense, midfield, and attack) as the ball constantly roams and reconfigures the coordinates of a living field.

This is the cutting-edge approach to soccer that all the runners-up and next-best teams (like the promising young German team, for example) are trying to emulate. It embodies a number of interesting 4.0 characteristics, including the shared awareness of an ever-evolving field of emerging possibility.

So while the best soccer teams on the planet are closing in on playing from a 4.0 type of shared awareness of the evolving whole, where is our global economy headed? Sadly, it is stuck at much earlier stages. The current economic situation reflects a system that reacts to 4.0 challenges with 2.0 or 3.0 responses.

IN SEARCH OF 4.0

What would it take to upgrade the operating system of our economy to 4.0? Here are four propositions to start this conversation.

1. *The antagonism of markets versus hierarchies is a myth.* Much of the twentieth century was wasted in a false discourse: markets versus

government, capitalism versus socialism. The complexity of the economic playing field and its developmental options was reduced to a discourse on "more markets" versus "more government." The Matrix of Economic Evolution depicts a gameboard of economic evolution and offers 390,625 possibilities, but we reduce the intellectual discussion to just two of these options.

2. *The answer to "either-or" is "both-and."* One of the mindsets that triggered the financial crisis in 2007–08 was the fatal "either-or" logic in economic thought that led to the mindless deregulation of the financial sector in the 1990s and 2000s. When we take a closer look at current economies, we see that we need both markets and governments.

Economies that are built on a "both-and" philosophy are stronger than ever. Examples include China, Singapore, South Korea, Brazil, Indonesia, and Germany and the other countries of Northern Europe. All of these countries came out of the 2008 crisis better and faster than many others. Their economies collaborate strategically across the sectors of government, business, and, in some cases, civil society. They have created multiple platforms of conversation where the strategic direction of the whole country or community is being discussed and strategized. When disruptive change hits, they tend to move together and cooperate more closely, rather than moving apart and deepening political divides.

3. *An economy is not a business.* There are at least two important differences between an economy and a business: (1) An economy cannot walk away from its community of citizens;[62] and (2) it has to internalize all of its externalities.

The traditional market idea argues that the goal of the corporation should be to maximize the financial bottom line while dumping all negative externalities onto others. Examples are Wall Street hedge funds and most of the financial services companies. Corporations acquire other companies in order to maximize profits. This might entail selling valuable assets at high profit margins, downsizing what remains, and leaving the social security costs to the government, and with that to society. An economy needs a different leadership than a company does, a leadership that owns and is fully accountable to reducing negative and increasing positive externalities.

4. *ABC closes the feedback loop between parts and whole.* The evolutionary threshold we are facing with capitalism today concerns the birth of a new coordination mechanism, one that complements the existing three mechanisms (hierarchy, markets, and negotiation) and builds the capacity of the whole system to see, sense, and regenerate itself. We call this new capacity ABC—awareness-based collective action—because it arises from places that facilitate the capacity of the system to see itself, to sense what wants to emerge, and to explore the future by doing (prototyping).

Where do we have spaces in our societies today where the key players in our economic eco-systems can come together to see, sense, and regenerate themselves? We are missing such spaces. It is an important institutional blind spot. We don't even create a space where we, as a whole society, make shared sense of current reality. We have *lots* of spaces for individual sense-making and strategizing. All organized interest groups come up with their own sense-making inside their own institutional silos. But we don't have places for co-sensing, for uncovering common sense and common will.

SEEING OUR FUTURE: ABC

The 4.0 economic revolution is all around us. It is the direction that we are heading, and it can be witnessed in many living examples today, not only on the soccer field.

But the problems are that (1) many of these initial examples are spontaneous rather than intentional; and (2) they tend to be micro or meso rather than macro and mundo, as we will discuss in more detail in the concluding part of the book.

One example of ABC coordination in action comes from Ohio. The introduction of checklists has been an innovative method to reduce mistakes and malpractice in hospitals. Just as airplane pilots do before takeoff, surgeons and the surgical team use checklists before performing a procedure on a patient. Research shows that the introduction of checklists in hospitals at first lowers the risk of mistakes, but gradually the error rate returns to near its former level. Noticing that pattern, Dr. Marc Parnes, an OB/GYN surgeon in Ohio, devised a different practice. Instead of using a checklist, he converses directly with the patient as she is rolled into the procedure room. They have a quick, personal "check-in conversation" that includes the patient and the entire operating team. Surprisingly, this check-in practice reduces the rate of errors in a more sustainable way than the simple checklist practice did.[63]

We consider this example highly interesting and relevant, since it literally *pulls away the cover* that is blocking the capacity of the *system to see itself*. The system in this case is everyone in the operating room, including the patient. When the system sees itself, it facilitates a conversation that lets each member of the group see the situation through the eyes of others, including the patient. Creating this awareness and seeing the system through the eyes of other stakeholders are key leverage points in all profound systems change.

8. Ownership: Relinking Ownership with the Best Societal Use

As economies develop, the structure of ownership rights also evolves. This has become especially visible with the development of the Internet. Open-source Wikipedia, or the creative commons with its new copyright model,[64] clash with legislation such as SOPA (the Stop Online Piracy Act) and PIPA (the Protect IP Act). Ownership is a bundle of rights and responsibilities. Like all matters of rights, ownership rights rise, evolve, and change in their social context as a function of their *legitimacy*. All legitimacy emerges from a felt sense of fair balance between rights and responsibilities among people in a community.

THE JOURNEY FROM 0.0 TO 3.0: OPEN ACCESS, STATE, PRIVATE, MIXED, AND COMMONS

Property rights are a bundle of rights and responsibilities that are legally enforceable. These rights include (1) access, (2) use, (3) management, (4) exclusion, and (5) alienation (the right to sell). These five elements can be viewed as five sticks in a bundle of ownership rights. Ownership can be viewed on a spectrum: One end of the spectrum holds just one stick (one right) and all five sticks are at the other end. All of these rights may be held by single individuals or by collective entities. Table 5 depicts how ownership forms have evolved from open access to state, private, mixed, and common ownership structures.

TABLE 5 Evolution of Property Rights by Economic Stage

Economy	Property Rights	Types of Goods	Bundle of Rights and Responsibilities	Institutionalization
0.0	Open access	Common pool resources: ocean fisheries, atmosphere (nonexcludable, rival)	No property rights	Communal ownership
1.0	State property rights	Public goods: national defense (nonexcludable, nonrival)	Property rights assigned by state	State ownership: four-year election cycles
2.0	Private property rights	Private goods: food, clothing, housing (excludable, rival)	Private property rights can be exchanged by market (access, use, management, exclusion, and right to sell)	Private ownership: quarterly results
3.0	Mixed (public-private) property rights	Mixed goods (public-private): eco-system services (excludable, nonexcludable, rival)	Mixed property rights that are managed and in part exchanged by markets (access, use, management, exclusion, and right to sell)	Mixed-stakeholder ownership (organized interest groups)
4.0	Commons-based property rights	Common goods: fisheries, eco-system services (nonexcludable and rival)	Property rights are jointly controlled by trust-based co-owners, stakeholders, and trustees (access, use, management, exclusion, and shared cultivation)	Shared eco-system ownership (trustees representing the whole system, including future generations)

In 0.0 economies, most assets were shared by the whole community, but a few assets were considered private property. Examples of shared assets include *common pool resources* such as air quality, ocean fisheries, and the *Allmende,* a German word for the local areas that were used collectively by villagers for agriculture. Regional forms of collectively used space such as the *Allmende* continue to exist in many rural areas worldwide, including in Europe.[65]

In 1.0 economies, more formalized property rights, such as those assigned to states or private entities, emerged. Examples of state property include national parks in the United States. The state emerged as an important economic player, particularly in regard to the production of *public goods.* Examples of public goods are national defense and IT infrastructures like the World Wide Web. The key characteristic of public goods is that they are accessible to all (nonexclusive) and that their consumption by one person does not reduce their benefit to someone else.

In 2.0 economies, we saw a profound shift to the primacy of *private ownership.* Private ownership has existed in all stages of economic and social development. But never before had it been the primary property concept framing much of public policy and economic development thought. The success story of private ownership happened in two waves. The first wave was based in the ancient *occupation theory* of ownership and was originally articulated by Cicero during the Roman Empire. This theory dominated the understanding and debate over private property in Europe almost up to the Industrial Revolution. Here are the cornerstones of that view: The world was given to all men in the first place, and whoever is the first to claim ownership holds the legal right (prima occupation), and with that the protection of the state. The main principles of this view include: (1) a starting point in which all men share common ownership of all property; (2) first occupation, which defines the right of individual ownership; (3) private ownership, which includes the social responsibility to provide for those who come later and have less; and (4) the state is permitted to intervene in the ownership of private property only when the well-being of society is at risk.[66]

The occupation theory paradigm was challenged by John Locke with the publication of his "Second Treatise of Government" in 1689. Locke introduced what was later referred to as the *labor theory* of property.

Locke's main argument is that man owns his own body and consequently the fruits of his labor. This idea transformed several cultural assumptions. Whereas earlier the accumulation of wealth had been criticized as greed, under the labor theory wealth was viewed as God's reward for men's work. The labor theory of property also created the underpinnings for the argument that poverty is the result of laziness. It thus weakened the ability of the state to intervene in private property rights for the well-being of society as a whole.

Private property rights became a success story throughout the era of the first and second Industrial Revolutions. Yet, as discussed earlier, successful growth and the accumulation of material wealth came at the expense of negative externalities in the form of poverty and environmental overshoot. The societal response to these negative externalities resulted in a set of institutional innovations that reflected the interests of other stakeholders (examples include social security, public education, environmental legislation, building codes, and public-private partnerships).

Yet none of these Economy 3.0 innovations could prevent what we are facing today: the three major divides that have emerged directly from the tragedy of the commons, which could also be called the tragedy of common pool resources.[67] These common pool resources include ecological commons such as water, topsoil, clean air, energy, and seed; social commons such as trust, software, and social networks; and cultural commons such as knowledge, wisdom, and learning infrastructures.

The crisis of our time is a crisis of our commons. The three divides reflect a massive attack on our commons through a host of unintended negative externalities that the current design of property rights facilitate. Creating a 4.0 economy requires us to rethink and update the essence of property rights.

In a twenty-first-century networked society where value is emerging from distributed relationships among people, what good does it do to ground property rights in a highly individualistic theory that reflects seventeenth-century British society rather than the twenty-first-century global world? Today we need to continue the success story of private property rights by taking it to the next evolutionary stage: a new class of commons-based property rights that hold trustees and multiple stakeholders accountable as stewards of the well-being of the eco-system and future generations of users.[68]

IN SEARCH OF 4.0

Let us launch the 4.0 ownership conversation by considering the following propositions.

All Ownership Forms Are Socially Constructed

All ownership forms are socially constructed and hence contingent on a felt sense of legitimacy. In the world of Locke, characterized by small populations, small-scale individual production, and seemingly unlimited resources, it made complete sense to think in terms of individual private property rights. In the twenty-first-century world, with seven billion people, massive distributed networks of co-creative production, and collaborative consumption, as well as increasing resource scarcity and a depleted set of commons, we have entered an era when insisting on the primacy of individual property rights is outdated and in conflict with the real needs of our time.

There is a growing recognition that any form of private property rights should also include responsibilities to other stakeholders that might be affected by negative externalities of the goods or services at issue. For example, one of the primary founding principles of the German Constitution *(Grundgesetz)* states: "Property entails obligations. Its use shall also serve the public good."[69] This is an example of a constitutional attempt to balance private property rights with the well-being of the society as a whole. But what we haven't seen yet is a real strengthening of commons-based property rights that could spark a third Industrial Revolution featuring co-creative production and collaborative consumption, just as individual property rights sparked the first and second Industrial Revolutions.

Two main myths have locked the understanding of property rights in what are now outdated tracks of thought:

Myth 1: *Only private property rights are efficient; other forms are not.* Yes, it is true that private property rights have been a huge success story and remain an integral component of the rise of modern capitalism 2.0 and 3.0. But it is not true that all other forms of property rights are ineffective. Three examples suggest a reevaluation of the primacy of individual private property rights: (1) the economic success of China, where a majority of the GDP is produced by state-owned companies;[70] (2) Germany, which bounced back from the 2008 crisis more quickly than other countries because companies, the government, and unions worked closely and collaboratively; and (3) the general decline of our global ecological commons, which reflects a lack of property rights that would create transparency and accountability for the overuse of scarce resources.

Myth 2: *There is no third form of ownership.* A second myth is that public and private are the only two forms of ownership and that there is no third form. In fact, much of the discourse of the past few decades has been shaped by an unholy alliance of special-interest groups that have used the interplay of state and private property rights to disenfranchise local communities from their commons-related de facto ownership rights. For example, farmers in developing countries have become dependent on genetically engineered hybrid seeds that no longer reproduce. What used to be a community-owned commons, seeds, was declared a public good (owned by the state) and then turned into a private good (owned by multinational companies like Monsanto). And before they knew it, millions of farmers in India and other places could no longer use their traditional practices of sharing and reproducing seeds because Monsanto had secured the patents on copies of local seeds. What used to be a cultural and economic practice (seed sharing among farmers) was illegal and could be prosecuted, leaving the farmers with a bad choice between economic dependence on Monsanto's GMO seeds and breaking the law, resulting in the major driver of what has been called the single largest wave of recorded suicides in human history, with 250,000 Indian farmers killing themselves over the past 16 years. This was referred to as "genetically modified genocide" by the press in India, but the Western press, particularly in the United States, continues to turn a blind eye to it.[71]

We Need Commons-Based Property Rights

In his book *Capitalism 3.0,* Peter Barnes suggests creating a third category of commons-based property rights that would augment existing state and private property rights. Commons-based property rights would be institutionalized through trusts and trustees accountable to all stakeholder groups in the eco-system, including future generations, to act as stewards of the whole. While financial benefits would go to the government in the case of state ownership and to shareholders in the case of private ownership, in the case of the commons the payoff would go to all citizens in the affected communities, providing, in effect, a "citizen dividend."

A feature of trust-based community property rights is that they don't operate like a company, which tends to be driven by profits over the short term, or like a government, which tends to be driven by special interests over the short and medium term (such as the run-up to the next election). A trust and its independent trustees are accountable for the long-term sustainability of the specific commons that they manage for the next generation.[72]

Shared Ownership Is Rising

There are many examples of trusts and other forms of shared property rights. Access to and use of the Internet is an example that has become an essential part of our daily life. Emerging forms of ownership rights compose a global movement with many faces that is not yet even fully aware of itself. This new breed of 4.0 sharing-based ownership is disruptive to the old ways of doing business. As Mark Levine writes in the *New York Times,* "Sharing is to ownership what the iPod is to the eight-track, what the solar panel is to the coal mine. Sharing is clean, crisp, urbane, postmodern; owning is dull, selfish, timid, backward."[73]

Along those same lines, author Rachel Botsman says, "I don't want stuff, I want the needs or experiences it fulfills! This is fueling massive shift, where usage trumps possession. I believe it will be referred to as a revolution, so to speak, when society, faced with great challenges, makes a seismic shift from individual getting and spending toward the rediscovery of collective good."[74]

Here are a few examples of the early stages of that seismic shift. Zipcar, a car-sharing service founded in 2000 in Cambridge, Massachusetts, had 670,000 members in 2012. Netflix, founded in 1997, allows its 23 million members to share access to DVDs. Zimride is a social network for ride-sharing at MIT that allows students, employees, and faculty to coordinate shared car rides. At "Powershopping Parties" in Germany, women swap clothes at parties of eight hundred or more. More and more consumers are moving from buying to "using"; Botsman calls this phenomenon collaborative consumption.[75]

Says Robert Henrich, CEO of Daimler's Car2go, a car-sharing company that operates in Vancouver, British Columbia; Austin, Texas; Washington, DC; San Diego; Amsterdam; Vienna; Lyons; and Hamburg, Dusseldorf, and Ulm, Germany, "In the beginning, especially young people wanted to try this out. [Now] all groups of society participate. Students, employees, self-employed, entrepreneurs, seniors."[76] In all of these examples, instead of owning a car, a DVD, or a tool, users share that resource.

Community-owned urban agriculture is also on the rise. The United Kingdom–based Landshare project connects people who have yards but no time or interest in using them with people who want to grow food. Launched in 2009, and with 71,000 members three years later, Landshare combines the concern for producing food locally with the creation of a social network. An interactive map and website create a network of local growers. Members are individuals and families as well as schools and retirement homes.

Taking this idea to a different level, the town of Todmorden in West Yorkshire has set a goal to become self-sufficient in vegetables, orchard fruits, and eggs by 2018. It has carrots in front of the police station, raspberries, apricots, and apples on the canal towpath, blackcurrants, redcurrants, and strawberries beside the doctor's office. Citizens are encouraged to harvest what they want. All produce is free.[77] Todmorden has inspired other towns to join the Incredible Edible model, which not only produces free local products, but also has fostered a new sense of community within the town. Interface, an Atlanta-based manufacturer of carpets, retains the ownership of its carpets and for a monthly fee maintains its products in the clients' location. This service, combined with a system in which Interface replaces (and recycles) worn-out carpet tiles, reduces the need to replace carpets by up to 80 percent.

The 4.0 forms of shared ownership do not stop at the level of products or resources. Shared ownership is also being applied to what in capitalism seems to be the crown jewel of all assets: industrial capital.

Case in point: The global automotive supplier Bosch has more than 350 subsidiaries in more than 60 countries and employs over 300,000 people worldwide; it had revenues of approximately €51.4 billion in 2011. Ninety-two percent of its ownership is held by the Bosch Foundation, a charitable foundation that receives a portion of the dividends.

Another model comes from employee-owned corporations where ownership is distributed and held by those who work for the company. The Mondragon Corporation is a corporation and a federation of worker cooperatives based in the Basque region of Spain. In 2011 it employed 83,000 people, with a revenue of €14.7 billion. The Mondragon cooperatives operate with a highly participative culture and business model, which have made it possible to develop a whole eco-system of collaboration that includes 256 different cooperative companies. The cooperatives are owned by their worker-members, and power is based on the principle of one person, one vote.[78]

In total, one billion people are involved in cooperatives as members-customers, as employees-participants, or as both. In 2008 the 300 largest cooperatives created a revenue of US$1.6 trillion, which is comparable to the GDP of the ninth-largest world economy.[79]

And, last but not least, the Internet has more than 2.1 billion users, almost a third of the earth's population. Without centralized governance, the Internet has two operating principles: (1) the Internet Protocol address space; and (2) the domain name system. The Internet Engineering Task Force (IETF), a nonprofit organization of loosely affiliated international participants that anyone may associate with by contributing technical expertise, standardizes the core protocols (IPv4 and IPv6).[80]

SEEING OUR FUTURE: RECLAIMING THE OWNERSHIP AND STEWARDSHIP OF OUR COMMONS

The evolution from open access to state, private, and mixed forms of ownership and from there to commons-based property rights is at the heart of our current global transformation. While we are seeing the emergence of many spontaneous forms of collaborative commons and distributed ownership, we also cannot ignore the profound impact of the three divides that will hit our societies in the next few decades. They will lead to major disruptions that will require us to rethink the design, from scratch, of property rights in our mainstream institutions and systems. It will not be sufficient to experiment with new forms of property rights on the outskirts of the system; we will be required to rethink and rebuild ownership rights in all mainstream systems that affect the regenerative capacity of our commons.

The current crisis of capitalism is a crisis of our outdated 2.0 and 3.0 frames of economic thought, which conceive of nature, work, and capital as commodities. Our belief in this commodity fiction allowed us to easily accumulate capital and organize industrial labor, and then, in fewer than two hundred years, to burn through almost all the fossil fuel that our planet had accumulated over millions of years.

If everything is a commodity, then I can take it, sell it, use it, dump it, and buy another one. And that is exactly what happens. Private property rights are brilliant in the case of commodities and less-distributed systems. But when they are applied to complex and distributed commons, they have a lot of baggage.

The ecological divide (overshoot), the social divide (inequity and poverty), and the spiritual-cultural divide (depression) emerge directly from the model of economic thought that frames the earth, human beings, and money as commodities. But the earth is not a commodity, and human beings aren't, either. We did not create the earth; it was given to us. Instead of just "take, make, sell, use, and dump," our role is to be good stewards who pass what has been given to us on to the next generation in the same or better condition as the one in which we received it.

We are at a turning point in history where the continued negative externalities that we collectively enact can no longer be absorbed by our surrounding ecological, social, and spiritual eco-systems. We are beginning to hit a wall, and the way we know this is the increasing rate of disruptions that we are facing as a global society. The present time is a profound moment in our evolutionary path: We can either wake up and redirect ourselves, or we can ignore what's going on and stay on a collision course that will cause catastrophic failures affecting billions of people just in our lifetime.

This is what is at stake when we consider the evolution of our economy and of economic thought.

Conclusion and Practices

This chapter focused on illuminating the blind spot that underlies the eight structural disconnects discussed in chapter 2. What is it that keeps us reenacting these structural disconnects? It is the outdated frames and paradigms of economic thought that decision-makers keep operating from.

We inquired into the evolution of the eight key concepts of economic thought that underlie the disconnects discussed in chapter 2: nature, labor, capital, technology, leadership, consumption, governance, and ownership. What we found throughout this reconstruction of economic thought is that each of these core concepts has gone through the same journey (see table 3). It is a journey that redefines the essence of these core concepts according to the meta-journey of economic thought that has moved through the paradigms of communal (0.0), state-centric (1.0), free-market (2.0), and stakeholder or social-market (3.0) thought, and that going forward might evolve into an intentional eco-system economy that creates well-being for all (4.0). This journey through various economic paradigms can be told as a tale of the movement of human consciousness from traditional (1.0) and ego-system awareness (2.0) to stakeholder (3.0) and eco-system awareness (4.0).

Summing up, the evolution of economic thought and our economy follows the evolution of consciousness. The essence of the new economy is to transform economic thought from ego-system awareness to eco-system awareness. Throughout this chapter, we exemplified this transformation for our eight issue areas or, to use another term, acupuncture points. The story of these acupuncture points is basically a story of going beyond the commodity fiction of land, labor, and capital in order to develop better and more intelligent ways of stewarding the commons and redirecting financial capital into the real sources of individual and collective entrepreneurship, creativity, and well-being.

JOURNALING QUESTIONS

Use table 6 as a mini-version of the Matrix of Economic Evolution (table 3) in order to assess your organization through the following five steps.

TABLE 6 Organizational Assessment

	Nature	Labor	Capital	Technology	Leadership	Consumption	Coordination	Ownership
1.0	Resource	Serfdom	Human	Tools	Authoritarian	Traditional	Central planning	State
2.0	Commodity	Commodity	Industrial	Machines	Incentives	Consumerism	Markets and competition	Private
3.0	Regulated commodity	Regulated commodity	Financial	System-centric automation	Participative	Selective conscious consumption	Networks and negotiation	Mixed
4.0	Eco-system, commons	Entrepreneurship	Cultural, creative	Human-centric	Co-creative	Collaborative conscious consumption	ABC: Awareness-based collective action	Commons: shared access

1. In each row, check one box (1.0, 2.0, 3.0, or 4.0) that best represents the currently dominant operating model in your organization and context.

2. Then draw a *current reality line* that links all the boxes that you checked.

3. What would be the most appropriate operating model for the future work that needs to happen to address the big challenges of the next decade or two? In each row, check one box, this time using a different color.

4. Now draw the *emerging future line* by connecting the second set of checked boxes with the second color.

5. Compare both lines, the current reality line and the emerging future line. Do they differ, and if yes, where, and what does it mean?

CIRCLE CONVERSATION

1. After completing the tasks above individually, have each member share with the group what the answers might mean going forward.

2. What interesting prototypes can you think of for exploring 4.0 types of operating models in the context of your own work and life right now?

4

Source: Connecting to Intention and Awareness

This chapter talks about the deepest level of the "current reality iceberg," which we call the Source level or the level of intention and awareness. The visible level of an iceberg is the area above the waterline. We equate this with "surface symptoms" in a society (see chapter 1). Beneath those visible symptoms are structural disconnects that give rise to the systemic limits that we are hitting as a global civilization today (see chapter 2). In chapter 3, we looked at the paradigms of economic thought that lead to these structural problems, which we summarized in the Matrix of Economic Evolution (see table 3). This chapter explores the source level of social reality creation—how to connect to the source of the future that is wanting to emerge.

The Blind Spot III: Source

In 1996, our MIT colleague and friend Peter Senge told us about a conversation he had had with the Chinese Zen master Huai-Chin Nan, also called Master Nan, in Hong Kong:

> In China he's considered an extraordinary scholar because of his integration of Buddhism, Taoism, and Confucianism. I asked him if he thought that the industrial age was going to create such major environmental problems that we would destroy ourselves and whether we had to find a way to understand these problems and change industrial institutions. He didn't completely agree with that. It wasn't the way he saw it. He saw things on a deeper level, and he said, *"There's only one issue in the world. It's the reintegration of mind and matter."* That's exactly what he said to me, "the reintegration of mind and matter."[1]

When those words had penetrated my mind, I (Otto) felt as if they had pierced a veil that had kept me from seeing reality more deeply. In a flash I visualized a social field that on its surface displayed the current symptoms of societal pathology, and beneath the surface contained the deeper sources from which these symptoms arose.

What if all symptoms at the surface level were a function of a split on a deeper level, which for now we are calling "the source"?

What does "reintegration of mind and matter" mean when we are talking about the social field, the levels of collective behavior that we enact as a global community? Does it mean reintegrating "action" and "awareness" in order to address the challenges of our time? Does it mean that we need to close the feedback loop among outcomes, action, and thought on the level of whole systems?

A Conversation about Mind and Matter

Three years later, in the fall of 1999, I had the opportunity to interview Master Nan in Hong Kong. He said that the twentieth century lacked a central cultural thought that unified society and life, and he saw the world sinking ever more deeply into a technology- and money-driven materialism. He also saw the beginnings of a new spirituality. He said: "It will definitely go this way, spiritual. But this path will be different from the spiritual path of the past, either in the East or in the West. It will be a new spiritual path. It will be a combination between natural science and philosophies." But this new spirituality, he thought, would still be deeply connected to the deeper dimensions of our humanity: "It will always go back to some of these questions. What is the purpose of life? What is the value of life? Why do we exist?"

Later that day I learned from his students that Master Nan had just published a reinterpretation of Confucius's "Great Learning" essay, one of two central texts in Confucianism. In its commentary, Master Nan points out that leaders, in order to do their best work, have to learn to access seven states of leadership awareness. The central section of the "Great Learning" essay reads like a U-in-action process from macro to micro and then back:

> The ancients who wished to illustrate illustrious virtue throughout
> the world, first ordered well their own States.

Wishing to order well their States, they first harmonized their
  families.
Wishing to harmonize their families, they first cultivated their
  persons.
Wishing to cultivate their persons, they first rectified their hearts.
Wishing to rectify their hearts, they first sought to be sincere in
  their thoughts.
Wishing to be sincere in their thoughts, they first extended to the
  utmost their awareness.
Such extension of awareness lay in the investigation of the
  underlying matrix of mind and matter.

The underlying matrix of mind and matter being investigated,
  awareness becomes complete.
Awareness being complete, thoughts then become sincere.
Thoughts being sincere, hearts then become rectified.
Hearts being rectified, persons then become cultivated.
Persons being cultivated, families then become harmonized.
Families being harmonized, states then become rightly governed.
States being rightly governed, everything under heaven then comes
  in balance.[2]

While Confucianism is often understood to emphasize good follow-
ership and not fighting authority, Master Nan claims that this is not how
"The Great Learning" should be interpreted. "The important part is to
actually understand yourself, understand your opening process."

The Tao of Leadership

Later that day we reconvened around a large dinner table, joined by a
dozen of his students. With delicious food coming and conversations
going, people were chanting, meditating, laughing, smoking, drinking,
and talking about cultivation practices, science, and topics as far-ranging
as research on the feelings of plants.

With the help of my translator, Professor Zhao, I tested with Master
Nan my understanding of what I had heard him saying in the afternoon.
I summarized and partly extended what he had shared with me by saying
that the blind spot of the twentieth century was related to our inability to

see the process of *coming-into-being* of social reality or, in different words, our inability to understand where our actions originate. Usually we perceive social reality around us as a thing, as something that is outside and separate from us. The blind spot means that we do not see *ourselves* bringing forth social reality in the first place, and with that we do not have an understanding of how our individual awareness and intention impact social reality around us. In order to illuminate this blind spot, we have to practice the seven meditational states of leadership that Master Nan identified in his new interpretation of "The Great Learning."

Master Nan agreed with this interpretation. After that, I kept asking different versions of the same question—namely, where does this stream of social reality creation really originate? Master Nan responded that the source is "the mind and thought." But I kept asking: "Where do mind and thought originate?" Master Nan responded by talking about different levels of consciousness and self. My final question concerned the sources of self: "Where do the self and the Self originate?," with the capital-S Self indicating our highest potential.

"The small self and the big Self come from the same source," responded Master Nan. He continued:

One origin for both of them. The whole universe is just one big Self. Religious people call it God. Philosophers call it the fundamental nature. Scientists call it energy. Buddhists call it the Atma. Chinese call it the Tao. The Arabs call it Allah. So every culture, in a sense, they know there's something there, an ultimate something. Religious people, they just personalize this. Make him like a person, like a God. Okay, so this God is supernatural, has all these super capacities, et cetera. That's religion. Philosophers use logic to analyze it. Scientists want to uncover or try to find the big Self in all of this, you know, the physical research, et cetera. If you really look at human culture, they say it starts with religion and then people begin to have doubts about religions, and why, and then they begin to do research on them. Then you come to philosophy. And then there's still doubt about it. It's all based on reason and logic. It's too abstract, it's not real. So they want to do experiments with it, and then that's how science came to evolve, to emerge. That is the Western civilization's development. From religions to philosophy to natural science. Religion, science, philosophy, they're all trying to look for this big

Self, this origin of life. This big Self was originally just one body, all together in one.

Master Nan then differentiated between the small self and the big Self. "So for cultivation, learning Buddhism, the first thing you do is try to get rid of this view of the [small] self. Once you reach the state of no self [let go of the small self], you reach the state of the big Self. Compassion, loving, et cetera, all of that originates from the big Self. You no longer will be selfish from that large Self."[3]

I left the encounter with Master Nan and his circle of students deeply moved and inspired. It struck me that the leverage point for overcoming the split between mind and matter had to do with the sources of Self. So what would it take to learn more about these sources?

The Blind Spot of Cognition Science

This question led to a 2000 meeting in Paris in the office of the late cognition scientist Francisco Varela, one of the most brilliant scientists and thinkers of his generation. If we had to identify the two or three most important interviews that gave rise to the development of Theory U, my (Otto's) interviews with Varela would be among them.

In my first interview with Varela, in 1996, he voiced an important insight: "The problem is not that we don't know enough about the brain or about biology; the problem is that we don't know enough about experience. . . . We have had a blind spot in the West for that kind of methodical approach, which I would now describe as a more straightforward phenomenological method. Everybody thinks they know about experience; I claim we don't."[4]

In the 2000 interview, I started by asking Varela whether he had any further reflections on this topic. He responded that this question had been a primary focus of his work since our 1996 meeting, and he pulled a special issue of the *Journal of Consciousness* down from a shelf.

Pointing at it, he said: "This would have been an unthinkable book three or four years ago." He went on to explain that he had been studying and synthesizing the three main methodologies that in his view addressed the blind spot of accessing experience: phenomenology, psychological introspection, and contemplative practices. He found that all three take an individual through the same fundamental process of becoming aware. He synthesized that fundamental process of becoming aware as a sequence of crossing three thresholds: *suspension, redirection,* and *letting go.*[5]

When he described these three thresholds and how crossing them changes the way we pay attention, I immediately recognized them. I had seen the same shifts of awareness and attention in groups and teams and during workshop retreats. Whenever the objective of the work of teams and organizations is to confront complex challenges that require innovative responses and collective creativity, these stages emerge:

1. *Suspension:* Stopping and suspending old habits of judgment and thought is a precondition for the first phase of the work. It requires breaking habitual patterns and starting to pay attention.

2. *Redirection:* After suspending the patterns of the past and the habit of downloading, there is a need to start seeing reality from a different angle. This requires listening to the views and experiences of others, taking them in as part of seeing current reality from a multiplicity of views.

3. *Letting go:* Then, if we are lucky, we will go through a profound moment of "quieting" that allows us to let go of our old self and connect with another state of being, a state that helps us to become aware of who we really are and what we are here for. This requires us to let go of everything that isn't essential and to drop our baggage when facing the eye of the needle. Entering this deeper state allows us to operate from a co-creative flow.

This conversation with Varela felt like a seed or a gift. Today, in hindsight, we would say what grew out of this seed is a summarizing framework of Theory U called the Matrix of Social Evolution, which links the essence of Theory U—connecting to source—back to Master Nan's dictum on the reintegration of mind and matter.

The Matrix of Social Evolution

One of the core ideas of Theory U is that form follows attention or consciousness. We can change reality by changing the inner place from which we operate. The Matrix of Social Evolution (and the rest of this book) spells out what this looks like for an individual (attending), a group (conversing), an institution (organizing), and a global system (coordinating). Table 7 shows how these different social fields (micro, meso, macro, mundo) transform according to the inner place—or the quality of awareness—from which we operate.

The first step in understanding the impact of attention on reality is to look at how we operate on the individual level. Consider the example of listening. On level 1, the quality of listening is called downloading. Same old, same old! The listener hears ideas, and these merely reconfirm what the listener already knows. Examples are manifold: (1) not seeing the new challenges by holding on to old theories; and (2) not sensing future opportunities by holding on to old frameworks or experiences from the past.

On level 2, listening is called factual listening, which is what good scientists do. They do not hold on to existing interpretations of reality, but they let the data talk to them. They try to listen to the facts even if those facts contradict their own theories or ideas. Factual listening connects people to the actual particulars of the world.

But what is missing from factual listening is getting inside social complexity. This happens at level 3, which we call empathic listening. Empathic listening allows the individual to see reality from the perspective of the other and sense the other person's circumstances. This does not imply that the two agree, but that they are able to acknowledge and respect each other's perspective. Empathic listening means seeing from the viewpoint of another stakeholder.

Level 4 is generative listening. Generative listening means to form a space of deep attention that allows an emerging future possibility to "land" or manifest. It is what great coaches do: They listen deeply in a way that allows you to connect to your emerging future self. Sometimes we also use the example of a jazz ensemble that is "in the flow" to illustrate this capacity. When individual players can listen to the whole and simultaneously attune their own instrument to an emerging pattern, they are able to co-create something new together.

As one's listening moves from level 1 (shallow) to level 4 (deep), the listener's field of attention passes through several turning points, from suspending (the gateway to level 2) to redirecting (the gateway to empathic listening) to letting go (the gateway to generative listening).

TABLE 7 The Matrix of Social Evolution

Field: Structure of Attention	Micro: *Attending* (Individual)	Meso: *Conversing* (Group)	Macro: *Organizing* (Institution)	Mundo: *Coordinating* (Global System)
1.0: habitual awareness	Listening 1: downloading habits of thought	Downloading: speaking from conforming	Centralized control: organizing around hierarchy	Hierarchy: commanding
Suspending				
2.0: ego-system awareness	Listening 2: factual, open-minded	Debate: speaking from differentiating	Divisionalized: organizing around differentiation	Market: competing
Redirecting				
3.0: stakeholder awareness	Listening 3: empathic, open-hearted	Dialogue: speaking from inquiring others, self	Distributed/networked: organizing around interest groups	Negotiated dialogue: cooperating
Letting Go				
4.0: eco-system awareness	Listening 4: generative, open-presence	Collective creativity: speaking from what is moving through	Eco-system: organizing around what emerges	Awareness-based collective action: co-creating

Columns 3 through 5 illustrate how this process of opening plays out in groups (conversing), institutions (organizing), and eco-systems or societies (coordinating).

Crossing the Threshold to 4.0 Societies

Still, moving social and economic systems to a 4.0 state of operating remains a huge challenge. It requires crossing a threshold of self-reflective meta-awareness on multiple levels. As individuals, we must begin to pay attention to our attention (self-awareness); as teams, we must begin to converse about our conversations (dialogue); as enterprises, we must begin to organize our organizing (networks of networks: eco-systems); and as eco-systems, we must begin to coordinate our coordinating (systems of awareness-based collective action, or ABC).

On each of these levels, the threshold requires a self-reflective turn. *Attending to your attention* means bending the beam of observation in order to see yourself. *Conversing about our conversations* means bending the beam of conversational attention to help a group see itself. *Organizing our organizing* means creating conditions that make eco-system-wide self-organizing more intentional, fluid, and self-aware. *Coordinating our coordinating* means creating a meta-level that allows a community of players to see itself and to adjust the portfolio of existing coordination mechanisms as needed—for example, by redrawing the boundaries between cooperation and competition in an industry.

Crossing this threshold requires social technologies, tools, methods, and leadership practices that allow us to shift from ego-system to eco-system awareness and consciousness.

Conclusion and Practices: Reintegrating the Matrix

The remaining chapters will introduce social technologies that expand on the columns of table 7 as they apply to the transformation of

1. the individual: from me to we (chapter 5);
2. relationships: from ego to eco (chapter 6);
3. institutions: from hierarchy to eco-system (chapter 7); and

4. capacity building: from old forms to creating a global action leadership school (chapter 8).

Each journey is a process of profound opening. The essence of this journey brings us back to Master Nan's new interpretation of Confucius.
According to that text, it's a journey that moves from outer fields (the
world, the state, the family) to the inner field: one's heart, one's thoughts,
and the awareness that extends to the investigation of the underlying
matrix of mind and matter.

This investigation leads to yet another new impulse, which is chan-
neled back into reality through renewed awareness, thoughts, hearts,
and families all the way to renewed nations and ultimately a renewed
world.

The questions that Master Nan and others ask invite us to take a
closer look at how mind and matter relate to each other—how our awareness and consciousness affect the pathways of enacting social forms,
how they impact and shape our ways of bringing forth the world. On
levels 1 and 2 of the Matrix of Social Evolution, the social field is based
on a separation between matter and mind; on level 4, these boundaries
collapse and open up a new field of co-creative possibility. It is that field
where the presence of the future begins. . . .

JOURNALING QUESTIONS

Use table 8 as shorthand for the Matrix of Social Evolution in order to
assess your current situation by answering the following questions.

1. What percentage of your time do you spend on each level of listening? Write down the percentage.
2. What percentage of your time do you spend on each level of
   conversing?
3. What percentage of your time does your institution make you organize around centralized, divisionalized, networked, or eco-systemic
   structures?
4. What percentage of your time do you spend on connecting to the
   whole through the mechanisms of hierarchy, competition, stakeholder negotiation, or ABC (shared awareness of the whole)?

TABLE 8 Personal Assessment

Awareness	Micro: Listening	Meso: Conversing	Macro: Organizing	Mundo: Coordinating
1.0: habitual	Level 1: downloading	Downloading	Centralized control	Central planning
2.0: ego-system	Level 2: factual	Debate	Divisionalized	Markets and competition
3.0: stakeholder	Level 3: empathic	Dialogue	Networked	Negotiation and dialogue
4.0: eco-system	Level 4: generative	Collective creativity	Eco-system	ABC: seeing/ acting from the whole

5. With a different-colored pen, indicate in the table what you would like the future to look like (using percentages).

6. Compare the two sets of percentages, notice the gaps, and develop ideas for bridging them.

CIRCLE CONVERSATION

1. After answering the six questions above individually, have each member of your circle share their insights, questions, and intentions in regard to their personal profile.

2. What interesting small prototypes can you think of for exploring 4.0 types of operating that can move your profile from actual to desired?

5

Leading the Personal Inversion: From Me to We

Stepping into the field of the future starts with attending to the opening of an inner crack. Following that crack requires us to let go of the old and "let grow" something that we can sense, but that we cannot fully know before we see it emerge. This moment, which requires us to move although we cannot yet fully see the new, feels like jumping across an abyss. At the moment we leap, we have no idea whether we will make it across.

As human beings, we are on a journey of *becoming who we really are*. This journey to ourselves—to our *Selves*—is open-ended and full of disruptions, confusion, and breakdowns, but also breakthroughs. It is a journey that essentially is about accessing the deep sources of the Self.

Man Is a Rope

The nineteenth-century philosopher Friedrich Nietzsche saw the tension between current reality and the possible future state of the human being.[1] In 1883, he wrote in *Thus Spake Zarathustra:*

> Man is a rope, tied between beast and Superman [*Übermensch*]—
> a rope over an abyss.
> A dangerous crossing, a dangerous on-the-way, a dangerous
> looking-back,
> a dangerous shuddering and stopping.
> What is great in man is that he is a bridge and not an end: what can
> be loved
> in man is that he is an overture and a going under.

I love those who do not know how to live, for they are those who
   cross over.[2]

We are a rope over an abyss. A bridge, not an end—a living embodiment
of crossing over. When Nietzsche wrote these lines, none of his readers,
colleagues, or even his friends understood the deeper existential crisis
that he was talking about. Nobody got what he was trying to say. Cer-
tainly the Nazis didn't get it when they started misusing his writings
more than thirty years after his passing. Nietzsche's writings mark the
beginning of a significant disruption or opening in human consciousness. He saw the abyss, and in his journey he failed to reach across it.

Today the presence of the abyss is no longer a singular experience of
an individual philosopher who 130 years ago anticipated and seeded the
great turns of twentieth-century philosophy by taking human thought
to the edge of death and rebirth. At the beginning of the twenty-first
century, probably for the first time in human history, the *living presence
of the abyss*—that is, the simultaneous existence of one world that is
dying and another one that is being born—is a widely shared experience for millions of people across cultures, sectors, and generations. It is
experienced in communities as well as in ministries, global companies,
NGOs, and UN organizations—wherever people are looking at the real
picture.

It's a felt sense that applies to relationships, institutions, and systems, but even more to the personal level of our journey from self to Self.

Cracking through the Wall

The other day we saw, at the edge of a parking space, a young sprout of
a tree that had just pierced the layer of asphalt above it. When you see
something so improbable, you can't help but wonder how it happened.

This image captures the essence of what we see so many people
doing today. Everywhere you look, you see remarkable individuals and
communities that have managed to break through the walls of trauma
and tyranny in order to connect to their deep sources of humanity. What
are the conditions that make these breakthroughs possible and allow
"miracles" to happen time and again?

Conditions of Possibility

Knowing who we are is impossible as long as we direct the beam of observation away from ourselves and onto the exterior world around us. In order to discover true self-knowledge, we have to *bend the beam of scientific observation back* onto the observing *self*—that is, back onto its *source*. Francisco Varela described this as the "core process of becoming aware": his three gestures of suspending, redirecting, and letting go that mark the downward slope of the U process.

We follow the movement of bending the beam of observation in the remaining chapters of this book: for transformation of the individual (this chapter), of relationships (chapter 6), of institutions (chapter 7), and of society (chapter 8). We will describe a new meta-pattern of transformation that we call inversion (*Umstülpung* in German), a deep opening process of turning a social field completely inside-out and outside-in, of upending things.

In our discussion of the Matrix of Social Evolution in chapter 4, we differentiated among four types of listening:

Listening 1 (habitual): projecting old judgments

Listening 2 (factual): directing the beam of observation onto the world around us

Listening 3 (empathic): adopting the other person's perspective and therefore seeing ourselves through the eyes of the other (bending the beam)

Listening 4 (generative): listening from the whole and the emerging new, which further turns the beam of observation onto the deep sources of Self

BENDING THE BEAM OF ATTENTION IN BERLIN

One example of these qualities of listening occurred in our advanced practitioner program at the Presencing Institute. In the last module of a two-year program, seventy-two participants from nineteen countries met in Berlin in June 2012. Our colleague Dayna Cunningham remembers one particularly affecting experience that demonstrates the power of bending the beam of attention:

Several of our group with a Jewish background had lost family during the Holocaust, while other members of our group came from a German background. Spending a week together in Berlin, visiting, among other places, the Holocaust Memorial, brought back painful and yet important memories to many. A group of us—Germans, American Jews, and an African American (me), all women—sat at dinner one evening talking about what it meant to be in Berlin. One of my very dear German friends began to describe the pain they have experienced as Germans, a sense that the whole world sees you in a very negative way. She talked about German society's determination to address the past head-on. Based on her own horror as a child when exposed to the graphic history lessons, my friend questioned whether some of the exposure was too early for some German children who perhaps are not ready to encounter the horror of that history.

As she told these stories, I could feel a sense of rage rising in me. All I could think about was that the Jewish children I know *must* confront the horror of the Holocaust from the earliest age because it is their own family history. It made me think of the many conversations I'd had with my white American friends who felt they needed to shield their children from the harsh truth about racism in the US until they were ready to hear it, while I was forced to talk to my own very young children about "driving while black," for instance, so they would not think that their father, who was regularly stopped by cops, was a criminal. From my earliest encounters with the random hatred of racism, I'd learned to cultivate anger as a form of self-protection.

So I could not listen quietly any longer to my friend's experience. "Really?" I said aloud, my rage right on the surface. "How old do you think Jewish children are before they are exposed to the horrible truth? Maybe from birth?" I then unloaded my stories of painful experiences with talking to my children about racism. I talked for a while before bothering to look at her to see the impact my words were having. When I did, I found her sitting so quietly and looking so sad that it brought me up short. As I understood it then, my lack of curiosity had visibly hurt her. I felt very bad, regretted that I had not listened with an open mind, and apologized for my insensitivity. I asked her what she would propose as a better way to address the dilemma of facing the pain of this history. Her answer was smart and humane: create a mode of dialogue that enabled everyone to heal.

Through that exchange, our conversation moved rapidly from level 1 (polite and conforming) to level 2 (blaming and confronting) and then to level 3 (reflecting and connecting) as my friend and I got beyond knee-jerk blame and shutting down. But we were not finished. I came home that night and called my son back in the US to describe what had happened. I still did not feel right about the exchange. I could not forget the image of sadness in my friend's face; something had begun to move in me, but I did not yet know what.

It all became clear the next day. Our whole group of seventy-two change-makers experienced a profound shift of the field that allowed Jews, Germans, Americans, Asians, Africans, Latin Americans, and Australians to connect to each other and themselves on a much deeper, more raw, and more vulnerable and essential level than any of us had experienced in such a group before.

Otto opened the conversation by bringing us back to the experience of being in Berlin. It was emotional for him, and his willingness to be raw and vulnerable opened a crack. Suddenly many people were sharing their own personal stories. One story shared by Gail Jacob, an American Jewish woman, deeply touched me. Her mother, a death camp survivor, had faced unspeakable horrors in the camp, but the only memory she had shared with her children was of seeing Germans weeping as they lined the streets outside the camp when it was liberated. For me, it was breathtaking that she chose only to highlight the humanity of a people whose country had committed such atrocities against her.

As the stories unfolded, the listening in the room dropped deeper and an incredible conversation started to take its course—a shift of the field that allowed each of us to see our life's journey from a different and more collective angle. There was a flow experience of speaking from the core, speaking from my not-knowing, speaking from what is moving through me and through us. Many of the stories were about intense personal suffering, but in the room, held by the collective listening, they were transformed into moments of powerful healing.

Another participant, Yishai Yuval, from Israel, remembers:

On the preceding day, we had visited the Holocaust Museum and had shared emotional experiences within our subgroup. Then in the evening our small coaching group met for dinner. Each of us shared our feelings with the others. This was the last opportunity for us to be together, face to face, in that week. We were very open to each other.

The next morning at some point, Otto stood up to suggest that we reopen ourselves to the meaning of convening in Berlin, [of] having Jewish colleagues, even Holocaust survivors, among us. People stood up and talked for more than an hour on suffering, cruelty, and the need to remember. I looked around at my fellow Jews in the room, expecting them to join the conversation. At the beginning, none did. It hit me that this type of discussion can't go on while the victims' voice is missing. So, contrary to my habit, I raised my hand to ask for the microphone. The ten steps from the corner where I was sitting into the group's circle were a very long journey. . . .

What happened was a personal defining moment. Everything slowed down around me. There was no need to struggle with words and sentences. They just came one by one in the right order. I felt the faces around me listening, radiating profound empathy, deep understanding, and love. It became easy to share with the group the notion that, prior to being exterminated, Holocaust victims struggled day after day to maintain their dignity as human beings in the midst of the surrounding horrors. Many of them realized that humanity and love didn't save them, concluding that anger, aggressiveness, even hatred might do better in that daily struggle for survival. As an Israeli, this is the heritage I was born into. One can count only on oneself to be strong and suspicious. I was proud as a soldier, trained to kill if necessary, blessed for protecting my own family and people; blessed for not being helpless; blessed for not being in the mercy of brutal killers like my mother's parents and sister [had been]. But time moved on and suddenly we, Israelis, have the power over other people, forced to face annoying questions: Are we strong enough not to exercise power and still remain safe? Had the time arrived to put aside suspicions and hatred, open our hearts, and offer real peace with our enemy? Or is it naïve, even dangerous, to expose humanity in the face of an opponent?

As I talked, looking around the circle, I felt I belonged and was connected to the whole. The deep listening and empathy radiated around me well after I stepped out of the circle. A little while later a young Jewish American woman stood up at the opposite corner of the big hall, asking just to sing a piece written by a young, brave Jewish woman who left Palestine in 1944, parachuted into Hungary on a rescue mission, but was caught by the Nazis, tortured, and killed:

Oh my God, my God
Let it never be stopped
The sand and the sea
Rustle of the water
Flash of the sky
Prayer of Man. . . . [3]

Yishai continued:

Hearing her gentle voice singing so emotionally, I couldn't resist standing up, at the other side of the hall, and joining her. Since then, whenever I hear that song I tremble inside. It touches me in an unknown land, in a way unrecognized to me before. I'll never forget that precious moment of connection with that wonderful young woman as well as with the whole group.[4]

Antoinette Klatzky of New York, the young woman who sang the song, remembers how that situation unfolded from her perspective:

At twelve years old, I attended Jewish day school and learned of Hannah Senesh, a young woman who was killed by the Nazis at age twenty-three while rescuing Jews from Nazi-occupied Hungary. At age twenty-six, sitting in the space with seventy-two change-makers, I listened deeply as each voice shared a personal story, and I felt a crack within myself open. Each time someone spoke, I could feel the crack widen, my heart beating harder, thumping in my chest for each drop of pain or ray of hopeful healing. I could feel the hymn, Hannah's prayer, rising from roots that I didn't know I had. I felt the words jump into my heart, the melody beat through my veins, and like an earthquake my body lifted me to a standing position. The world was in this room—the past, the present, the future—and it was as if I had lived every moment of my life to sing this song. The lyrics, in a language I hadn't spoken in years, began to flow with my tears as each word was a crescendo of its own. Voices seemed to fly in to join us through the windows, the room was filling with rays of light and sound, and I could feel Hannah there with us in Berlin. The song finished. The song ran its way through me like electric current in the wires above. I melted back into the chair, feeling completely held.[5]

Shortly after that, Tho Ha Vinh of Vietnam and Bhutan stood up and shared a poem by Thich Nhat Hanh. "The name of the poem is "Please Call Me by My True Names,'" said Tho and reached into his pocket to pull out a small journal that helped him to keep this poem close to his heart. Tho started reading:

Don't say that I will depart tomorrow—
even today I am still arriving.

Look deeply: every second I am arriving
to be a bud on a Spring branch,
to be a tiny bird, with still-fragile wings,
learning to sing in my new nest,
to be a caterpillar in the heart of a flower,
to be a jewel hiding itself in a stone.

I still arrive, in order to laugh and to cry,
to fear and to hope.
The rhythm of my heart is the birth and death
of all that is alive.

I am a mayfly metamorphosing
on the surface of the river.
And I am the bird
that swoops down to swallow the mayfly.

I am a frog swimming happily
in the clear water of a pond.
And I am the grass-snake
that silently feeds itself on the frog.

I am the child in Uganda, all skin and bones,
my legs as thin as bamboo sticks.
And I am the arms merchant,
selling deadly weapons to Uganda.

I am the twelve-year old girl,
refugee on a small boat,
who throws herself into the ocean
after being raped by a sea pirate.
And I am the pirate,
my heart not yet capable
of seeing and loving.

I am a member of the politburo,
with plenty of power in my hands.
And I am the man who has to pay
his "debt of blood" to my people
dying slowly in a forced-labor camp.

My joy is like Spring, so warm
it makes flowers bloom all over the Earth.
My pain is like a river of tears,
so vast it fills the four oceans.

Please call me by my true names,
so I can hear all my cries and laughter at once,
so I can see that my joy and pain are one.

Please call me by my true names,
so I can wake up
and the door of my heart
could be left open,
the door of compassion.[6]

Stillness. Tho sat down. We all felt that the walls between us had been melting away. Time had been slowing down and elevating our own experience of that moment. We started experiencing the situation from multiple angles. I am the girl. The pirate. The child. The weapon seller. I am the victim and the perpetrator of the Holocaust. I am in you. You are in me. I begin to feel the we. The we is something in me that isn't me. What brings us together here on this earth? Why are we here? "What struck me most deeply," remembers Dayna,

> was the level of connection and compassion people expressed toward others who had been life-and-death adversaries or who had done violence to them: the soldiers, survivors of assault and neglect, the Jewish descendants of Holocaust survivors, and, yes, the young Germans facing a world that blamed them. I now could see that the night before I had been unable to open my heart, not just my mind. Gail captured precisely what was moving through me at this time: "I am sixty-three years old. I've spent my whole life as a Jew thinking I was alone in this world, thinking that if anything happened to me or my people, no one would help. Now, in this room in Berlin, I understand that I am not alone."[7]

Condition 1: Bending the Beam of Observation

What are the conditions of possibility that allow a profound collective shift like the one in Berlin to happen? What allows a seedling to pierce a ceiling of asphalt, or a movement to bring down the Berlin Wall?

Probably the first and most important condition has to do with bending the beam of observation. It happened to Dayna when she saw the sad face of her friend and realized that she had caused it by reacting in a way that was habitual. It happened to Yishai when he joined the conversation and words flowed in unexpected ways. And it happened to Antoinette, who was moved to stand up and sing a song she hadn't heard or thought about in years.

Each of them described the same social grammar of opening, of cracking the wall of asphalt that separated them from one another and from the deep levels of their humanity. They each tell the story of bending the beam of attention back onto its source. The beam first radiated into the outside world (level 2), then bent back onto the self (level 3), and then found the sources of self, of becoming present in the moment, in the now (level 4). That is the first condition of shifting the field: bending the beam of attention back onto its source.

Condition 2: A Holding Space for Embracing the Shadow

The second condition of possibility concerns the holding space. The bending of the beam happens in a social holding space formed by true listening from the heart. Dayna turned the beam of attention back onto herself at the moment she felt the pain of her friend. When Yishai, in his words, "felt the faces around me listening, radiating profound empathy, deep understanding, and love," he was empowered to make his courageous move. At that point Antoinette remembered "feeling the true presence of what each heart is holding."

The cultivation of a holding space allows a shift of the social field to happen—the mind and the heart begin to open. The holding space that was created in Berlin had started to form six months earlier in a small gathering; each participant in the seventy-two-member master class had met monthly in this small-group coaching circle for two years. The purpose of the coaching circle was to provide a level 4 listening environment for each person's personal and professional journey. Gail remembers:

When we met in our coaching group six months earlier, I shared my trepidation about going [to Berlin] and using that as an opportunity to visit where I was born—the displaced persons' camp near Dachau, from where both my parents were liberated.

Before I knew what I was going to say, I was talking about going to Berlin and taking my family to where I was born for the first time. I started crying and then the group wept together for a long time and there was this amazing knowing in the group about healing—not only me, but knowing also how the world needs to heal from our collective trauma of war and genocide.

There I was sitting next to Otto, a German, and two Buddhists: Tho, a Vietnamese; Julia, of Korean descent; also Yishai, an Orthodox Israeli Jew; Jim, a former military person; and Antoinette, the next generation. . . . They were able to be my holding space. . . . I felt the earth shift. I've carried the wounds of the Holocaust in my DNA and in my being every day of my life. Somehow for the first time I began to see the possibility of transforming that energy into something else.[8]

After that experience in our coaching group, we all carried that moment of transcending connection with us when we arrived in Berlin six months later. When I (Otto) sensed that something wanted to happen, it was because of that coaching circle. When I stood to open up and hold the space on that morning, it was because of the presence of our circle in the room—of directly feeling the connection to Gail, Yishai, and the others.

"The field shifted during that morning with the class," remembers Gail, referring to the quality of the holding space. "We were open to each other and we were one. It was as though *collectively we needed to embrace the shadow in order to glimpse what is needed to heal the world.* And for me, the fear was gone."[9]

Healing, health, and *holy* all share the same word root, *hal,* which means to "make whole." The Berlin experience provided a holding space for making whole at a collective level unknown to us before. As Gail put it: Collectively we needed to embrace the shadow in order to glimpse what is needed to heal the world.

Condition 3: Going to the Edge of Letting Go

The third condition of possibility concerns the willingness to go to the edge of the abyss, to let go, to lean into the unknown—and take the leap.

When Yishai, against his nature, took the microphone, he took that leap. So did Antoinette and Gail, and many others. The holding space enabled us to go to the edge without pulling back.

The condition of going to the edge comes in two different forms. Sometimes it means that you have to take the leap, to jump off the cliff from the known into the unknown. Sometimes, when you feel that something is beginning to emerge, it can also mean to not jump away, but to stay with what wants to emerge. In both cases we deal with a deep trust in reality and self, in connecting to the deep levels of the field. Going to the edge means having the courage to not hold on to the old, to let go and lean into what wants to emerge through us. And then, as Martin Buber put it so beautifully, "to bring it [the new] into reality as *it* desires."[10]

The story of the Berlin master class is just one example of people connecting in small coaching circles with the presence of letting go and letting come, of dying and rebirth. It's a movement that is starting to happen all over the world and that has many different faces, forms, and practices. Let's look at another inspiring example.

MINDFULNESS-BASED STRESS REDUCTION

Jon Kabat-Zinn is professor of medicine emeritus and founder of the Stress Reduction Clinic and of the Center for Mindfulness in Medicine, Health Care, and Society at the University of Massachusetts Medical School. He is also the developer of mindfulness-based stress reduction (MBSR), the program upon which the Stress Reduction Clinic is based. Since its founding in 1979, the clinic has trained over twenty thousand medical patients. The MBSR program has been replicated and institutionalized in over 720 medical schools, hospitals, health-care systems, and stand-alone clinics worldwide and has given rise to a number of other mindfulness-based interventions closely modeled on it for particular medical, psychiatric, and social conditions. The success of MBSR is one of the principal drivers of the heightened interest in mindfulness in health and cognition sciences at the beginning of the twenty-first century (see figure 9).

So how did this success story of MBSR come into being? What are the origins of this movement that is touching the lives of hundreds of thousands today, and that thirty years ago no one had even heard of?

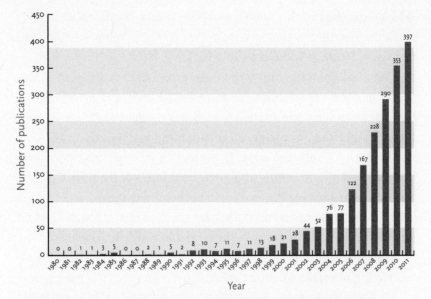

FIGURE 9. Research publications on mindfulness, 1980–2011. Figure prepared by David Black, MPH, PhD, Cousins Center for Psychoneuroimmunology, Semel Institute for Neuroscience and Human Behavior, University of California, Los Angeles. Source: J. M. G. Williams and J. Kabat-Zinn, eds., *Mindfulness: Diverse Perspectives on Its Meaning, Origins, and Applications* (London: Routledge, 2013), 2.

The driving forces behind the rapidly growing interest in mindfulness include (1) the crisis of the old paradigm; (2) successful interventions like MBSR that have pioneered a new approach to medicine, blending medical science, clinical application, and mindfulness; (3) training programs in MBSR for health professionals that seeded the field over many years; and (4) the establishment of the Center for Mindfulness along with an ongoing research program that helped to turn this momentum into published scientific studies and nurture a new field in medical science and a vibrant new research community. Jon recalls:

> In the year 2000, during a meeting in Dharamsala, India, organized by the Mind and Life Institute, in which the Dalai Lama and a group of psychologists, neuroscientists, scholars, and contemplatives explored together the subject of destructive emotions and what might be done to mitigate the enormous personal and societal harm that so often stems from them, the Dalai Lama, amazingly and yet characteristi-

cally, challenged the scientists to come up with non-Buddhist, secular methods for working with and transforming the energies of these said emotions. He acknowledged that Buddhism might have a lot to offer, in terms of its elaborate and detailed understanding of what he termed *afflictive emotions,* including a range of meditative practices that have been utilized for centuries and millennia in monastic settings to work with them in skillful ways. At the same time, he was saying that the real hope lay in a non-Buddhist, a truly universal and secular approach that would make use of whatever elements of Buddhist understanding and methods were found to be helpful, but only combined with and integrated into Western culture, its understanding of the psyche, and, in particular, its scientific understanding of emotions, emotional expression, and emotion regulation. . . .

It was also pointed out at that meeting that there already was an approach that had been doing much of what the Dalai Lama was calling for in clinical settings, primarily hospitals, for twenty-one years at that point, namely mindfulness-based stress reduction and the family of mindfulness-based interventions that have arisen around it. . . .

Of course, it was well known by many of the participants in that meeting that the curriculum of MBSR and other mindfulness-based interventions is deeply rooted in a universal expression of the Buddhadharma [the foundational teachings of Buddha], and that the curriculum features the cultivation of mindfulness of mind states and body states, including in particular awareness of reactive emotions, as well as how to deploy specific strategies to respond mindfully rather than react reflexively when they are triggered.[11]

Jon recounts a part of his personal journey, beginning in his early student days: "Even as a graduate student at MIT, I had been pondering for years, 'What is my job with a capital J?,' my 'karmic assignment' on the planet, so to speak, without coming up with much of anything. It was a personal koan for me and became more and more a continuous thread in my life, day and night, as those years unfolded. 'What am I supposed to be doing with my life?' I kept asking myself. 'What do I love so much I would pay to do it?'"

He knew that it wasn't his destiny to pursue a career in molecular biology, even though he loved science and knew he would disappoint his

Nobel laureate thesis adviser at MIT, Salvador Luria, and his own father, also an accomplished scientist. In 1979, still searching for the right path to link his livelihood (his job) with his sense of essential purpose (his Job) in a way that felt aligned with the needs of the time, he went on a two-week meditation retreat. Jon recounts:

> While sitting in my room one afternoon on about day ten of the retreat, I had a "vision" that lasted maybe ten seconds. I don't really know what to call it, so I call it a vision. It was rich in detail and more like an instantaneous seeing of vivid, almost inevitable connections and their implications. It did not come as a reverie or a thought stream, but rather something quite different, which to this day I cannot fully explain and don't feel the need to.
>
> I saw in a flash not only a model that could be put in place, but also the long-term implications of what might happen if the basic idea was sound and could be implemented in one test environment— namely that it would spark new fields of scientific and clinical investigation and would spread to hospitals and medical centers and clinics across the country and around the world, and provide right livelihood for thousands of practitioners. Because it was so weird, I hardly ever mentioned this experience to others. But after that retreat, I did have a better sense of what my karmic assignment might be. It was so compelling that I decided to take it on wholeheartedly as best I could.

After his meditation retreat, Jon returned to the hospital and met individually with three physicians, the directors of the primary care, pain, and orthopedics clinics, to find out how they viewed their work, what their clinics' successes were with their patients, and what might be missing in the hospital experience.

> When I asked what percentage of their patients they felt they were able to help, the response was typically 10 to 20 percent. I was astonished, and asked what happened to the others. I was told that they either got better on their own or never got better.
>
> I asked whether they would be open to referring their patients, when appropriate, to a program that would teach them to take better care of themselves as a complement to whatever the health-care system was or was not able to do for them. It would be based on relatively intensive training in Buddhist meditation without the Buddhism, as

I liked to put it, and yoga. Their responses were very positive. On the basis of those meetings, I proposed that a program be set up under the auspices of ambulatory care in the hospital, which would take the form of an eight-week course to which physicians would refer patients they were seeing who they felt were not responding to their treatments and were, in some sense, falling through the cracks of the health-care system. And so MBSR came into being in the fall of 1979.[12]

For many years, Jon and his team worked with groups of patients in their windowless room in the basement of the hospital. At first little noticed, their work at the hospital turned into a holding space for birthing a different paradigm of medicine. "Although our patients all come with various problems, diagnoses, and ailments," explains Jon, with the MBSR approach, "we make every effort to apprehend their intrinsic wholeness. We often say that from our perspective, as long as you are breathing, there is more 'right' with you than 'wrong' with you, no matter what is wrong. In this process, we make every effort to treat each participant as a whole human being rather than as a patient or a diagnosis or someone having a problem that needs fixing."

Jon's story is an amazing example of what a small group of committed citizens is able to do. It also exhibits some of the same enabling conditions that we witnessed in the Berlin story. Bending the beam of observation, of course, is what happens in all practices of mindfulness. But what was the holding space that allowed him to lean into the crack and to leap after returning from the meditation retreat? "My decision to leap," remembers Jon, "was in part based on years of meditation practice and inquiry on the one hand, as well as training in science [on the other], so I was at home in the language and thinking of medicine and medical science."[13] So again, the seeds for this moment had been germinating over many years.

Turning Yourself into a Vehicle for the Future

Jon's story exemplifies the presence of the abyss (what is my Job?), of letting go (of a career in science) and then crossing the abyss (following his heart). His experience in the retreat and his conversation with the three physicians helped him to see the opening or the crack and to follow that emerging path. His many years of practice in mindfulness and science gave him the confidence to sense and actualize the moment of opportunity. Working with his core team in a windowless basement for many years established the holding space for co-creating the seeds of a profound revolution that a few years later would spread around the world.

The Berlin experience and Jon's story share a feature: the human spirit breaking through the asphalt-hard surface structure of habituated action and thought. In these moments of breaking through, the new starts coming into being. When you watch this process of coming into being, it's interesting to see how the field enters the space through certain individuals first—as if the field of possibility chooses these individuals as gateways to come into being. Jon is one of them. He opened the gate—he became the vehicle. And that allowed the next circle of people to also connect. And so on. So we are learning here how to become a vehicle for what is emerging from the other side of the abyss.

In this chapter we have described a different way of connecting to a deep source of creativity, humanity, and self. Although we have given only a very few concrete examples, we know that the deep conditions of possibility explored here—bending the beam of attention, cultivating a holding space, going to the edge of dying, and turning yourself into a vehicle for the future that is wanting to emerge—can be observed at work in many other places around the planet. It's the social grammar of emergence. It's what you feel when talking to change-makers like Jon. It's what we experienced in Berlin, when, in Gail's words, we collectively embraced the shadow in order to function as a vehicle through which healing may come into the world.

Conclusion and Practices: Twelve Principles

One interesting development over the past several decades has been a subtle shift in the balance of power between individuals and institutions in favor of individuals. As the entrepreneur Nick Hanauer puts it:

> One of my favorite sayings, attributed to Margaret Mead, has always been "Never doubt that a small group of committed citizens can change the world. Indeed, it's the only thing that ever has." I totally believe it. You could do almost anything with just five people. With

only one person, it's hard—but when you put that one person with four or five more, you have a force to contend with. All of a sudden, you have enough momentum to make almost anything that's imminent, or within reach, actually real. I think that's what entrepreneurship is all about—creating that compelling vision and force.[14]

Hanauer names an important shift in the world that helps small groups of citizens to have a big impact on where the world is going. Think about the impact of Jon and his team—and the ripples keep coming. The good news is that the world has enormous unexploited potential in the form of inspired, intentional, and collective entrepreneurship. But we will need to be much more methodical about tapping this dormant force to bring about global movements for good.

We conclude this chapter with twelve principles and practices that can help advance our individual journey from self to Self, from me to We, as exemplified in the stories shared above. They reflect various pockets of our and our colleagues' experiences over the past years.

1. *Practice, don't preach.* Apply the U by practicing, not by preaching. Start by listening. Listen to others, to yourself, and to the whole. Listen to what life calls you to do. Connect with people where they are and then look for cracks or openings from these viewpoints; then be helpful.

2. *Observe, observe, observe: Become a blackbelt observer and listener.* The U process extends what is the core work of science—namely, "Let the data talk to you"—from the exterior realm (the third-person view) to the more subtle levels of human experience (the second- and first-person views). Thus the practice of letting data talk to you applies not only to objective, exterior data (through the open mind), but also to empathic, intersubjective data (through the open heart) and to the transsubjective realm of self-knowledge (through the open will). Attending to all three types of data requires refined observation and listening skills. The impact of the deeper levels of listening is profound: They function like a welding flame on the process of social reality creation. They can melt the walls of habitual interaction that keep us separate from the world, from one another, and from ourselves.

3. *Connect to your intention as an instrument.* Brian Arthur, an economist with the Santa Fe Institute, once said in one of our research interviews: "Intention is not a powerful force. It's the *only* force."[15] Connecting to the intention of our life's journey establishes a vertical alignment: "Who am I?" "What am I here for?" "How can I link my work with my Work, or my job with my Job?" The more we can connect to that deeper place—to what is essential for us—and the more we can clarify what we want to be in service of, the better we can act as instruments for bringing that emerging future into being.

4. *When the crack opens up, stay with it—connect and act from the now.* Applying the latter two principles (observe, observe; intention) connects you both horizontally and vertically with a higher level of presence and readiness. When opportunity presents itself, it often feels as if time is slowing down and a crack to a field of future possibility is opening up. These moments ask for some courage, but mainly for full attention. When such a moment occurs, stay with it, connect with it, and then *act* from the *now*—that is, from what wants to emerge. Put differently, when you find yourself beginning to connect with a significant future opportunity, first say yes, then *do* it, and only then ask whether it's possible.

5. *Follow your heart—do what you love, love what you do.* As we've noted, Steve Jobs once said the only way to do our best work is to do what we love and to love what we do. It's the only reliable way to connect to our emerging future path. Make sure that at least some of the projects and activities in your portfolio are things you love doing. When this element is missing, you are in danger of losing your way or living someone else's life.

6. *Always be in dialogue with the universe.* As Alan Webber said, "The universe is a helpful place." This is an important guiding principle. It means that the universe—in other words, the larger context that surrounds us—provides useful feedback. This feedback comes in different forms. Sometimes that feedback sucks. But we need to learn to listen and identify those elements of the feedback that are helpful to further evolve our idea.

7. *Create a holding space of deep listening that supports your journey.* The most important leadership tool is your Self—your capacity to access

your highest future possibility. Two of the most effective mechanisms to strengthen your capacity to access your emerging Self are cultivation practices and deep-listening-based circle work. A daily cultivation practice—a moment of stillness or contemplation in which you filter out all the noise from outside and focus on what's essential for you—can be performed in many different ways, drawing on whatever works best for you. The point is that you do it every day. A circle practice usually involves a small group of up to seven participants who meet a few times a year to support one another through deep listening, by attending to the calling and journey of each of their personal lives and work.[16]

8. *Iterate, iterate, iterate.* What "observe, observe, observe" is for the left-hand side of the U, "iterate, iterate, iterate" is for the right-hand side of the U. It's about practicing and adapting to what we see emerging. Where in your life is the windowless basement room that allows you to practice, practice, practice in order to explore the new by doing?

9. *Notice the crack to the field of the future.* All change takes place in a context. It can be personal, relational, institutional, or global. Attending to the opening of a crack requires exploring the edges of the system and the self. At these edges, when we are lucky, we can sense a field of future possibility that is wanting to emerge.

10. *Use different language with different stakeholders.* Innovation in complex systems requires us to be multilingual, to connect to the various stakeholders about the issues that matter to *them*. Complex problems require complex solutions. That means that single-focus approaches are almost certain to fail. Instead we need to master the art of broadening and deepening the definition of the problem to get all of the relevant parties—who need one another to change any system—committed to participate.

11. *If you want to change others (other stakeholders), you need to be open to changing yourself first.* If you need to change the system but you cannot use hierarchy to do it, then the main leverage you have is the quality of your relationship with the other stakeholders. That's what you must build and strengthen. And that means being open to changing yourself *first*.

12. *Never give up. Never give up. You are not alone.* Every profound journey of innovation and renewal takes an enormous amount of perseverance. Important ideas often take many years of failed effort—or practice—before they produce something concrete in the real world. The key is never giving up. Always figure out what you can learn from failure, get back on your feet, and try again. Allowing yourself to be discouraged by failed efforts is a waste of energy. It leads to being trapped in your own (and other people's) Voice of Judgment, Voice of Cynicism, and Voice of Fear. Leading change requires courage most of all: the courage to go to the edge and leap into the unknown. That courage is an important condition that connects us with the deep dimensions of our being—with who we really are. Courage resides in the trust that we are not alone. Or, as one experienced change-maker once put it: "The collective always delivers."

JOURNALING QUESTIONS

Take a journal and some quiet time to answer these sixteen questions. Spend about one to two minutes per question.

1. What in your life and work is dying or ending, and what wants to be born?

2. Who have been your "guardian angels," the people who have helped you to realize your highest potential?

3. Where, right now, do you feel the opening to a future possibility?

4. What about your current work and/or personal life frustrates you the most?

5. What are your most important sources of energy? What do you love?

6. Watch yourself from above, as if from a helicopter. What are you trying to do at this stage of your professional and personal journey?

7. Watch the journey of your community/organization/collective movement from above. What are you trying to do in the present stage of your collective journey?

8. Given the above answers, what questions do you now need to ask yourself?

9. Look at your current situation from the viewpoint of yourself as a young person at the beginning of your journey. What does that young person have to say to you?

10. Imagine you could fast-forward to the very last moments of your life, when it is time for you to move on. Now look back on your life's journey as a whole. What would you want to see at that moment? What footprint do you want to leave behind on this planet?

11. From that future point of view, what advice would your future Self offer to your current self?

12. Now return to the present and crystallize what it is that you want to create: your vision and intention for the next three to five years. What vision and intention do you have for yourself and your work? What are the core elements of the future that you want to create in your personal, professional, and social life? Describe the images and elements that occur to you. The more concrete, the better.

13. What would you have to let go of in order to bring your vision into reality? What is the old stuff that must die? What "old skin" (behaviors, thought processes, etc.) do you need to shed?

14. Over the next three months, if you were to prototype a microcosm of the intended future in which you could discover "the new" by doing something, what would that prototype look like?

15. Who can help you make your highest future possibilities a reality? Who might be your core helpers and partners?

16. If you were to take on the project of bringing your highest intention into reality, what practical first steps would you take over the next three days?

CIRCLE CONVERSATION

Invite each person in your group to share the most meaningful things that surfaced through this sixteen-step journaling experience. Listen deeply and go with the flow of the conversation.

CHAPTER 6

Leading the Relational Inversion: From Ego to Eco

The next revolution has to be a relational one: a revolution that transforms the quality of communicative action throughout social and economic systems. To make that shift, we need to bend the beam of conversational attention back to its source. Instead of just seeing others, we need to learn how to see ourselves through the eyes of others and of the whole.

One of the biggest challenges we face in moving toward an eco-system economy is to act collectively in ways that are intentional, effective, and co-creative. Over the past several years, I (Otto) have watched executives participate in a climate change simulation game at MIT, designed and led by MIT Professor John Sterman. He splits the group into small teams, with each team representing a key country group in the ongoing United Nations–sponsored negotiations over carbon emissions. The negotiators' agreements are fed into a simulation model using actual climate data. After the model calculates the likely climate change outcomes, the negotiators go back to the table for a second round. After three or four rounds, they are presented with what is inevitably the devastating and destabilizing impact of their collective decisions on the climate worldwide.[1] Then the group reflects on what they have learned.

Three Obstacles: Denial, Cynicism, and Depression

During their postnegotiation reflection session, I noted that the participants had three habitual reactions of avoidance that prevented the consequences of their actions from sinking in deeply: (1) denial, (2) cynicism, and (3) depression.

The most common strategy for reality avoidance is denial. We keep ourselves so busy with "urgent" issues that we don't have time to focus on the one that may in fact be the most pressing. We are simply too busy rearranging the deck chairs on the *Titanic*. . . .

The second response is cynicism. Once the outcomes of an agreement become obvious, cynicism is an easy way out. A cynical person creates distance between himself and the consequences of his actions by saying, "Hey, the world is going to hell anyway; it doesn't really matter what *I* do."

But even if these first two strategies of reality avoidance are dealt with, there still is a third one waiting: depression. Depression denies us the power to collectively shift reality to a different way of operating. Depression creates a disconnect between self and Self on the level of the will—just as cynicism creates a disconnect on the level of the heart and denial creates a disconnect on the level of the mind. And into that void slips doubt, anger, and fear. Fear inhibits us from letting go of what is familiar, even when we know it doesn't work and is holding us back.

Conversations Create the World

Learning how to deal with these three types of reality avoidance requires self-reflection and a conversation that bends the beam of attention back onto ourselves. We call this Conversation 4.0—a conversation that allows for embracing the collective shadow, as we heard in the Berlin story of the last chapter, and for unleashing our untapped reserves of creativity, as we will discuss later in this chapter.

The main problem today is that we try to solve complex problems like climate change with traditional types of conversation, which results in predictable outcomes. The collapse of the climate talks in Copenhagen in 2011 and of the MIT climate simulation game are just two of many, many examples.

All complex modern systems—health, education, energy, sustainability—deal with both individual and collective entities, the latter

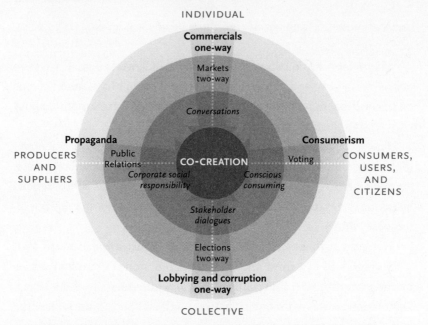

FIGURE 10. Four levels of stakeholder communication in economic systems.

often through government. Accordingly, figure 10, which shows how stakeholders communicate within our society's systems, differentiates between individual and collective entities on the one hand, and suppliers and consumers on the other hand. The four levels of conversation are represented by four rings.

The most common types of conversation, represented by the outermost ring, are

1. unilateral and linear;
2. low on inclusion and transparency; and
3. organized by an intention to serve the well-being of the few.

At the center are the rarest and most precious types of conversation, which offer a major acupuncture point for future change. They are

1. multilateral and cyclical;
2. high on inclusion and transparency; and
3. organized by an intention to serve the well-being of all.

LEVEL 1: UNILATERAL, ONE-WAY DOWNLOADING, AND MANIPULATING

Level 1 stakeholder communication is unilateral, one-way downloading with the intent to manipulate, rather than to serve the well-being of, the other side. Most of what we call corporate or professional communication strategy in business and election campaigns is organized this way. Market research segments citizen and consumer communities into specific target groups that are bombarded with customized messaging and communication strategies. The flood of commercials that hits consumers and citizens every day is mind-boggling. According to a survey in 1993, the average child in the United States sees twenty thousand commercials per year. The average sixty-five-year-old in the United States has seen two million commercials.

One-way communication focuses on "selling," on making the target buy something or vote in a particular way. But the target has no opportunity to talk back. Lobbyists and special-interest groups operate the same way. Their influence often is based on privileged access and excluding other relevant parties from the conversation.

LEVEL 2: BILATERAL, TWO-WAY DISCUSSIONS, AND EXCHANGE OF VIEWPOINTS

Level 2 stakeholder communication is a bilateral, two-way discussion with the intent to provide and receive information, and includes a response or feedback mechanism. In markets, the buyer talks back with her money. In democratic elections, the voter talks back by casting her vote. Both are excellent examples of two-way communication.

LEVEL 3: MULTILATERAL STAKEHOLDER DIALOGUE: SEEING ONESELF THROUGH THE EYES OF ANOTHER

Level 3 stakeholder communication is a multilateral conversation characterized by reflection, learning, and dialogue.[2] Dialogue is a conversation in which you see yourself through the eyes of another—and in the context of the whole. The examples are manifold, from roundtables and "world cafés" to interactive social media. The conversations need a form, a process, and a holding space to operate well. Some companies, like

Natura, Nike, and Unilever, have internalized level 3 communication to their benefit.

For example, Eosta, an international distributor of organic fresh fruit and vegetables in the Netherlands, and also one of the first companies to be climate-neutral and use compostable packaging, wants its customers to see the "invisible" processes behind its products. A three-digit code on each of its products leads the consumer through the Eosta website to the producer. For example, the code 565 on a mango leads to Mr. Zongo in Burkina Faso, who then responds to the consumer comments online on his wall. This mechanism is an excellent example of level 3 communication because it allows consumers to see themselves in the context of the whole value chain.

Examples of multilateral stakeholder communication also include town hall meetings in New England, where citizens discuss local issues, and UN efforts such as the Framework Conventions on Climate Change. To work well, these stakeholder communication require enabling technologies and facilitation.

In the end, all of these approaches deliver the same result: They help stakeholders in a system to see themselves in the context of the other stakeholders and the larger whole. They bend the beam of attention in ways that help these distributed communities to *see themselves* as part of a bigger picture.

LEVEL 4: CO-CREATIVE ECO-SYSTEM INNOVATION: BLURRING THE BOUNDARY OF EGO AND ECO

Level 4 stakeholder communication is a multilateral, collectively creative eco-system conversation that helps diverse groups of players to co-sense and co-create the future by transforming awareness from ego to eco. Examples include transformative multistakeholder processes like the World Commission on Dams and the Sustainable Food Lab, which we will describe in more detail later in the book.[3] The outcomes of these processes deliver not only astonishing breakthrough results, but also a shift in mindset and consciousness from ego-system awareness to eco-system awareness—from a mindset that values one's own well-being to a mindset that also values the well-being of one's partners and of the whole.

LEVERAGE POINTS

Although there are some inspiring examples of level 4 innovations, it is quite clear where the main leverage points are today for shifting the system to a better way of operating:

1. We need to get rid of the toxic layer of level 1 communication (bribery, soft money, commercials, and other forms of propaganda and manipulation that keep intoxicating the communication channels of our society today).

2. And we need to develop new spheres of level 4 co-creative stakeholder relationships, in which partners in an eco-system can come together to co-sense, prototype, and co-create the future of their eco-system.

The question is how to do it. How can we build the deep capacities that will allow us to build and scale these level 4 arenas of co-creation? Here are three stories that offer some inspiration.

Girl Scouts—Arizona Cactus Pine Council (ACPC)

The CEO of the ACPC, Tamara Woodbury, sees the Girl Scouts as a part of the larger global movement that recognizes the importance of women leaders in the transformation of intractable societal issues. Since 2005, she and Presencing Institute facilitator Beth Jandernoa and her colleague Glennifer Gillespie have been experimenting with a process called Circle of Wholeness, designed to dive deeply into the qualitative practice of wholeness and well-being in the council and in the larger Arizona community. The circle, a group of eighteen, is composed of Girl Scout staff and volunteers, as well as business, nonprofit, and civic leaders, men and women, young and old (late teens to early eighties), from a range of social and ethnic backgrounds.

In October 2012, after a day spent immersing themselves in experience and research around well-being and wholeness, the group began a round of check-in, touching base with where people were in their own learning process. Beth and Glennifer felt a tension between the group's urge to take action and the need to slow down and listen internally to what was wanting to emerge. A breakthrough moment came when John, the former CEO of an international heavy construction equipment company, shifted the action-driven momentum. He spoke slowly of his difficulties in the early phase of becoming a philanthropist. John's quality of speech opened the group's listening and evoked a sense of curiosity and palpable spaciousness.

Moments later, ACPC executive Carol Ackerson began to speak. Carol is known for her capacity to conceptualize and articulate complex issues so that others can easily understand them. This time, instead of taking a rational approach, she paused and said: "I know I usually speak from my head, but this time, even though it's not comfortable, I feel it is important for me and for all of us to slow down and listen and speak from our hearts. I feel a new sensation in my body, and the meaning I make of it is, if we can be patient and keep from jumping into action, there's a new possibility present."

A deep silence descended on the group. As people sat quietly together, someone said, "This is amazing. What is going on?" Glennifer answered calmly: "At the beginning of a group's gathering, silence is often awkward. As we drop into a deeper space together, we can have that rare experience as a collective that 'silence is golden.' Let's keep sitting with this and let it do its work." Beth describes her experience, in those moments, as one in which "both I and the collective were being *rearranged* internally—somehow transformed." Later Carol said, "I felt as though the presence of Juliette Gordon Low, the founder of the Girl Scouts, was in the room."

The quality of the conversation that followed this silence was alive and fresh with ideas that the group had previously never considered. They began to explore how they might define the ACPC's "signature" conversation (the atmosphere and process) and "signature" narrative (the content of its unique principles and practices). During that meeting they identified "creating conversations that generate the experience of love" as one of the unique future competencies of ACPC.

Shifting the Conversation on Climate Change

Martin Kalungu-Banda, co-founder of Presencing Institute Africa, shares the following story:

After the Copenhagen Climate Change Conference in December 2009, there seemed to be a feeling and perception that the world had let itself down by failing to reach the kind of international agreement and commitment that would significantly and urgently begin to tackle issues of climate change. For many people and organizations, Copenhagen also exposed a disconnect between climate change discourse and development thinking and practice.

In mid-2010, the Climate and Development Knowledge Network (CDKN) began to think about how to strengthen the nexus between climate change and development. A consortium of organizations was convened to create an event that could bring new life into the climate-development nexus. This thinking culminated in the CDKN Action Lab Event, which took place in Oxford in April 2011.

Preparation for the event was led by a cross-sector group of process designers and facilitators. The intention was to create an event wherein two hundred participants from over seventy countries, covering public, private, and civil society sectors, could think and interact together in ways that could generate actionable ideas at the nexus of climate change and development. Participants' experience and expertise were gathered using online tools. Guest speakers were identified to illuminate key aspects of the challenge. Weekly meetings were held between facilitators online over a period of four months to design and test the process for hosting and conducting the event.

The hosting environment, Oxford University, was carefully chosen for its capacity to provide the space and atmosphere required for breakthrough thinking. The best practices in human interaction and systems thinking were tapped into and brought into the design. The entire process was a mix of plenary conversations, small-group discussions, and individual moments of reflection. To maximize the creativity of the participants, various tools and techniques in creative processes, such sculpting, drawing, painting, systems games, and journaling, among others, were used.

The conference began with three days of "sensing the field," seeking to understand and share as much as they could about the brutal facts of climate change. Next, participants went for an hour of deep reflection in the Oxford Botanic Gardens. The two questions that guided the reflection were "If I suspended all that is not essential, who would be my best future Self?" and "What is life asking me/us to do to create a different future for the world?" At the end of the reflection period, the two hundred participants returned to the plenary room. The group of two hundred somehow felt like a small group that had been seeking solutions to a common challenge together for a long time.

With unusual ease, they listened to each other's insights arising from the hour of silence. Much of the sharing sounded like people singing from the same page of a hymnal. We had become one in seeing what was at stake, and, even if we did not say so to one another, we seemed to have glimpsed a common future through the one-hour reflection period. The experience brought a new feeling of hope after the disappointments of Copenhagen. One participant from Ghana, Winfred, said, "Copenhagen had dampened my spirit. Now I know I do not need to be a politician to make a difference. It is our turn to provide leadership to the politicians."

Working in small groups created on the basis of interest and work/organizational focus, participants collaborated to come up with twenty-six prototypes as a way of creating the landing strips for the common future we envisioned together. Equally profound were the different collaborative relationships and networks that emerged during the four-day event.[4]

What is so interesting about Martin's story is that the voices of denial, cynicism, and depression seem to have been somewhat transformed. These networks have gone on to implement some initiatives that are proving to be cutting-edge in responding to issues of climate change, as may be seen on the CDKN website, http://cdkn.org/.

One promising development that emerged from the Oxford meeting was a similar engagement in 2012 with top national leaders in Ghana, including the vice-president, cabinet ministers, members of parliament, and many others. These leaders were invited to reflect on what climate change meant to them personally. They watched a theater performance put on by local students that demonstrated the impacts of climate change, along with a documentary that showed Ghanaian citizens asking their leaders to take action. The secretary to the cabinet reflected, "All along, we have looked at climate change as an issue far from our day-to-day work. We must use the instruments of government to create a different future for our children. How could we have let this go on for so long?" To date, over four hundred additional government officials were invited to participate in a similar process, and have committed to change in their regions.[5]

ELIAS: Emerging Leaders Innovate across Sectors

A third story brings us to Cambridge, Massachusetts. Around 2004 we started to get frustrated. Reflecting on the bigger picture, we realized that in spite of our modest progress on this project or that one, we were not having any real impact on the three big divides. We also realized that most of our work had been focused on what went on inside individual organizations, while the biggest societal problems tended to reside in the space between institutions and individuals, among sectors, systems, and their citizens.

One day, during a conversation about this with our friends Peter Senge and Dayna Cunningham, we finally decided to do something about it. Otto would go out and talk to some of the key organizations that we had been working with over the years. Starting in 2005, Otto met with some key stakeholders in these organizations and presented the issue as follows in order to recruit them as founding partners into our idea for ELIAS:

> Okay, we don't know what the future will bring, but we all pretty much know one thing: We are entering an age in which the leaders of the future will face a series of disruptions, breakdowns, and turbulence that will be unparalleled by anything that has happened in the past. So what matters now is how we prepare the people who will end up in key leadership positions over the next decade or two, how well they are networked across systems and sectors, how well they listen, how creative they are in turning problems into opportunities. And given that no single organization can build these critical capacities alone, are you willing to experiment? Are you willing to ask some of your best high-potential leaders for four or five weeks' time, over twelve months, to join a global group of young leaders from government, business, and the nonprofit sector in exploring the edges of both their systems and their selves?

Very much to our surprise, with only one exception, all of them said yes.

In March 2006, twenty-seven high-potential young leaders from ELIAS partner organizations, including Oxfam, WWF, Unilever, BASF, Nissan, UNICEF, InWEnt (Brazil), and the Ministry of Finance in Indonesia, began an innovation and learning journey that followed the U process of co-sensing, co-inspiring, and co-creating. While continuing in their day jobs, they joined us in developing and learning how to use a new set of innovation tools, including deep sensing journeys, stakeholder dialogues, strategy retreats, design studios, and rapid-cycle prototyping of their ideas in order to explore the future by doing.

By the end of the journey, we saw the following results:

1. profound personal change
2. deep relational change within and beyond the group
3. prototypes that showed a variety of new approaches. Some of them were really inspiring. Others simply seemed, at the time, like valuable learning experiences for everyone.

But what no one expected is that this mini-eco-system of small seedlings, or mini-prototypes, would continue to grow over the following years into a global ecology of innovation that is nothing short of amazing. Without anyone making much noise around this, these initiatives have organically replicated themselves multiple times and now involve dozens of institutions and thousands of people who continue to co-initiate new platforms of collaboration.

Here are some examples.

ELIAS Prototypes: A Global Innovation Ecology

- Participants from South Africa, the "Sunbelt team," wanted to explore methods for bringing solar- and wind-generated power to marginalized communities using a decentralized, democratic model of energy generation to reduce CO_2 emissions and for fostering economic growth and well-being in rural communities. Today the project has changed the strategic priorities of a global NGO and resulted in the formation of a mission-based company called Just Energy that operates in South Africa and helps local communities to participate in the rapidly growing market for renewable energy.[6]

- In Indonesia, an ELIAS fellow from the Indonesian Ministry of Trade applied the U process to establishing new government policies for sustainable sugar production. His idea was to involve all key stakeholders in the policymaking process. The results were stunning: For the first time ever, the ministry's policy decisions did not result in violent protests or riots by farmers or others in the value chain. Now the same approach is being applied across ministries to other commodities and to standards for sustainable production.

- Also in Indonesia, a trisector U-based leadership program was launched on the model of ELIAS (now called IDEAS), involving thirty leaders from all sectors. They are working on several prototype initiatives, one of them being the Bojonegoro case, discussed later. IDEAS Indonesia now has about one hundred graduates and started its fourth program in spring 2013.

- An ELIAS fellow from GIZ (the German Ministry of Development Cooperation) developed and launched a lab for combating climate change with emerging leaders in South Africa and Indonesia.

- Using ELIAS and IDEAS as a model, in 2012 the first China-based IDEAS program was launched, involving senior government officials and executives from Chinese SOEs (state-owned enterprises). The second IDEAS China program, working with some of the biggest SOEs on this planet, will be launched in 2013.

- At MIT, two ELIAS fellows teamed up to create a collaborative research venture that resulted in the founding of the MIT CoLab (Community Innovators Lab). The CoLab has since emerged as a hotspot for innovation around field-based action learning for students at the MIT Department for Urban Studies and Planning, putting Theory U and related methodologies into practice.

We have also become aware of initiatives that were inspired by ELIAS, among them the Maternal Health Initiative in Namibia and the Coral Triangle Initiative (CTI), which has produced a six-country treaty linking sustainable fishing practices with revenue-sharing and economic opportunities.[7] What's so interesting about the ELIAS network is that it continues to generate an ongoing flow of ideas and initiatives.[8]

So what did we learn from the ELIAS project about building presencing platforms for co-creative entrepreneurial initiatives?

Five Learning Experiences
ELIAS has challenged many of our deeply held assumptions. First, we now realize that although it might well have been our most powerful and influential initiative to date, ELIAS was not born out of a client-

driven relationship. No one asked us to do it. It was born out of our deep frustration and aspiration.

Second, we learned that the framing around "problem solving" that surrounds most multistakeholder work may be limiting. The deep principle should be "Energy follows attention." A mindset that is only about fixing a problem or closing a gap puts limits on creativity. In our case, it worked well to simply bring together young high-potential change-makers from diverse systems, sectors, and cultures, throw them into a broad set of unfiltered, raw experiences at the edges of their systems, equip them with good contemplation and reflection practices, and then let them make sense of what they saw and experienced together. Out of that, interesting new ideas were sure to emerge. With a supporting infrastructure, the result of such a process will be powerful—if the leaders have the opportunity to prototype what they believe in.

Third, we learned that individual skills and tools are usually overrated. While methods and tools have been a very important part of the ELIAS journey and the projects would not have been successful without them, it is also clear that the deep journey we were on made all the difference. Disconnected individuals became part of a co-creative network of change-makers. That journey seems to have switched on a *field of inspired connections* that helps people to operate from a different place, a place that is more relaxed, calm, inspired, and focused. Igniting this flame of inspired connections is the heart and essence of all education and leadership today. Everything else is secondary. In the case of ELIAS, the flame was sustained long after the program ended, and we also see it sparking outward and being reignited in many other areas. Overall it feels as if we touched a source of collectively creative power—and of karmic connections—that even today we do not fully understand.

Fourth, we learned that cross-sector platforms of innovation, leadership, and learning require a high-quality holding space. Part of that holding space is process, part of it is people, part of it is place, and part of it is purpose. But the most important ingredient is always the same: a few fully committed people who would give everything to make it work. Sometimes it's just one or two people. But if you have four of five, you may be able to make mountains move.

Fifth, we learned to attend to the crack—an opening to a future possibility that everyone can support. All cross-sector platforms suffer the same problem: The people you need are already overcommitted in their existing institutions, which explains why in most multistakeholder platforms there is a lot of talk and little action. So the only chance of building a successful platform for cross-sector, cross-institutional innovation is to pick a topic that all of the participating individuals and their institutions value very highly.

Growing the Co-Creative Economy

ELIAS, the CDKN Action Lab Event, and the Girl Scouts—ACPC Leadership Circle have other lessons to teach as well.

First: Redraw the boundaries between cooperation and competition. Capitalism 2.0 is constructed on the logic of competition. The 3.0 economy adds government action on top of that (an example is the welfare state). Today we face challenges that are characterized by simultaneous market and government failure. These problems invite us to redraw the boundaries of competition and cooperation by introducing arenas of premarket cooperation among all sectors.

Second: The most efficient way to redraw the boundaries between competition and cooperation is to build arenas or platforms of co-creation within existing eco-systems in business and society. Eco-systems are societal systems plus their enabling social, ecological, and cultural context. Examples include education systems, health systems, food systems, energy systems, and specific business systems. The stakeholders in an eco-system share some scarce resources (the commons) that all partners have a material interest in preserving and sustaining instead of overusing.

Third: The platforms and arenas of eco-system innovation need new social technologies that help stakeholders shift their collaboration from ego-system to eco-system logic and awareness. One of these social technologies is Theory U. From a Theory U point of view, it would be key to build the following five types of innovation infrastructures:

1. *Infrastructures to co-initiate.* Successful multistakeholder projects are built on the same currency: the unconditional commitment from one

or a few local leaders who are credible in their own communities. If the eco-system is highly fragmented, the core group that co-initiates the project must reflect the diversity of the overall eco-system.

2. *Infrastructures for co-sensing.* The simplest and most effective mechanism for changing our mindset from ego-system to eco-system awareness is to take people on sensing journeys to the edges of the system, where they can see it from other perspectives, particularly that of the most marginalized members. Shadowing practices and stakeholder interviews are other activities that help participants learn to see the system from the viewpoints of multiple stakeholders and from the perspective of the whole.[9] Effective co-sensing infrastructures are the ones we lack most.

3. *Infrastructures to co-inspire.* Another increasingly powerful leverage point in the area of distributed leadership concerns the use of mindfulness and presencing practices that help decision-makers to connect to their deep sources of knowing, both individually and collectively.

4. *Infrastructures for prototyping, or exploring the future by doing.* Prototyping is a process. You stop worrying about what you don't know and start acting on what you do know. A successful prototyping process requires a dedicated core group that is aligned around the same intention; a network of supportive stakeholders and users; a concrete "0.8 prototype" (one that is incomplete but elicits feedback from partners throughout the system); a firm resolve by the core group to push forward while integrating feedback from stakeholders; and review sessions that look at all the prototypes, conclude what has been learned, take out what isn't working, and strengthen what is working.

5. *Infrastructures for co-evolving.* Micro- and frontline prototype initiatives are seeds that leaders can plant and support in selected parts of the system. Growing, sustaining, scaling, and evolving these initiatives in the context of the larger system require cross-functional, cross-level, and cross-institutional leadership learning and hands-on innovation initiatives. In order to provide this support, the team at the top also requires a helping infrastructure to progress on their own leadership journey from ego- to eco-system awareness.

Conclusion and Practices

Working with the U process has taught us that breaking through patterns of downloading and connecting individuals to their Self (with a capital S) is essential for an open process of co-creation. Taking a diverse group of stakeholders through a U journey bends the beam of conversation across the following stages of conversation:

Level 1: conforming, or projecting and confirming your existing judgments onto others;

Level 2: confronting, or surfacing the differences that stakeholders hold as they view the issue from very different angles;

Level 3: connecting, or holding these different views simultaneously, thereby bending the beam of attention back onto the observing self—helping a system to see itself (dialogue);

Level 4: co-creative flow, or bending the beam of attention back onto the sources of creativity and self—helping a system to connect to its emerging future Self.

TOOL: STAKEHOLDER INTERVIEWS

At the end of the earlier chapters, we offered you journaling questions as tools to explore the relevance of the chapters' content to your own work and life. At the end of this chapter, we suggest a different tool: stakeholder interviews. The purpose of a stakeholder interview is to develop the capacity to see your work from the perspective of your most important stakeholders. It's an example of the sensing tools that we emphasized so much in this chapter. Find the complete tool description online on www.presencing.com/tools/u-browser.

If you cannot go online, here is a short summary: Identify three to five really important stakeholders in your life and/or work. Invite each of them to a conversation in which you pose the following seven questions (modify the questions as needed for your particular situation):

1. What are you seeking to accomplish in your work, and what is my contribution to that work?

2. Can you give me an example of a time when my contribution has been helpful to you?

3. Which criteria do you use to gauge whether or not my contribution to your work has been successful?

4. Which two things, if changed in my arena of influence or responsibility within the next three to four months, would create the most value for you?

5. Which issues have made it difficult for us to work together effectively in the past?

6. What best possible future would you like to see in regard to our collaboration going forward?

7. What might be a first practical next step that will move us onto that path of desired future possibility?

CIRCLE CONVERSATION

1. Invite each person to share some key insights from the stakeholder interviews.

2. Reflect on some emerging themes.

3. Invite those who want to share a story of when they experienced of a shift in the social field, like the one in Berlin or the one that Beth Jandernoa shared in this chapter. Share a story of a time when you saw a social field shift from one state to another—what changes did you notice in the field in how people interact? What changes did you notice in yourself?

7

Leading the Institutional Inversion: Toward Eco-System Economies

The next social revolution has to be an institutional one. A revolution that helps us to bend the beam of institutional attention all the way back to source—that is, to a place where the institutional system can see and renew itself.

Shifting the Locus of Leadership

What do you do when you are part of a system whose vital components operate in separate silos? Answer: You connect them. *You shift the locus of leadership from the center to the periphery*—that is, from one place to many places. You connect these places in ways that facilitate sense-making in more distributed, direct, and dialogic ways.

We witness this process of shifting the locus of leadership from one place in the center to many places on the periphery in numerous institutions today. The process is driven by globalization, the rise of the World Wide Web, and the blend of new information and communication technologies that allow for distributed and decentralized ways of organizing. We witnessed a first wave of this process when global companies and organizations started to decentralize their decision-making processes according to functions, divisions, and geography.

Today we see a second wave further shifting the locus of leadership. Decision-making is being pushed even further out, beyond the boundaries of the organization. This process is referred to by different names: extended enterprise, innovation eco-system, crowdsourcing, swarm intelligence. What is happening in organizations today is what has happened to nation-states in a globalized world before: Both became *too small for the big problems* and *too big for the small problems*.

The result is an inversion of the old model. The pyramid is flipped upside-down so that the cultivation of *co-creative relationships* among stakeholders is at the heart of the new eco-system model of organizing.

Institutional Inversion

Before we begin discussing different examples of institutional inversion, let us briefly review the four main logics of institutional power and organizing.

We will track the journey from 1.0 to 4.0 through the concept of inversion, which is a translation of the German *Umstülpung* (inverting and upending). Otto came across the concept of *Umstülpung* when studying the work of the German avant-garde artist Joseph Beuys in Germany. The simplest example of inversion is this: Hold a sock in one hand and with the other reach deep inside it, pulling the toe back until you have turned the whole thing inside out. The completion of that movement is inversion, or *Umstülpung*.

The same principle applies to transforming the field structure of an institution. Here it means inverting the geometry of power. The following four figures present a graphical depiction of that process: The source of power shifts from the top-center of the pyramid (1.0) to closer to the base (2.0), then to the periphery (3.0) and to the surrounding sphere of a system (4.0). The resulting structural journey of transformation is marked by a complete inversion.

In 1.0 structures, power is located at the top of the pyramid. The organizational structure is centralized and top down. Coordination works through hierarchy and centralized regulation or planning. The 1.0 structures work well as long as the core group at the top is really good and the organization is relatively small. Once organizations or companies begin to grow, they need to decentralize in order to move decision-making closer to markets or citizens. The resulting 2.0 structures are defined by both hierarchy and competition.

In a 2.0 structure, decentralization enables the source of power to move closer to the real work in the periphery. Coordination works through markets and competition. The focus shifts from inputs to output. The result is a functionally or divisionally differentiated structure

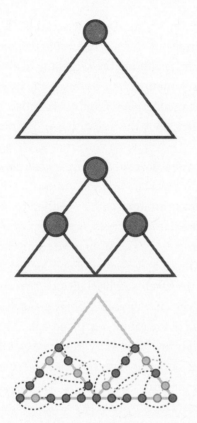

FIGURE 11. Structure 1.0: pyramid. Power is centralized and resides at the top. Solid lines here indicate traditional vertical leadership structures.

FIGURE 12. Structure 2.0: decentralized. The source of power moves closer to the base.

FIGURE 13. Structure 3.0: networked. Sources of power turn relational. Dotted lines here and in the following figures indicate networked and relational leadership, rather than hierarchical structures.

in which decisions are made closer to markets and consumers or to communities and citizens (figure 12). The good thing about 2.0 structures is the entrepreneurial independence of all of its divisions or units. The bad thing is that no one is managing the space between the units.

Which brings us to 3.0 structures, in which the source of power moves even farther from the top and originates *beyond* the traditional boundaries of the organization. The result is a flattening of structures and a networked type of organizing. Coordination works through negotiation and dialogue among stakeholders and organized interest groups. Power emerges from the relationships between players across boundaries (figure 13).

The good thing about 3.0 structures is their networked connections. The bad thing is the increase in vested interests. Special-interest groups use their networked connections to benefit their ego-interests while compromising the well-being of the whole. Examples include Wall Street (making taxpayers pay for its own risk-taking), Monsanto (displacing farmers in India from their cultural property rights), big energy companies (funding pseudo-science around climate change that is designed to confuse the public), the health industry (keeping health-care costs outrageously high), labor unions (often paying little attention to the well-being of unemployed nonmembers), and environmental organizations (often paying little attention to the well-being of communities in protected areas).[1]

In 4.0 structures, the source of power moves to the *surrounding sphere* of co-creative relationships among individuals and institutions in the entire eco-system. Coordination works through shared attention to the emerging whole. In 4.0, power emerges from the presence of that whole (we-in-me) rather than the mere ego-presence of its members (I-in-me) in a given eco-system. Figure 14 shows that the flattening of the hierarchy from 1.0 to 3.0 continues below the baseline. The U-shaped territory below the baseline of the flipped pyramid represents the transformed relational space through the opening of the mind, heart, and will.

The journey from 1.0 to 4.0 is an inversion story in two respects. First, it is an inversion of the source of power from the top and center (1.0) to the base/periphery (2.0) to beyond the organizational boundaries (3.0) to the surrounding eco-system (4.0). This journey is a profound opening process of a closed pyramid (1.0) until it is completely upended and inverted (4.0).

And, second, it is an inversion that concerns the reintegration of mind and matter. In 1.0, the mind-matter split is the defining feature of the system: Leadership power originates at the top, and there is maximum distance between the top and the base of the pyramid—that is, between mind (governing, leading) and matter (frontline work). The rest of the journey reduces and transforms the distance between the top and the base of the system (the pyramid) as follows. In 2.0 structures, the vertical split is somewhat reduced through decentralizing and divisionalizing. In 3.0 structures, the vertical split is further narrowed through horizontal networked organizing at the base of the system. Networked organizing is effective at reducing the vertical distance, but is less effective at transforming habitual mindsets. The final shift, to 4.0, is a move from the base of what used to be a pyramid to a "negative space" below the former pyramid's base—that is, to a space that allows the system to see itself in order to facilitate the shift from ego-system to eco-system

FIGURE 14. Structure 4.0:
inverted pyramid. Transforming
relationships from ego (I-in-me)
to eco (we-in-me).

awareness. Any system or community that wants to become aware of itself has to cultivate that negative space below the former base; that is, it has to cultivate the soil of the social field, the root system of the emerging new 4.0 types of organizing.

Institutional inversion can thus be described as a profound opening process that shifts the source of power from the top/center to the surrounding sphere. It can also be told as a story of overcoming the vertical mind-matter split between leadership and frontline work in a system by inverting the pyramidal structure into a U-shaped holding space that cultivates the root processes of the social field: attending, conversing, organizing, and integrating.

Leading the 4.0 Revolution across Sectors

In spite of the importance of personal and relational change, we all know that none of the change initiatives discussed in earlier chapters will make a dent in the global challenges that we face unless we succeed in transforming the key institutions that constitute our society's systems.

The way we do this is by helping them to advance to 4.0. This requires a process of institutional inversion that replaces and supplements the old mechanisms of hierarchy and competition. The cultivation of dialogic and co-creative relationships will allow the stakeholders in each eco-system to innovate at the scale of the whole.

This chapter outlines a developmental roadmap for the institutional transformation that our generation is called to bring about. We can do it proactively, or we can leave it to our children after a long series of painful external disruptions and shocks. It's a transformation that has been in the making for many years. The journey to 4.0 is the next stage of a process that has been continuing over several centuries, and which differs

TABLE 9 Sectors of the Current Institutional Transformation

Stage	Government	Health	Schools	Companies	NGOs	Banks
1.0 Traditional Awareness: *Hierarchy*	Dominating state	Authority and input-centered: *institution-driven*	Authority and input-centered: *teacher-driven*	Centralized: hierarchy: *owner-driven*	Program-focused: *reactive-driven*	Traditional banking: *owner-driven*
2.0 Ego-System Awareness: *Markets and Competition*	Dormant state	Outcome-centered: *managed care–driven*	Outcome-centered: *testing-driven*	Decentralized: divisions: *shareholder- and target-driven*	Policy-focused: *advocacy- and campaign-driven*	Casino banking: *speculation-driven*
3.0 Stakeholder Awareness: *Networks and Negotiation*	Welfare state	Patient-centered: *need-driven pathogenesis*	Student-centered: *learning-driven*	Matrix or network: *stakeholder-driven*	Strategic initiative–focused: *stakeholder-driven*	Socially responsible banking: *stakeholder-driven*
4.0 Eco-System Awareness: *Awareness-Based Collective Action (ABC)*	D-4: direct, distributed, democratic, dialogic	Citizen-centered: *well-being-driven, salutogenesis*	Entrepreneurial-centered: *co-sensing- and co-creating-driven*	Co-creative eco-system: *intention-driven*	Eco-system-focused: *intention-driven*	Transformative eco-system banking: *intention-driven*

in form based on place, sector, and culture. The 4.0 revolution will look different in China, South America, and Africa than it looks in the West. It will also differ somewhat across systems of health, education, energy, and agriculture. Yet in essence our experience has been that all sectors and systems deal fundamentally with the same challenge: to develop the capacity to act from the whole.

Table 9 provides an overview of this chapter: It shows how all of society's systems have been walking on parallel paths from 1.0 to the emerging possibility of 4.0. The rest of the chapter focuses on how to move each system from ego- to eco-system awareness—that is, from organizing around special interests to organizing around common intention. The walls of the silos that have contained these systems for so long will gradually but inevitably open up as we progress on our journey toward 4.0.

GOVERNMENT AND DEMOCRACY 4.0:
DIRECT, DISTRIBUTED, DIGITAL, AND DIALOGIC

The journey to Government 4.0 is an institutional transformation from

1.0: a centralized ruler-centric system (*l'état c'est moi*—"the State, it's me"); to

2.0: an abstract, differentiated machine bureaucracy (à la Max Weber); to

3.0: a networked government that pays more attention to citizens; to

4.0: a distributed, direct, dialogic system that operates by connecting to and empowering its citizens to co-shape the whole.

This journey to Government 4.0 is highly intertwined with the journey to Democracy 4.0, which moves from

1.0: one-party democracy (centralized); to

2.0: multiparty indirect (parliamentary) democracy; to

3.0: participatory indirect (parliamentary) democracy; to

4.0: participatory direct, distributed, digital, and dialogic (4-D) democracy.

The transformation to Democracy 4.0 entails shifting the source of power from the habitual actions of the center to the real needs and aspirations of the communities on the periphery—from a top-down leadership to a shared process of co-sensing and co-shaping the new.

Here are two examples that offer some glimpses of that emerging future.

Bojonegoro, East Java, Indonesia: Shifting the Field of Democracy to 4.0

The IDEAS Indonesia program that Otto chairs at MIT is a nine-month innovation journey based on systems thinking and presencing that guides diverse groups of high-potential leaders from government, business, and NGOs through a deep immersion journey to the edges of society and self. In the second half of that program, participants develop prototype initiatives to explore the future by doing. One prototype generated in one of the recent programs addressed the issue of government corruption.

Led by Bupati Suyoto, the regent of Bojonegoro, the prototype's goal was to reduce corruption and improve the quality of government services in the district. In a move from Government 1.0 to 2.0, in 2005 Indonesia shifted from centralized governmental decision-making to a more decentralized model that empowered the four hundred regencies in the country and their directly elected Bupatis (regents).

Bojonegoro, one of these regencies in East Java, had long been known for high levels of corruption and low service quality. But in 2011 and 2012, Bojonegoro emerged as one of the *ten best* regencies nationwide according to various quality assessments, and received multiple prestigious awards for low levels of corruption and high levels of service quality. What happened?

Bupati Suyoto, a 2010 graduate of the MIT IDEAS Indonesia program, came into power without any support from established interest groups. With no money and no budget for his election campaign, at first no one gave him a chance. But he did the only thing he could: He went to the villages and listened to the citizens. In a surprise victory, he removed the incumbent Bupati from his post. In 2012, he was reelected by an even wider margin, even though other candidates were backed by powerful industrial interests (the region has one of the biggest oil reservoirs in the country) and ran very expensive advertising campaigns against him. So again, what happened? How is it possible that a single person with no big-business support could run and win against power-ful vested interests like the oil industry?

On his first day in office, Bupati Suyoto called for a general assembly of all government employees in his regency. Many of the senior people expected to lose their jobs because they had actively worked against him during the campaign. In his address to them, Suyoto delivered two main messages. First: Everyone would keep their jobs. He said that he didn't want to look backward but to look forward, building a future that would be different from the past. The other message consisted of three things he didn't want them to do: (1) Don't take any money; (2) don't complain about your job; and (3) don't say, "This is not my job" or "This is not my responsibility."

When he delivered these messages, people were surprised. They lis-tened politely, but hardly anyone believed that he really meant what he said. According to some of the participants, probably 80 percent of them remained skeptical. After all, most public servants and politicians had had to borrow money to "buy" their current positions and hence needed bribes to repay these loans.

So how did the Bupati manage to shift the mindsets of the skeptics who surrounded him in office in spite of all these economic forces work-ing against him? In the beginning, he made three primary moves.

First, he continued to communicate the three don'ts and embodied these principles in his own everyday behavior. For example, in his offi-cial residence, he opted to use the small guest quarters for himself and his family while offering his official guests (and sometimes his driver) the larger space. With this unusual move, he demonstrated that the State House didn't belong to him personally; he was just there as a guest, like everyone else before him and after him.

Second, he developed a series of intense offsite leadership retreats with his core team. These retreats facilitated the letting-go of old mind-sets and tuning in to new inspirations, intentions, and identities.

Third, he started to close the feedback loop between people and their government officials. How? By activating four simple mechanisms:

1. *Text messaging:* He gave his cell phone number to citizens and told them that they could text him at any time. Since then he has received

hundreds of text messages every day. He responds to many of them personally. Many others he forwards to his directors and department heads. Everyone in his administration is expected to respond to a message from a citizen within a day or two.

2. *Open door:* Anyone can walk into his office at any time.

3. *Town hall:* Every Friday afternoon he conducts a town hall community dialogue meeting to which all citizens are invited and which all his top civil servants are required to attend. I (Otto) attended one of these meetings. First a farmer raised his issue: He had no access to fertilizers. When he sat down, the microphone went to the head of the Department of Agriculture to explain the problem and say what could be done to fix it. The department head was a bit defensive. But he also knew that next week he would be back there facing the same people and the Bupati. So he had every incentive to fix the problem within a week's time. Next came a woman in her twenties wearing a hijab, the Muslim head scarf. She said she was an educator and needed books to support her teaching in the villages. The classes that she wanted to teach included sex education for girls, and there were no instructional materials available. She completed her request without any sign of fear or hesitation (I had to remind myself that I was watching a town hall meeting in the biggest Muslim country on earth). The Bupati responded by telling her how to find the resources she needed. He said that one of the big US oil companies had come to his office earlier that day and asked what they could do to help the community. The Bupati told the teacher to submit to him a summary of the program and also pose her request directly to the oil company. There is no doubt that she will get what she needed. Nevertheless, if she stumbles into unexpected delays from the oil company or even his own staff, she should come back to him. Everyone in the community was listening to the exchange between the young woman from the village and the Bupati—and that shared listening turned her initiative into a legitimate community project.

4. *Village visits:* Fourth, *every single day* the Bupati takes his key officials to villages where they conduct a similar dialogue on a local level.

What do these four mechanisms add up to? Listening. Listening by government officials to the everyday experiences of their citizens. Listening by different citizen groups to one another. And listening by the community to itself (dialogue).

When I saw these different types of listening closing all the feedback loops, I thought, "Boy, that's exactly what's missing in our democratic institutions in the West and other parts of the world today." In the West, elected officials spend all their time listening to the lobbyists and organized interest groups who finance their election campaigns. For example, in the United States, members of Congress spend about 50 percent of their time fundraising for their *next* election campaign. The system works by turning lawmakers *away* from listening to real citizen needs. In contrast, the Bojonegoro story worked by interrupting that toxic cycle (the "three don'ts") and then establishing four direct feedback loops. The promulgation of Law 23/2011, passed in 2011, evidenced that the four direct feedback loops can be written in stone and applied not only in Bojonegoro but also have greater implications at the national level of greater Indonesia. This is another great example of how leaders can efficiently listen to constituents. It also proves that political parties are actually manageable when the leader is independent, sound, and solid.

In a nutshell, what we saw in Bojonegoro was a profound shift in the field of government and democracy from primarily 1.0 to what may have been 3.0, with the first elements of 4.0. That shift deepened democratic forms by making government more direct, distributed, digital, and dialogic. I felt that community's presence when I was asked, at the end of the gathering in the town hall, to address the group. It was an intimate and grounding experience. I felt the power of community for a moment or two—a power that in most places today is shockingly underused.

Without significant strengthening of 4-D citizen connections, Western democracy could soon find itself in the same situation that an American colonel faced in 1975 when he debated a North Vietnamese colonel. "You know you never defeated us on the battlefield," said the American colonel. The North Vietnamese colonel pondered this remark a moment. "That may be so," he replied, *"but it is also irrelevant."*[2]

To stay relevant to the challenges of our time, we have to advance our institutions of democracy and government to 4.0. Examples like Bojonegoro can give us some seeds of inspiration for that. Another seed of inspiration for Government 4.0 comes from Brazil.

Brazil: Transforming the Secretariat of the National Heritage

Alexandra Reschke served as Brazilian Secretary General for National Heritage (SPU) during President Lula's term. Upon taking office, she saw that the organization was becoming obsolete, a result of disregard on the part of previous administrations. Reschke also noticed that the way people communicated within the organization was harming relationships. She saw this as a leverage point for sparking change within the organization. This strategy proved so successful that eight years later, the changes Reschke set in motion are still visible and felt. What did she do, and how?

As a woman in a very powerful position, she purposefully chose what she called "a feminine leadership style" and recommended that decision-making happen through circles of conversation. Thus began a new era at SPU.

The idea was to shift away from people not saying what they were feeling and thinking and toward a way of conversing where the conversation itself would become the field for collaboration and generative action. She put a process into place to change existing communication habits, adding moments of stillness and retreat before the circles. She immediately started preparing for the first National Strategic Management of SPU, which occurred in early 2004, bringing together all the leaders in Brasília and several of SPU's partners for the first time in its 150 years of existence.

Over the years, SPU managed to change the very structure of the organization, from an authoritarian, pyramid model to circles of conversation. SPU went from being "obsolete" to being recognized as an outstanding public agency by 2007. It brought together different sectors of society to create an innovative and legal participatory way to ensure regularization of land for thousands of riverside communities in the Amazon.[3]

Reschke summarizes her journey with three lessons: (1) Dare to be different; (2) believe in people; and (3) invest in cooperation. "We moved together [as people]; as a result the institution came along."[4] For her, the learning came from the willingness of people at SPU to exercise the values of authentic conversation and empathic listening as a new way of co-shaping their collective future.

Another interesting example is the participatory budgeting model that the city of Porto Alegre, Brazil, pioneered starting in 1989. It allows its citizens to discuss, identify, and prioritize public spending projects. It has been an inspiration to many and has been replicated in more than

140 municipalities in Brazil. According to a study by the World Bank, it has led to better matching of social services with community needs. However, it has been also criticized for not sufficiently involving the most marginalized groups (people living in poverty as well as young people) and for the susceptibility of the process to hijacking by existing vested interests.[5]

The two regions with the most efficient governments and public services in the world are the Confucian cultural sphere in East and Southeast Asia (Singapore, Korea, Japan, China, Taiwan, and Vietnam), and Northern Europe. The Nordic countries (Denmark, Sweden, Finland, and to some degree Norway) and Singapore are at the top of the rankings for government efficiency, education, health, competiveness, and wellbeing. The Nordic countries faced a perfect storm in the 1990s when all their eastern markets disappeared with the collapse of the Soviet Union, and their 3.0 welfare state model faced a severe financial crisis. Nonetheless, since then, these countries and their public sectors have reemerged with a leaner, better, and more transparent model of government that focuses on empowering citizens to be entrepreneurial and inventive (for more detail, see the story about the Danish health system later in this chapter).[6]

HEALTH 4.0

The institutional transformation of the health-care system follows roughly the same journey from 1.0 to 4.0 that we have described in other areas. It is a journey from

1.0: input and authority-centered institutional care; to

2.0: outcome-centered managed care; to

3.0: patient-centered integrative care; to

4.0: citizen-centered holistic-integral care.

Here are two examples that shed some light on transforming a health-care system in light of the above framework.

Namibia

Our work on the health-care system in Namibia started as a partnership among the Synergos Institute, McKinsey and Company, and the Presencing Institute. In the early stages of the process, in the fall of 2010, Otto conducted a three-day workshop with the cabinet of Namibia. On the first day, the prime minister explained the core issue they were confronted with, as he saw it: "We need to reconnect our political process to the real needs of the communities. Right now our political process is largely disconnected from the real needs in the villages."[7]

One of the ministers added: "Here is what our situation is like. You must understand that we have all these planning routines. We have our vision 2030. We have our five-year plan. We have our strategic plan. And we have our annual budget plans. To develop all of these plans takes a lot of time. The problem is that these plans do not talk to each other and they all do not connect to what is really going on." All of the government leaders in the room agreed that this was a major issue they were dealing with: the disconnect between their government routines and services on the one hand and the actual needs of the village communities on the other hand.

The second disconnect they described involved the top of the pyramid. "We cannot really talk to our top civil servants," one minister explained to me; "they do not really take us seriously. They feel they got into their job through professional qualifications, but that we, the ministers, are just political appointees. You know, just because we have political connections, not because we are competent." Other ministers in the room nodded in agreement.

Then another minister explained a third disconnect, the pervasive silo issue that fragments the work of government agencies in many places. "The silo issue starts right here, between us," she said and looked into the faces of her colleagues, "because we do not really talk straight with each other. It starts with us and then the same behavior gets replicated throughout our ministries." The silo issue impedes communication between as well as inside ministries.

Our work with the Ministry of Health and Social Services confirmed the existence of these divides. We started with a joint assessment of the situation that identified weak leadership, work processes separated into silos, dysfunctional structures, no strategic planning, no proper data collection, and no clear targets, and we found that the ministry was off track to meet the UN's Millennium Development Goals (MDGs).

After three years of collaboration, several of these problems have been successfully addressed, though many will require further work. Throughout this process, however, something very important has changed. Namibia's leaders have begun to recognize their own role in perpetuating the problems and are taking initiative and responsibility in working on innovative solutions.

Here are a few lessons we identified from their journey of transforming the system beyond 1.0:

Co-initiation. The first phase established common ground and a shared intention among the Namibian Ministry of Health's key players. The international partners wanted to develop cross-sector platforms of innovation and leadership. The ministry leaders, however, were more interested in getting their civil servants to work as a team. We (the international and Namibian facilitation team) therefore abandoned our original plan and started by attending to the stated needs of our partners on the ground. We realized that if you want to change others, you first need to be open to change yourself.

Co-sensing. A successful sensing journey breaks down outdated and artificial boundaries. In Namibia, we had to open health leaders' eyes to the system as seen through the eyes of patients, nurses, and remote communities. This type of sensing journey is conducted in small groups of five to seven persons (so everyone can fit into one car or van) over multiple days.

Co-inspiring. The most important change in any transformation journey is the change of heart. That change requires deep reflection and contemplation practices along with a supportive infrastructure, including workshops, coaching, and peer coaching. These activities address both individual needs and the team or organizational culture: reconnecting to the deeper purpose, developing team spirit, prioritizing, and encouraging personal responsibility.

Co-creating. All deep cultural changes and institutional innovations require learning by doing. The prototyping stage in the Namibian health project generated the idea for Regional Delivery Units (RDUs). A small cross-sector group of leaders, including nurses, doctors, and the regional director, hold weekly meetings as a way of learning by doing. Their objective is to improve maternal health. Each discussion begins with a review of the week's data and events. These meetings allow professionals of different ranks to communicate, question one another, and exchange views in a supportive and nonjudgmental environment. At one of the RDU team meetings I (Otto) attended, they discussed a situation of concern to the nurses. At one point in the discussion, a junior nurse, a young woman, turned to the most senior leader at the table (the director of the entire region), who had not participated in the discussion before. She said: "I gather from your body language that you do not agree with what is being said here." And then it was the director's turn to explain his reading of the situation. When I heard that junior nurse draw out the most senior person in the group, I knew that something was working—they had established a constructive communication and learning culture.

Today (in 2013) these RDU team processes are being rolled out throughout Namibia's thirteen regions. This work is being performed by and is owned by Namibians, without any of the international partners. The RDU process helps leaders in the regions to focus on accountability for improved outcomes. The teams then drive policy implementation, coordinate service delivery, manage progress on goals, and solve problems to ensure the effectiveness of health interventions. Discovering what makes these groups effective is an ongoing process of learning by doing.

Co-evolving. "I used to think that the Permanent Secretary in Windhoek had to take final responsibility for health. But now I understand that *I* am the permanent secretary of my region and I have to take responsibility," says Bertha Katjivena, regional health director of Hardap Region. She is one of twenty-five existing and emerging leaders who meet regularly in Leadership Development Forums (LDFs). Deputy Permanent Secretary Dr. Norbert Forster smiled when he recounted the progress of that team. "There was a rigidity in the way that the department worked, with different departments in silos, and there was a disconnect between the national level and the thirteen regions," he says. "The process we went through focused on breaking down barriers through workshops and retreats. People have gotten to know each other. Through joint sense-making and visioning, we have developed a cohesive team we didn't have before. By the end of this process, there will be a major change in organizational culture, from working in silos to working in teams."

Overall, the Namibia process helped to get the system from 1.0 (each part contained within its own silo) to 2.0 (being more responsive to patients) and 3.0 (cross-silo collaboration in the RDUs).

Moving to 4.0, to a system driven by the goal to strengthen the sources of health of the whole community, of all citizens, is still a task for the future. Which brings us to the next stop: Denmark.

Regional Health Transformation in Denmark

In the fall of 2010, the leadership team of a large Danish university hospital came to Boston to conduct a leadership workshop. Supported by our Danish colleague Karen Ingerslev, the group conducted stakeholder interviews before arriving in Boston. Stakeholder interviews help decision-makers to see their roles through the eyes of their stakeholders. One of the main insights that the leaders took away was that their role as hospital leaders was not limited to their own hospital, but was connected to the quality of health in their entire region.

The following year the group suggested a follow-on workshop with the entire leadership team in central Denmark, including the management teams of all the smaller hospitals in the region. It was a very interesting process that allowed me (Otto) to observe a rapid transformation from ego-system awareness to eco-system awareness up close.

The stakes for these leaders were very high. Hospitals were being merged and/or closed left and right in order to reduce square footage amid stagnating budgets and increasing performance pressures from stakeholders. As Ole Thomsen, the leader of the group, put it: "The problem is we have systems that we cannot put more money into. Our challenge is how we can develop more quality with less resources."[8]

Every one of them felt enormous pressure to fight on behalf of their home organization to hold on to existing positions, functions, and funding streams. How do you build trust in an environment where competitive and survival genes are hypercharged?

We started with sensing. Over several weeks the group conducted stakeholder interviews and sensing journeys. The workshop started by synthesizing their insights from the sensing activities through café conversation, modeling, and stakeholder mapping. Later we asked them to use Social Presencing Theater to enact how they saw the current system and how they saw the future that wanted to emerge. Social Presencing Theater is a method developed under the leadership of Arawana Hayashi at the Presencing Institute; it blends elements of mindfulness, theater, dance, dialogue, social sciences, and constellation work.

When they mapped out current reality—which we call Sculpture 1— they quickly formed a constellation that looked very institution-centric, with the management teams of each hospital in control at the top. Then, when we ask them to draw Sculpture 2, another constellation that represents the future of the system that they feel is wanting to emerge, the group moved the relationship between patient and care provider into the center of the health-care system. Interestingly, we noted that Sculpture 2 showed two interconnected spheres. The first sphere was related to health care and put the *patient* at the center; the second, adjacent sphere was related to sources of health and put the *citizen* (not the patient) at the center, surrounded by relationships with family, civic organizations, and community.

As they morphed from Sculpture 1 to Sculpture 2, the management teams of the hospitals saw their own role changing. In Sculpture 1, the hospital managers were between the department heads and the nurses and physicians, blocking the direct connection between health-care providers and citizens (not patients). In Sculpture 2, one part of the hospital management teams left their position and reached out to citizens, communities, and civil society, while others moved in the opposite direction in order to jointly form a holding space for the new relationship between health-care providers and patients and citizens.

In the language of table 9, we can see Sculpture 1 as an enactment of managed care (health 2.0), with the patient experience fragmented by many competing hospitals and entities. Sculpture 2 has elements of health 3.0 (integrating the various provider institutions to optimize a seamless patient journey) as well as 4.0 (reaching out to the citizen space and citizen journey and creating a holding space for the entire health eco-system).

Although this started as an exercise, what was most inspiring was that these health-care workers then put some of their ideas to work. They told their leaders: "We appreciate your leadership, but you could better use our expertise if you asked us some key questions instead of just imposing solutions on us. That way we could co-create the solution together." After hearing that suggestion, Ole Thomsen was inspired to change the way the regional leadership team operates by conducting several regular meetings in the form of case clinics.[9]

The workshop ended with the group developing five prototype initiatives. In only two months they achieved some astonishing results, including taking the first steps toward replacing the financial model, based on activity and productivity targets ("the more procedures we perform, the more money we bring in"), with one that puts the health of citizens and patients first. This required a shift in mindset from ego-system ("the more for us, the better") to eco-system awareness ("the better for patients and citizens, the better for all of us").

When I (Otto) saw the same group present this and other prototyping results two months later, I understood a little better why the Danes, Finns, and Swedes rank so highly, as mentioned before. It's their leadership culture. They are not afraid to challenge one another. And when challenged, they listen to one another. The leaders are willing to listen to subordinates and to conflicting stakeholders and to give credit to useful points of view. They are willing to put their egos aside for just a bit and to listen and think about what might be in the best interest of the entire region. It's not easy. It's hard work. But it's possible. I saw it happen as I watched. And that may well be the most important message from Northern Europe to the rest of the world today: It's possible. Just do it!

EDUCATION 4.0

Just as the transformation of a health-care system revolves around transforming the relationship between patient and health-care provider from doctor-centric (1.0) to co-creative (4.0), the education system is likewise going through a transformation process that revolves around the relationship between learner and educator (see table 9).

Accordingly, the institutional transformation of the education system is a journey from

1.0: an input- and authority-centered, teacher-driven way of organizing, to one that is

2.0: outcome-centered and testing-driven, to one that is

3.0: student-centered and learning-driven, to one that is

4.0: entrepreneurial-centered, co-creative, and presencing-driven.

Vienna: Reinventing the Educational System

One of the first times I (Otto) met the Austrian minister of education and culture, Claudia Schmied, and her ministry team, was during a half-day workshop. We were sitting at a long rectangular table. The minister and her dynamic young assistants sat opposite me at the head of the table. Next to them, on one long side, were all her department heads, people who had spent most of their careers inside the ministry; across from them, on the other long side, was a group of school innovators from Germany and Austria. As I looked at the school innovators and the department heads facing each other, it felt as if the twenty-first century were meeting the nineteenth, with the minister and her team in between. The minister was full of energy and inspiration. She came to her job from a business and organizational change background—not a typical party career. I silently wished that her good energy would never dissipate.

Fast-forward a year. I was back in Vienna, this time for a country-wide network meeting of education innovators from throughout the system. Instead of 10 grassroots innovators, there were now 250. There were fewer ministry people, but they were still visible. Somehow the whole educational system seemed to be present. During that meeting we asked everyone to reflect on three aspects of the educational system: the changing learner-teacher relationship; the school as a learning organization; and the countrywide system as a whole.

It took the local innovators only an hour or two to establish that they all agreed on 80 or 90 percent of the changes the system needed, but that none of these changes were reflected in the political discourse in the country. There was a complete disconnect between the education innovators at the school level and the national political discourse.

Fast-forward another year. This time another group of 250 change-makers met in Alpbach, Austria. Before Minister Schmied arrived, we held a first session in which we asked participants where they saw a world that was dying and where they experienced a world wanting to be born. What was dying, they said, was "the teacher who transfers knowledge, who acts as a single player. . . . " What was being born was "the teacher as coach and team player."

"What is dying is a pedagogy that revolves around techniques and recipes. What is being born is a pedagogy that revolves around sensing and actualizing the best potential in students."

"What we need to let go of," added others, is "thinking of school in terms of lessons or periods" and "a culture of regulation and control. What we need to develop is a new form of equal collaboration among parents, teachers, and students."

A third cluster of statements focused on evaluation. "There are many good things in the system, but the focus on standards and outputs is killing the new; the old standards of evaluation impose their stamp on the new."

And a fourth cluster focused on the system as a whole: "We are constantly tinkering with rebuilding the school; we are replacing a window here and another door there—but what we really need is a *new foundation for the entire house.*"

When I heard these comments, I realized that the minister's efforts had not been in vain. Somehow she had managed to bring all of the players into connection with one another. The practical outcomes and accomplishments were nothing short of amazing. Against the combined resistance of the conservative establishment and the teachers' union, the minister and her team managed to first prototype and then scale her concept of the New Middle School, one among several key initiatives that she used to bring the Austrian education system into the twenty-first century. She also focused on building individual and collective leadership capacity throughout the system.

Claudia Schmied, who travels the country on regular listening journeys, embodies a new breed of political leadership: independent, professional, self-reflective, inspired, courageous, and playful in taking on powerful vested interests in her country. To me she demonstrates that there are no limits to how big our impact can be if we connect to the deep intention of our journey.

Minister Schmied reflects on the journey of systemic change she has been witnessing and leading:

> The school system in Austria still has many System 1.0 elements, including a culture of centralized regulation and control. The authorities are supposed to fix the problems. Moreover, we increasingly see elements of System 2.0, where demographic changes (fewer students) or choices by parents create competition among schools. Elements of System 3.0 are very strongly developed in the Austrian educational system, for example in the political power that the teachers' union has over all key educational topics in the country.
>
> But the goal should be to realize the qualities and mental models of System 4.0. If we succeed, all school partners will focus on creating a successful school; teachers will see themselves as "Zubin Mehtas," as conductors and orchestrators of the highest creativity in their students; students will experience co-shaping the system. The foundation of System 4.0 is the common will. That means moving the relational dimension to center stage. This is what matters most. It's about what our schools of the future will be able to perform in order to serve the individual and communal well-being.[10]

Reinventing an education system for the now-emerging 4.0 world requires more than improving test scores or adding some new classes to the curriculum. It requires a common will, as Claudia Schmied puts it, to renew the very foundation of the whole house, of our entire educational system. It requires an understanding that the essence of all real education is transformation, tapping our deep capacities to create and providing resources for "transformative literacy."[11]

Wherever you go, people believe their educational systems are in crisis. Some systems see a crisis of performance: They want students to perform better on standardized tests (Education 2.0). Others see a crisis of process: They want to make learning more student-centered, turn teachers into coaches, and so on (Education 3.0). And a few want to provide learners with the chance to achieve their highest future potential as human beings, to have access to their best sources of creativity and entrepreneurship. They see a crisis of deep human transformation (Education 4.0).

It's a transformative journey that today is more readily available and more called for than ever before. Nietzsche captures the essence of that journey with a few simple and beautiful lines in *Thus Spake Zarathustra*, where he talks about the three metamorphoses of the spirit:

> Of the three metamorphoses of the spirit I tell you: how the spirit becomes a camel; and the camel, a lion; and the lion, finally, a child. . . .
>
> What is difficult? asks the spirit that would bear much, and kneels down like a camel wanting to be well loaded. What is most difficult, O heroes, asks the spirit that would bear much, that I may take it upon myself and exult in my strength?
>
> All these most difficult things the spirit that would bear much takes upon itself: like the camel that, burdened, speeds into the desert, thus the spirit speeds into its desert.
>
> In the loneliest desert, however, the second metamorphosis occurs: here the spirit becomes a lion who would conquer his freedom and be master in his own desert. Here he seeks out his last master: he wants to fight him and his last god; for ultimate victory he wants to fight with the great dragon.
>
> Who is the great dragon whom the spirit will no longer call lord and god? "Thou shalt" is the name of the great dragon. But the spirit of the lion says, "I will." "Thou shalt" lies in his way, sparkling like gold, an animal covered with scales; and on every scale shines a golden "thou shalt."
>
> My brothers, why is there a need in the spirit for the lion? Why is not the beast of burden, which renounces and is reverent, enough?
>
> To create new values—that even the lion cannot do; but the creation of freedom for oneself and a sacred "No" even to duty—for that, my brothers, the lion is needed. . . .
>
> But say, my brothers, what can the child do that even the lion could not do? Why must the preying lion still become a child? The child is innocence and forgetting, a new beginning, a game, a self-propelled wheel, a first movement, a sacred "Yes." For the game of creation . . . a sacred "Yes" is needed.[12]

The crisis of our educational system is that, at best, it treats our students as burden-laden camels. Missing is a deeper understanding of the human journey, needed in order to co-create learning environments that enable the learners to shift their state of operating from a burdened camel to "the praxis freedom" that is, from "Thou shalt" to "I want," and then from the state of the lion ("freedom from") to the state of the child, the sacred Yes ("freedom to") that allows us to access the deepest level of creativity.

Some people say, "Oh, well, maybe this 4.0 thing, this transformation of the human spirit—maybe that's just for the elite—the few, not the many."

Well, that's not *our* experience, or our belief. When you invite people to moments of stillness in order to investigate their deep developmental journey—their "evolving self," as Harvard's Robert Kegan would put it[13]—you find that most people today are very open to such an inquiry. We have been very surprised how open and interested younger leaders in particular are in inquiring into deep layers of awareness and knowing. We have experienced almost no pushback when introducing these concepts, methods, and tools in our work with farmers, teachers, health workers, communities, companies, and governments across generations and cultures—even though most of them didn't know any of these methods beforehand.

So what does all this suggest? We think it suggests that the real limitation is not "out there" in the world but in our heads, in our assumption about what might be possible. The common will that Claudia Schmied talks about to regenerate the entire foundation of our educational system has never before been more accessible and possible.

Table 10 depicts the parallels in the systemic transformation of education and health. Both systems go on a journey from an authority-centered, input-driven way of organizing (1.0) to one that is testing-centered and output-driven (2.0), then to one that is student-centered and learning-driven (3.0) and to one that is entrepreneurial, co-creative, and presencing-driven (4.0). Throughout this journey, the core axis of the system—that is, the axis between student/patient/citizen and teacher/doctor/nurse—shifted from being teacher/doctor-driven (1.0) to transactional (2.0) to dialogic (3.0) and then to co-creative (4.0). In the language of Nietzsche's three transformations of the human spirit, we can relate the burden-carrying camel ("Thou shalt") to the first two

TABLE 10 Parallels in Education and Health Systems Transformation

Stage	Health	Schools	Relationship	Learner/ patient	Teacher/ physician
1.0 Traditional Awareness: *Hierarchy*	Authority- and input-centered: *institution-driven*	Authority and input-centered: *teacher-driven*	Doctor-/ teacher-centric	Recipient	Authority
2.0 Ego-System Awareness: *Markets and Competition*	Outcome-centered: *managed care–driven*	Outcome-centered: *testing-driven*	Transactional	Customer	Expert
3.0 Stakeholder Awareness: *Networks and Negotiation*	Patient-centered: *need-driven pathogenesis*	Student-centered: *learning-driven*	Dialogic	Client	Coach
4.0 Eco-System Awareness: *Awareness-Based Collective Action (ABC)*	Citizen-centered: *well-being-driven salutogenesis*	Entrepre-neurial-centered: *co-sensing-, presencing-, and co-creating-driven*	Co-creative	Co-creator	Midwife

relationships, while the lion relates to 3.0 ("I want") and the child or self-propelling wheel belongs to 4.0 (the sacred "Yes").

Beijing: Leading Learning Communities in the Chinese Government

This may sound hopelessly idealistic, and some of you may be tempted to roll your eyes as you read this. But we believe that the few emerging 4.0 examples that we report on in this book are just exemplary pieces of a much larger shift that is starting to happen around the world. That shift is essentially a shift in consciousness by leaders and change-makers.

The transformation journey of the educational system led by Minister Claudia Schmied in Austria, the transformation of the regional health-care systems in Denmark and Namibia, the transformation of corruption and government services in Bojonegoro, Indonesia, and the transformation of the Secretariat of National Heritage, a quasi-ministry of the federal government in Brazil, are all unlikely stories and examples of a larger pattern. Consider also a group of senior Chinese government officials whom Otto and Peter Senge began working with in 2012.

What touched us in working with them was the sincerity with which they participated in a six-month U process journey. It started with a workshop in China, continued for two weeks at MIT and on related learning journeys on the East and West Coasts of the United States, and then took them back to China for a weeklong retreat workshop. During the second half of the process, they worked in small teams to co-create five prototype initiatives. When they first explored their prototype initiatives through the method of Social Presencing Theater, they realized that they needed to change or evolve the role of government in the system. The old role of government was to be at the center and provide solutions that would meet the needs of the citizens. The new role of government, which these leaders learned more about in their prototyping work, started with a space of deep listening, in which they heard the concerns of the citizens and all other relevant stakeholders. In this co-creative space, stakeholders could co-generate the solutions that best met their needs.

Everyone was impressed when the Chinese officials shared their results and learning experiences. But especially moving was a three-hour circle in which they shared their personal thoughts, reflections, and takeaways at the end of their six-month journey (during which each of them continued working in their usual day jobs). Here are several quotes that Peter recorded while we sat in the closing circle:

"The changes I notice in myself, to be calmer, may be subtle, but they are profound."

"Can I really let go?"

"Am I open?" "Is my heart open?"

"What is moving me is this group." "Everyone is my teacher here."

"What is moving for me is the authenticity in ourselves; the harvest [of this] is real community."

"What moved me was the dissolution of boundaries."

"I can feel my inner self changing. I can feel it . . . to think and feel from the inner self."

"The most important lesson to me is to listen."

"The more we learn here, the more we question ourselves."

"This is not just learning something tangible; it is learning to change the state of ourselves."

"As citizens of the earth, [we] can feel incapacitated [by the magnitude of the problems]. But when we are connected to our world, we feel strong."

"I believe this will have a long-lasting impact for my country."

"The problems that appear [in our work] are a chance for deeper thinking."

These reflective observations have led us, and Peter, to explore with our Chinese partners how this type of work could be organically developed, localized, and scaled in the Chinese context as needed. With the possible exception of global business, there probably is no institution on this planet other than the Chinese government that could have a more significant positive impact on pioneering a sustainable economy that works for all.

COMPANIES 4.0

What does this emerging shift in context and consciousness mean for transforming and revolutionizing what many consider to be the most powerful institution on this planet: business? Many companies have gone out of business because they stopped being adaptive and relevant; and even more are at risk of going that same route. So what does the journey to a possible 4.0 enterprise look like?

Here is a nutshell version of the journey to 4.0 in business, which we illustrate with real-life examples below. It moves from, generally speaking,

1.0: owner-driven with centralized control; to

2.0: shareholder-driven and decentralized and divisionalized; to

3.0: stakeholder-driven and networked and matrixed; to

4.0: an intention-driven co-creative eco-system.

BALLE: Creating a Nationwide Movement Out of the White Dog Café

The Business Alliance for Local Living Economies (BALLE) has twenty-two thousand members and is the fastest-growing network of socially and environmentally responsible businesses in North America.[14]

The origins of BALLE lead us to the White Dog Café in Philadelphia, and to its founder and owner, Judy Wicks, author of the memoir *Good Morning, Beautiful Business*.[15] Over the course of twenty-five years, Wicks pioneered a series of groundbreaking business practices, including direct partnering relationships with local farmers and sustainable and local sourcing. The White Dog Café paid all its staff a living wage, took customers on learning journeys to the farms that supplied the café's food, and organized eco-tours to show customers where waste from the restaurant went, where municipal water in Philadelphia comes from, and where the energy they use is generated. The White Dog Café became the first business in Pennsylvania to source 100 percent of its electricity from renewable energy.[16]

As she adopted these practices, the White Dog Café became more prosperous and successful. But instead of resting on that success, Wicks decided to do something different. She realized that if she really cared about the well-being of her community and environment, she needed to share her business practices and *help her competitors* learn how to do what she was already doing. Wicks remembers the moment when she realized that Business 3.0, doing socially responsible things, just wasn't good enough anymore: "It was a transformational moment when I realized that there is no such thing as one sustainable business, no matter how good the practices were within my company, no matter if I composted and recycled and bought from farmers and used [renewable] energy and so on, that it was a drop in the bucket. I had to go outside of my own company and start working in cooperation with others, and particularly with my competitors, to build a whole system based on those values."[17]

In order to move into this 4.0 environment, Wicks established the White Dog Café Foundation, which she funded with a portion of the profits from her restaurant. The first thing she did was ask the farmer who supplied her restaurant with two organically raised pigs each week what he would need in order to be able to supply other restaurants as well. When he told her that he needed a refrigerated truck, she loaned him US$30,000 (from her own restaurant's profits) to buy the truck so he could begin to supply all of her competitors with the same quality of pork.[18] The first project of the foundation was Fair Food (www.fairfood philly.org), which had the original purpose of providing free consulting to White Dog's competitors—chefs and local restaurant owners in Philadelphia—to teach them how to buy humanely raised pork and other products from local family farms and why it was important.[19]

Also under the umbrella of the foundation, in 2001 Wicks launched the Sustainable Business Network (SBN) of Greater Philadelphia in order to spread the business practices of the White Dog, and in that same year she partnered with others to co-found the Business Alliance for Local Living Economies (BALLE) to build a network of place-based businesses using these practices that could grow into a viable alternative to the corporate, chain-store economy.

The BALLE movement demonstrates how local businesses can succeed through increased cooperation rather than competition. The pioneers and entrepreneurs who are willing to share proprietary information about their operations, their practices, and the needs of their businesses while helping others in their sector are improving the well-being of the larger eco-system while also advancing the well-being of their own enterprise.

Natura: Shifting the Field of Business

Natura is a multibillion-dollar Brazil-based skin care and cosmetics company that has been a leading innovator in sustainable development in Brazil and Latin America. When the company sources raw materials from Brazil's forests, Natura makes sure extraction happens in an environmentally and socially sustainable way and that the activity does not disrupt local cultural traditions. The company has also created profit-sharing arrangements that make sure some of the surplus is reinvested in the sustainability and cultural resilience of the Amazon communities who work at the very beginning or origin of Natura's value chain. These profit-sharing arrangements with communities in the Natura eco-system are operated through self-governed community foundations in the communities themselves. Natura also invests in education and capacity building throughout its eco-system of partners and stimulates their partners to also work with other companies, so communities do not become economically dependent solely on Natura.[20]

In the 1970s and 1980s, Natura developed a direct sales model that empowered community members. Today its products are sold through 1.5 million micro-entrepreneurs and beauty consultants who resell Natura products in their own communities.

Just as the BALLE movement can be traced back to kitchen conversations in the White Dog Café, the origin of Natura can be traced to inspired conversations in a tiny generative space many years back. In 1969, then twenty-six-year-old Luiz Seabra stood in front of his studio in São Paulo, handing out white roses to women passing by on the street. Then he walked them, white roses in hand, from the street into the studio to engage them in conversation and provide a free consultation on the new skin-care and cosmetic products that he just had prototyped. "I fell in love," remembers Luiz, "with relationship and beauty."

And he has been in love ever since. I (Otto) met Luiz in November 2011 in São Paulo. Luiz is now in his late sixties, but his youthful, joyful energy still radiates from his whole being. Relaxed and dressed in jeans in the office building that he shares with his two Natura co-founders, he remembers how it all began.

"When I was twelve years old, I observed my sister using skin care. I had a strong feeling in my heart that one day *I would create these products*." Fourteen years later he was passing out white roses, inviting women into an inspirational relational space that enchanted them with a different kind of connection to their bodies, to their beauty, to one another, and to themselves.

"The white rose," explains Luiz, "is a symbol of what we would like to offer. What is your gift? What is our gift? Like the caterpillar that morphs into a butterfly, the gift that we bring into this world also morphs and changes." It needs, says Luiz, *loving attention* to find "its own path to beauty, the path to a butterfly." That loving attention, according to Luiz, is the essence of Natura. "It's about a conversation and relationship where we are touched by presence and beauty."

Listening to Luiz, I felt the presence of a worldview that values beauty and truth equally. That really struck me. It's what I like about Nietzsche. Most people today don't understand that beauty is primary to truth. They don't see that the essence of mathematics is beauty, that the essence of science is beauty. To find that essence, you have to follow math and science all the way to their source. Luiz is that guy: He went straight to the source. As a twelve-year-old, he began listening to his sister from an open-heart connection.

But how did Luiz apply this deep level of attention and listening to the task of building a US$4.5 billion company with 1.5 million resellers and touching the lives of more than 100 million consumers on any given day? You do that, replies Luiz, by not only focusing on managing numbers or managing others, but by "facing yourself" with an open mind and an open heart—in other words, by bending the beam of observation back onto yourself. The problem in many organizations today, says Luiz, is fear. And "the only antidote to fear is love." When we judge others, we create an atmosphere of coldness that opens the space for fear. Transforming that atmosphere of fear requires us "to connect with our sources of presence, our open heart."

Listening to Luiz is a joyful experience because he clearly enjoys the moment. He is very visibly still enchanted by the world; he is still in love with relationships and beauty. It's rare for a man (or anyone else) to so powerfully embody the presence of the open heart.

So, I wonder, how did he get here? What process brought him to this state?

"I am very shy," he responds. Really? "But I am enchanted with the world." That was quite visible. But how did he get here?

"I too had too much noise in my head," recounts Luiz. "So it was essential to find a silence within myself." He first found that silence by experiencing a shift of mind and heart while reading a philosophical text as a sixteen-year-old. In that text Plotinus suggested that "the One is in the Whole, the Whole is in the One." It dawned on Luiz then that this deeper level of reality that Plotinus referred to requires a deeper level of thought—a thinking that is powered by the intelligence of the heart. This moment of insight opened up a whole new world for him. It was an intellectual and also a spiritual experience that allowed him "to find a silence within myself." Connecting to that place was like "finding a new life inside myself, a new birth."

Ever since, he has tried to operate from that connection to essence in that quiet place. Many of the normal management tools, like managing by the numbers or managing by market share, are just a perpetuation of noise. "The use of these traditional management instruments makes us less intelligent." Good point, I thought when writing this down—it means that normal business schools are dumbing us down. So why would you pay for that?

"It's time to listen to our silence; to share it, we need a kind of massage." And in order to cultivate this inner silence, "we must have filters against excessive banality." That will help us to "transform fear into love."

Later that morning, I met his business partner, Guilherme Leal, another co-founder of Natura. After merging his own company with Natura in 1979, Guilherme helped build Natura into the largest direct-sales cosmetics company in Brazil. What struck me most was seeing how these two men interacted with each other. Often very successful and high-net-worth people tend to go it alone. Instead these two men seemed to have a relationship that was delicate, respectful, caring, appreciative. None of these words really get to the essence. If I had to choose a single word, maybe it would be *selfless*. They seemed to genuinely enjoy their differences and to support each other in them.

For all of the company's success, today it faces a new set of opportunities and challenges. Like all companies, Natura faces disruptive challenges in business and society. Additionally, the founders are playing a less active role in its everyday leadership. One current challenge, therefore, is how to keep the essence of Natura alive in this new context. Another challenge is to reinvent the direct selling strategy in the age of Web 2.0 business models. How can Natura become a platform that allows the entire eco-system of suppliers and consumers to co-sense and co-create to their highest future potential?

"Natura is a collective phenomenon," says Marcelo Cardoso, senior vice-president for sustainability and organizational development, "and today we are [on] the threshold of a new evolution cycle." The new evolutionary cycle that Natura and the whole business community face concerns the emerging 4.0 co-creative eco-system economy. The heart of the future eco-system-based company is no longer a particular product offering; instead it is a cultivated web of "multiple connections and relationships that we have with each other as partners, producers, users, owners, shareholders, and community. The radical vision we try to bring about puts the sacred relationship to our partners and customers into the very core of the company."

Marcelo suggests that three main principles characterize the 4.0 way of organizing. The first one concerns the need to influence by attraction rather than control. The second concerns tolerance for uncertainty. And the third concerns removing the 2.0 system of bonuses. "We found that in Silicon Valley no one is using bonuses linked to individual targets," Marcelo says. "In the future we will replace our individual target and bonus system with five goals for the entire company that tell the story of the company. In the future we will have more fixed and less variable compensation."

This shift in Natura's compensation system is backed by a lot of scientific evidence that suggests that individualized remuneration is doing more harm than good to the performance of companies, except in cases of very simple and mechanical routine operations with little creativity involved.[21] In essence, Marcelo sees the current transformation of Natura in terms of outside-in and inside-out. Outside-in means making the cultivation of relationships the center part of the future company. Inside-out means to let go of control, to let go of individualized targets and bonuses, and to come up with more intrinsic and co-creative mechanisms of motivating, direction setting, and innovating, often done jointly with the eco-system partners. Is that an easy process? It's not, and Marcelo will be the first to point out that he sees himself and Natura at just the beginning of that journey.

Food Lab: Shifting the Field of Food

BALLE and Natura are great examples of partially mission-driven enterprises that are moving in the direction of 4.0. But what about more traditional companies? What will it take for them to make the shift to 4.0?

The Sustainable Food Lab is pioneering solutions in this domain. The Food Lab is a forum for leaders across the system to address the most pressing and significant problems of food and agriculture.

In the summer of 2002, Hal Hamilton, Don Seville, Adam Kahane, and Peter Senge met over breakfast at a global leadership conference. They started exploring the possibility that the polarized debates over agricultural sustainability might benefit from the application of Theory U. The conversation later expanded to include leaders from Unilever and the Kellogg Foundation, who described their ongoing investments in sustainable agriculture projects and their desire to influence the mainstream. They noted, however, a sense that neither the Kellogg Foundation nor Unilever was powerful enough to do this alone.

In the year and a half that followed, Hal, Adam, and their colleagues interviewed dozens of system leaders in the United States, Europe, and Brazil. From these interviews, individuals were invited to join the Food Lab. Incorporating advice and experience from many interviews and meetings, the Sustainable Food Lab was launched with the purpose of making mainstream food systems more sustainable.

The lab brings together leaders from more than sixty businesses, governments, farm groups, and NGOs with this explicit focus. Although a sustainable food system is at the heart of its work, the group realizes that perspectives on what it means to be sustainable differ substantially among the institutions, businesses, and organizations represented in the lab. One of the challenges for the lab team is to use these differing perspectives and priorities as a catalyst for shared learning and significant innovations in the system.[22]

We asked Hal, now the co-director of the Food Lab, what he has learned from recreating infrastructures that help organizations to collaborate and innovate their way to 4.0. "What we have learned," Hal says,

> is that to move a whole eco-system of food suppliers toward sustainability takes a new type of leadership support structure. We have found three particular leadership or learning infrastructures to be effective. The first one we call learning journeys. We take diverse groups of stakeholders to the interesting spots and edges of their system and give them a deep immersion experience for a day or two.

That has always been so successful, regenerative, and in part even transformative.

Second, we have found that it is mission-critical to engage our members in concrete prototyping projects on innovation issues that link well with the strategic agenda of these organizations. If these projects are just of personal interest but not institutionally relevant, then these initiatives can't be sustained and can't go to scale.

And last, we found that there is a deeper personal or human dimension at work in all of this. I am not sure how to name this. But it has to do with the fact that we have created a deeper web of human relationships that crosses all these institutional boundaries. This different web of human relationships is not just about feeling better and having more energy. It is essentially about having a different relationship to our own journey, to the journey of your community, and to the journey of our planet. So it's a field that allows you to reconnect with your essence.

In addition to these three learning experiences articulated by Hal, there is a fourth one that he didn't mention: Get the right people with a 4.0 mindset into the core group of such an enterprise. The people must embody the essence of the initiative with everything they do—like all of the change-makers whose stories we've told in these pages: Jon, Suyoto, Alexandra, Claudia, Judy, Michelle, Luiz, Guilherme, Marcelo, Hal . . .

Summing Up

Table 11 outlines how the evolution of the corporation is embedded in the evolutionary stages of economic development and its underlying logic. The purpose of the 1.0 company is control over the entire value chain. The logic revolves around economies of scope; the focus is on vertical integration (for example, the old IBM). The purpose of the 2.0 company is profit. The logic revolves around economies of scale, and the focus is on horizontal integration (for example, Intel and Microsoft). The purpose of the 3.0 company is eco-system domination. The logic revolves around network economies. Examples are Apple, Facebook, and Google. The purpose of the 4.0 company is eco-system stewardship. The logic revolves around

TABLE 11 Stages of Economic Logic and Corporate Development

Stage of Economic Development	Coordination mechanism (power)	Pivotal sector	Dominant economic logic	Purpose of business	Company examples	Stakeholder relationships
1.0: Centralized State Economy	Hierarchy, regulation, control (sticks)	First sector: public	Economies of scope: vertical integration	Control over entire value chain	Old IBM	Controlling
2.0: Free-Market Economy	Market and competition (carrots)	Second sector: private	Economies of scale: horizontal integration	Profit and shareholder value	Intel, Microsoft	Transactional
3.0: Social-Market Economy	Networks and negotiations (norms)	Third sector: social	Economies of networks (and scope): circular integration	Eco-system domination	Apple, Facebook, Google	Empathic but dominating: no shared ownership
Co-Creative Eco-System Economy	ABC: awareness-based collective action (presencing of the emerging whole)	Fourth sector: cross-sector collaboration	Economies of presencing: spiral integration	Eco-system stewardship: co-creative relationships with self, other, nature, whole	Emerging examples: Natura, BALLE, Alibaba	Generative: co-sensing, presencing, and co-creating highest future potential

economies of presencing—that is, around sensing and actualizing emerging futures. Emerging examples of this category include BALLE, Natura, and the Chinese e-commerce giant Alibaba. The difference between 3.0 and 4.0 companies is intention: 3.0 companies are driven to dominate their eco-system, while 4.0 companies try to serve the well-being and shared ownership of all. The 3.0 and 4.0 corporations are a new breed of hybrid companies that have two main characteristics: They function as a business, and they are inspired and energized by a social mission (in 4.0 companies, the mission is more strongly embodied). This is not just a marginal feature of the business community. Think about what inspired visionary founders like Steve Jobs at Apple; Eileen at Eileen Fisher Inc.; Luiz, Guilherme, and Pedro at Natura; Judy and Michelle at BALLE; and Hal at the Sustainable Food Lab. These ventures are exemplars of an emerging "new essence" of what it means to run a successful enterprise. In this emerging business paradigm, success is defined not only by profit, but also by its relevance to the larger eco-system and its practical contributions toward bridging the ecological, social, and spiritual divides. Interestingly, some of these hybrid, social-mission-driven companies increasingly look and feel like some of the more innovative NGOs.

NGOS 4.0

With the collapse of the Berlin Wall and the end of the Cold War, a transition to a new era began that has seen the rise of an emerging new superpower: global civil society.

Since the late 1980s, millions of NGOs and CSOs (civil society organizations) have emerged on all continents. This movement, in the words of Paul Hawken, is the largest the planet has ever seen.[23] The NGO and civil society sector is the most recent arrival on the global stage. With the founding of the United Nations after World War II, governments went global, and with the surge of globalization, particularly after 1989, business went global in successive waves. In a nutshell, here is how civil society expresses itself through this new class of institutions and its developmental journey:

1.0: NGOs: alleviating actors, donor-dependent

2.0: NGOs: policy advocates, donor-dependent

3.0: NGOs: multistakeholder or social mission enterprises, partly
self-funding

4.0: NGOs: eco-system innovation enterprises, partly or fully
self-funding

WWF

The World Wide Fund for Nature (WWF; formerly the World Wildlife Fund) is an international NGO whose purpose is the conservation of our environment.[24] With over 5 million supporters, WWF is working in more than 100 countries worldwide and is the world's largest independent conservation organization. Its mission is to halt and reverse environmental destruction.

During my (Otto's) first visit to the US headquarters of WWF, COO Marcia Marsh explained the evolution of the organization's work. She said:

> First we were all about conserving the *environment*. Then we realized that in order to do that, we needed to include the *communities* that were living in these areas. We cannot do it without them. Then we realized that even that is not enough. We realized that the real forces that destroy our habitats and commons have little to do with the local communities and a lot to do with the forces of *global markets*. So we realized that in order to protect the environment, we had to work both with local communities and with global markets—that is, with global companies as well as with conscious consumer groups that would help to shift the corporate sourcing practices toward sustainability.

The three stages that Marsh described track the evolution of WWF from 1.0 (environmental protection only) to 2.0 (including the communities) to 3.0 (including the markets). In terms of challenges, that means that the closer you get to the current edge of the work, "the more you deal with complex, system-wide multistakeholder issues that no individual sector, let alone institution, can change alone." Says Marsh: "That is why we need multi-stakeholder initiatives to make it happen."

One example of the new type of multi-stakeholder work is the Coral Triangle Initiative (CTI). The Coral Triangle in Southeast Asia is unrivaled among the world's ocean environments for its biological significance and its beauty, and it is prized even more for its economic value to the 125 million people in the region, which includes six countries: Indonesia, the Philippines, Malaysia, Papua New Guinea, the Solomon Islands, and Timor-Leste. In May 2009, the leaders of these six countries committed to the ten-year Coral Triangle Initiative Regional Plan of Action, one of the most comprehensive, specific, and time-bound plans ever put in place for ocean conservation.

This initiative, which has since generated hundreds of millions of donor pledges, started as any other high-impact initiative does: small. And it emerged from a set of inspired conversations that helped to turn a growing frustration about things being stuck into a powerful intention to create a different future.

In this case, some of the first conversations happened to be sparked by the ELIAS initiative, which Marcia Marsh and others co-created with us at the Presencing Institute and MIT. Says Kate Newman, the first WWF program director for CTI:

> It was during those years that the big idea of the ELIAS program—to bring together all key players that need each other in order to shift a system, and then to give them methods and tools that would allow them to make it happen—influenced our thinking on how to approach a problem like the one that we saw in the Coral Triangle region. I still remember the breakthrough that we had one night after a long discussion with several other stakeholders, when it suddenly dawned on us that we would never be able to successfully deal with these issues one region at a time. But if we could combine all of these adjacent regions into one spectacular eco-region—one that most didn't realize hosts the highest levels of marine biodiversity on earth—and if the limited resources of each Coral Triangle government could be joined together, then we could probably pull in other major players who suddenly would have a very material interest in being part of making real change happen at scale. We would connect all these players and help create a platform that would allow them to shift the system for the better.

In 2007, WWF joined forces with the Nature Conservancy and Conservation International. Together they expanded their conservation efforts in the Coral Triangle—which is home to 75 percent of all coral species known to science and is, after the Amazon, the second most biodiverse region on the planet—and they mobilized hundreds of millions in donor money to implement the CTI agreement. In spite of plenty of problems in implementing the ten-year targets of the initiative on schedule, CTI remains a huge inspiration and role model for many other initiatives that are trying to better organize for the protection and intentional cultivation of our commons.

Organizing for 4.0 means to shift from organizing around special-interest groups to organizing around common intention. An eco-system economy starts by identifying, protecting, and cultivating the scarcest and most critical commons. Shifting the relationship of companies and NGOs from antagonistic and transactional to co-creative is one of the biggest success factors for moving our economy to a thriving 4.0 operating system.

BANKING 4.0: BANKING AS A VEHICLE FOR POSITIVE CHANGE

As intermediaries between borrowers and lenders, banks hold a unique position in an economy, and with that in society. All entrepreneurial ideas require financial capital; businesses need a banking partner, and citizens use financial services. Banks deal with a very special product, money. Money is a legal construct that can be used in almost any economic transaction. It rarely expires, is easily transferable, and everybody wants it. Real-economy products, like apples or Apple computers, are used by specific customers and are usable only for a certain period of time. Money, however, is used by every actor in an economy and happens to be usable almost anywhere, anytime. It also does not diminish in value (except if inflation surpasses the interest rate). As a result, banks and the financial sectors hold a competitive advantage over all other actors in the real economy.[25] Here, in a nutshell, is how the banking sector has evolved into its role in society to date:

1.0: traditional banking

2.0: casino banking

3.0: socially responsible banking

4.0: transformative eco-system banking

Throughout history, every financial crisis was followed by an increase in regulation of the financial sector, as well as public debate over the power and risks of banks. But once the crises and their impacts are forgotten, regulation of the financial sector is typically loosened again. From an evolutionary perspective, the debate over regulating the financial sector reflects the transition from banking 2.0 to banking 3.0.

But missing from the debate is a discussion of the real potential of banks—the potential to turn them into transformative, intention-driven financial institutions that become enablers in the evolution toward Society 4.0. As banks evolved from 1.0 to 3.0, a parallel, but much less noted, innovation process was occurring as well. Some communities, interest groups, religious organizations, and concerned citizens realized that their objectives, intentions, and visions required access to banks that served their particular needs.

Over the past few decades, a different breed of financial institutions slowly emerged, one that combines profitability with a social mission or, in today's language, one that operates according to the triple bottom line (measuring success by financial, social, and environmental performance). Some of these banks succeeded, others failed, and many bigger banks also used the concept of the triple bottom line as window dressing while continuing their main business with primarily one bottom line: profitability.

But several banks began to innovate around the idea of becoming a vehicle for transformative change by focusing on innovations in selected eco-systems. Banks, after all, decide which innovations and initiatives receive funding. Some banks started to question whether this decision should be based solely on potential profit or also on concern about social and environmental well-being.

For any bank, it is much more efficient to loan US$300 million to one established multinational corporation than to loan US$1 million to each of three hundred social and green entrepreneurs. But what if small loans are really what we need to address the pressing challenges of today?

Making three hundred loans to green entrepreneurs would be a conscious decision based not only on a concern for the bank's profitability, *but on an awareness of a societal need.* Such decisions have internal impli-cations, of course. A bank would need not just one loan officer for a US$300 million loan, but a team of loan officers who understand bank-ing *and* such things as renewable energy and social entrepreneurship.

Such financial institutions already exist. They are known as credit unions, lending circles, community banks, nonprofit financial organiza-tions, crowdfunding platforms, and banking cooperatives. In 2009, ten socially and environmentally responsible banks met at Triodos Bank in the Netherlands to found the Global Alliance for Banking on Values, an independent network of banks with the mission of "using finance to deliver sustainable development for unserved people, communities, and the environment."[26] In 2012, this network had twenty members with assets of more than US$40 billion, operating in all regions of the world. These banks see finance as a vehicle for social transformation.

Here are just a few examples of how these banks operate.

Transformative Eco-System Banking

BRAC Bank, introduced earlier in this book, is located in Bangladesh. A BRAC loan officer in the Old City of Dhaka will walk from client to client, visit a loan applicant's store, talk to his neighbor, and get to know the community around the applicant. In this way BRAC can decide whether to loan money to entrepreneurs who have no financial history, much less a bank account. Why this hassle? BRAC believes that these small businesses create employment and a way for people to pull them-selves out of poverty.

Triodos Bank and GLS Bank in Europe created funding options for wind energy decades ago, when no conventional bank would even consider a wind park. Their loan officers are uniquely specialized in renewable energy projects. But both banks also fund community living projects, alternative schools, organic farming, and cultural initiatives, all projects that would not find a partner in a conventional bank but that contribute uniquely to society. Because the banks' customers expect all funded projects to live up to high standards for green and social innova-tion, they make the recipients of all of their loans public on a website.

As a network, the Global Alliance for Banking on Values is moving beyond socially responsible banking toward using banking as a vehicle for transformation. Its message is clear: We cannot address the pressing issues of today without financial institutions that support these new corporations, NGOs, and communities of innovators.

Shifting the Center of Gravity of the Economic Field

The financial and capital movements in an economy create more than just a market exchange. Figure 15 describes how the financial economy relates to the real economy, and how both of them embody a different form of social-economic relationship that is very similar to our earlier description of the different levels of conversation and consciousness. According to the intention that underlies its use, we differentiate among four types of money:

1. casino money: used for speculative purposes

2. purchase money: used to buy goods and services

3. loan money: used to provide loans to entrepreneurs

4. gift money: used to cultivate commons or help social entrepreneurs

The four types of money (figure 15, upper left) differ in terms of the *intention* with which the money is passed on.[27] In the upper right quadrant of figure 15, you'll notice the different options for using money:

1. speculative investments in derivatives or assets of the real economy

2. purchasing goods and services

3. loan giving for entrepreneurial equipment

4. gifting for cultivating creative commons

Any transfer of money from one hand to another is an economic and communicative action that creates a social reality. For instance, if I use money to purchase something from you, our relationship is over the moment I leave the store. But if I lend money to an entrepreneur, the result is an established connection that lasts for the duration of the loan. Money empowers. Money is a means of communicating among agents in an economic system. The four circles or spheres tell us something about the quality of these communicative relationships, about how much they empower and how they differ. As spelled out in the lower half of figure 15, these relationships range from one-way downloading,

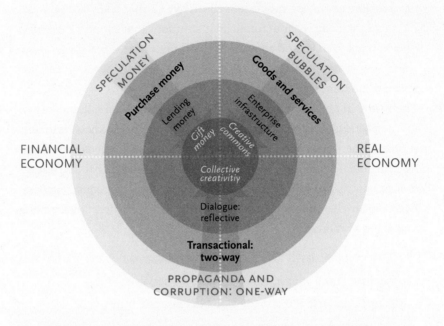

FIGURE 15. Shifting the center of gravity for economic and conversational action.

such as propaganda and corruption, in the outer sphere to co-creative relationships in the innermost sphere.

The problem of our economy today is that too much money circulates in the toxic outer sphere, which includes speculative profit extraction that fuels more speculation bubbles as well as corruption and propaganda. Furthermore, too little money moves into the innermost sphere, which is the heart and source of all social, economic, and cultural life. It is in that inner heart where the sources of all economic value and creation and of all human creativity are found: education, community, and the cultivation of the eco-system commons. And it is here where gift or seed money is most required.

OK, so there's too much money in the outer sphere and too little money in the inner sphere. But how big is that problem, really? It's big. Remember the $1.5 trillion in foreign transactions, not even 5 percent of which is connected to anything in the real economy? That's how big it is. It's a huge problem—and there is a lot of money at stake for very tiny but powerful special-interest groups that feed themselves from the oversized extractive bubble in the outer sphere. Estimates of how much private wealth is brought to offshore tax havens in order to (often illegally, but in some cases legally) avoid taxes that should have been paid are US$20 trillion (US$20,000 billion!).[28] Redirecting the flow of this money to serving the global commons would have an amazing instant impact globally. It's possible. But it takes common will.

The path to the future, to Economy 4.0, requires a shift at the gravitational center of our economy from primarily 1.0 and 2.0 communications (the outer two spheres) to 3.0 and 4.0 conversations and relationships (the inner two spheres). This implies that we have to redesign the system of money so that speculation money (in the outer sphere) will naturally be redirected and turned into gift money (in the inner sphere) that helps to cultivate the creative commons at the core. Transformative eco-system banking, featured in this section, is one answer to this challenge.

Another one is the idea of "aging money." According to this concept, money, just like products of the real economy, should lose its value over time. It means that money has, like yogurt, a finite period of usability. In the Middle Ages, Europe had such money systems. As a result, money flowed into, for example, the cultural sector instead of being invested in speculative bubbles—witness the massive churches that still form the face of European cities today, many centuries later.[29]

While a twenty-first-century solution is not yet clear, what is more clear than ever is the problem: We need to rebalance the playing field between the real and the financial economy so that the financial serves the real economy, and not the other way round.

An Emerging Fourth Sector: A Cross-Sector Platform for Eco-System Economies

Each living example of the emerging 4.0 intentional eco-system economy operates out of its own context and with its own inspirational heartbeat. We see this occurring in the Namibian health initiative, the 4-D government in Indonesia, the Danish health eco-system, the educational reforms in Austria, Brazil's Natura, China's Alibaba, the Sustainable Food Lab, BALLE, ELIAS, the WWF's Coral Triangle Initiative, and the first small examples of transformative eco-system banking. What do all these stories have in common?

Each initiative was started by a small core group of people who share a deep common intention to create a future that is different from the past. Whether it be at a kitchen table or in a windowless room in the basement, they share a holding space where inspired and yet brutally honest conversations can take place, a melting pot where the highest aspirations and everyday practices meet, connect, check each other, and evolve. They also share similar methods and tools, relying on methods that allow large, complex groups and systems to turn their institutional tensions into shared awareness and collaborative innovation.

The stories told here illustrate a set of principles of emerging eco-system economies that we believe should be institutionalized more intentionally and systemwide in the future. Here is our first attempt to articulate some of these emerging key principles:

1. *Openness:* Leadership shifts from inside an organization to the surrounding sphere.

2. *Transparency:* Information must be transparent, not secret.

3. *Sharing:* Ownership of goods must be accessible and intelligently shared.

4. *Intention:* Organizing revolves around common intention, not structures.

5. *Holding space:* Co-creative communities require high-quality core groups and holding spaces.

6. *Conversation:* Shift from levels 1 and 2 (toxic, transactional) to levels 3 and 4 (dialogic, co-creative).

7. *Awareness:* Shift the primary mode of operating from ego-system to eco-system awareness.

8. *Commons:* Identify, protect, and cultivate the commons as base of the whole eco-system.

9. *Playfulness:* Create a culture that values playfulness, entrepreneurship, and co-creation.

10. *Diversity and symbiosis:* These are the twin principles that allow eco-systems to thrive.

What we see today is the rise of a fourth sector that creates cross-sector platforms that connect people by embodying the above principles and applying them in the context of specific eco-systems such as health (Namibia, Denmark), education (Austria), sustainable food (Food Lab), specific industries (Natura), small entrepreneurs (Alibaba), governments (China), and local, place-based economies (BALLE).

Conclusion and Practices

This chapter described the process of institutional inversion. Using examples from society's major systems and sectors, we showed that the leadership challenge and transformation journey in different contexts are essentially the same: They're a journey from 1.0 to 4.0, a journey of inverting the social field to cultivate new qualities of co-creative relationships that bring the new into being.

JOURNALING QUESTIONS

1. How can you shift your conversational relationships from levels 1 and 2 to levels 3 and 4—that is, from downloading and debate to dialogue and collective creativity? Be specific. Name one or two examples.

2. Consider figure 15. How could you and your organization shift your economic and financial relationships from the outer to the inner spheres—that is, from speculation and consumption to entrepreneurial initiative and to cultivating the creative commons in your current context and community? Name one or two examples. Where are you contributing to the commons? Where do you take or enable entrepreneurial initiative?

3. How do the first two questions relate to each other? Be specific. Think about them in the context of your examples.

4. How can you keep cultivating your own sources of capital—that is, your own sources of creativity?

5. Consider table 11. What would your company or organization look like if it chose to operate as a 4.0 co-creative eco-system venture? Use the above list of ten key principles as input for developing concrete images and ideas.

6. What small prototype could you create that would allow you to explore your most interesting idea for a possible 4.0 venture?

CIRCLE CONVERSATION

Go to the website of the Presencing Institute, choose the tool section, www.presencing.com/tools/u-browser, and download the case clinic tool. It's a great process that takes a small group through a highly co-creative seven-step U-based process in seventy minutes. Each session focuses on one case-giver. We suggest that you start with just one session and case-giver and do additional sessions in the upcoming meetings of your group. Enjoy the process and share some of your experiences on the Presencing Institute website, which will have dedicated social networking space for this.

8

Leading from the Emerging Future: Now

We have entered the age of disruption. And we've taken you on a journey through some of the most inspiring projects we know in the world. In closing, we will invite you to explore how you can apply these 4.0 principles to your own life, close to home, and to the emerging journey and movement we all participate in on earth.

At the outset of this book we posed three questions:

1. In the face of disruption, how do we lead from the *emerging future?*
2. What *evolutionary economic framework* can guide our journey forward?
3. What *strategies* can help us to function as vehicles for shifting the whole?

In exploring these questions, we laid out three big ideas. The first is that there are two fundamentally different modes of learning: learning from the past and *learning from the emerging future.* In order to learn from the emerging future, we have to activate a deep learning cycle that involves not only opening the mind (transcending the cognitive boundaries), but also opening the heart (transcending our relational boundaries) and opening the will (transcending the boundaries of our small will). The U process of learning from the emerging future follows three movements: "Observe, observe," "Retreat and reflect: allow the inner knowing to emerge," and "Act in an instant."

The second big idea concerns the Matrix of Economic Evolution (table 3). The matrix suggests that *the evolution of economic structures follows the evolution of human consciousness*—or, to be more precise, that they are highly interdependent. The matrix offers four grammars or paradigms of economic thought. The evolution of the matrix has been embodied by different civilizations in different journeys over the centuries. The bottom line is that today's transformation of economic structures requires the transformation of human consciousness from ego-system awareness to eco-system awareness.

The third big idea is that the next revolution will require a multi-point strategy that, from a mundo or system perspective, focuses on all eight acupuncture points laid out by the Matrix of Economic Evolution. At the same time, from an agency perspective, the strategy must concentrate on the *inversion journey (Umstülpung)* that institutions and players have to go through when evolving from 1.0 to 4.0. This inversion journey requires actors on all levels to bend the beam of attention back onto themselves and the sources of Self. That means opening the mind, heart, and will (micro), moving conversations from downloading to generative dialogue (meso), and converting hierarchical silos into eco-creative fields that connect the eco-system as a living whole (macro).

Closing the Feedback Loop of Matter and Mind: Economy 4.0

What is the essence of this amazing evolutionary journey in which we are all engaged?

This question brings us back to the words of Master Nan in Shanghai, who spoke of the reintegration of mind and matter (chapter 4). It also brings us back to a lesser-known scientific tradition in the West that aims at transcending the mind-matter split in science, social science, and philosophy—an intellectual tradition that is connected to the names Varela, Husserl, Steiner, and Goethe, among others, and that is defined by bending the beam of *scientific observation* back onto the observing self—back onto the source.

The source is, from a systems view, where the feedback loop between mind and matter closes in the now, both individually and collectively. We have called these "closing-in" points or acupuncture points. This is how it happens for each of the eight acupuncture points:

1. *Nature:* Close the feedback loop of production, consumption, reuse, and recycling (through "earth-to-earth" or closed-loop design).

2. *Labor:* Close the feedback loop from work (jobs) to Work (passion) by building new entrepreneurship infrastructures that ignite the connection between self and Self.

3. *Capital:* Close the feedback loop in the flow of capital by redirecting speculative investment into ecological, social, and cultural-creative renewal (through gift money and intentional capital).

4. *Technology:* Close the feedback loop from technology creation to societal needs, particularly in underserved markets (through needs assessment and participatory planning).

5. *Leadership:* Close the feedback loop from leadership to the emerging future of the whole (through practices of co-sensing, co-inspiring, and co-creating).

6. *Consumption:* Close the feedback loop from economic output to the well-being of all (through conscious, collaborative consuming and new indicators such as GNH, or gross national happiness, discussed later in this chapter).

7. *Coordination:* Close the feedback loop in the economy from the parts to the whole (through ABC, awareness-based collective action).

8. *Ownership:* Close the feedback loop from ownership rights to the best societal use of assets (through shared ownership and commons-based property rights that safeguard the interests of future generations).

Thus the journey from 1.0 to 4.0 that we have been exploring throughout this book is a journey toward reintegrating matter and mind not only individually, but also collectively, across all eight acupuncture points of the matrix.

Our Dream

In chapter 5 we described the principle of perseverance as the twelfth principle: Never give up, never give up! For all of the eighteen years we have lived in the Boston area, we have pursued the same intention or dream. Not that we talked about it much. It often felt too distant—so different from our current reality. But every now and then it also felt possible, even close at hand. Finally, when we were almost ready to give up on it, we began to notice that something had happened: We noticed the seeds of the future sprouting around us, piercing through the layers of asphalt everywhere we turned.

The simple dream that we always had is about creating a global action leadership school that integrates science (the third-person view), social transformation (the second-person view), and the evolution of self (the first-person view) into a coherent framework of consciousness-based action research.[1]

In other words: We want to build a holding space that (1) applies advanced scientific methods to (2) the transformation of societies to 4.0 while (3) shifting from an ego-system to an eco-system awareness both individually and collectively.

Traditional institutions of higher education face the same problem that the ailing U.S. car industry did during the crisis of 2008 (and beyond): It has a product that is overpriced; it is disconnected from real needs of individuals and institutions; it is unable to reach out to the entire potential user base; and it is increasingly irrelevant to addressing the major global challenges of our time.

With a massive revolution in online learning platforms underway, we know that the old model of higher education is probably on its way out. As one example, MIT, Harvard, and Berkeley have teamed up to create an online learning platform called edX that will offer all courses online for free or for a very minor fee.[2] What no one knows today, however, is what the new model of higher education is going to look like.

U.school: Putting Students into the Driver's Seat of Profound Societal Innovation

To close this book, we want to share some of the images of the future that we have been co-developing and holding over the years with many of our colleagues and friends. We propose to integrate seven core elements that could constitute a new learning and innovation ecology that could help change-makers from all sectors and cultures to pioneer new pathways to 4.0. Here are the seven elements that we see merging in what could be called University 4.0:

1. *Global classroom.* A blended technology approach that creates an intense, personal learning relationship among a global, multilocal community of learners and a world-class faculty by combining live-streamed classroom sessions and mini-lectures with highly interactive small-group practice sessions. Social media–supported conversation spaces would continue the classroom dialogue between sessions.

2. *Deep dives into inspiring local, regional, and global hot spots of innovation.* Deep dives are total immersion journeys (actual, not virtual) that allow the learner to feel, empathize, and connect with multiple new perspectives (e.g., marginalized communities) and that connect the learner to a global web of inspiring living examples that address critical challenges in promising new ways.

3. *Awareness-based leadership technologies.* The capacity to facilitate processes of profound societal innovation is grounded in mindful leadership and awareness-based leadership technologies that link the intelligences of head, heart, and hand. These methodologies combine state-of-the-art organizational learning tools with participatory innovation techniques and blend them with awareness-based leadership practices. Mastery of these blended new leadership technologies, such as presencing, to sense and actualize emerging future possibilities is the methodological backbone of the school.

4. *Presencing coaching circles.* One of the most important mechanisms for holding the space for deep learning is peer circles that use deep listening–based coaching practices. A coaching circle usually consists of five to seven members and applies a version of the case clinic process that we described at the end of chapter 7. We have found that the power of these peer group circles is simply amazing. They hold the space for individual and shared renewal. As one member of Otto's peer group put it in a recent coaching call with his colleagues: "You [the whole circle] are the cradle of my rebirth." This may sound

airy-fairy or sentimental to some, but it is in fact an accurate description of a subtle experience that all of us—and many others in their
circles—have experienced.

5. *Action learning.* Students participate on the frontlines of profound
societal innovation through access to a global innovation ecology,
and by being challenged to co-create hands-on prototype solutions
that are helpful to a specific community or stakeholder constellation.
These real-world prototypes are embedded in and guided by a global
network of mentors and change-makers that operate in or collaborate
with their living examples of institutional renewal.

6. *Innovation hubs.* Innovation happens in places. Innovation hubs prototype the globally distributed campuses of the future. While a traditional campus is organized around discipline-based schools that deal
separately with societal challenges and issues, an innovation hub is
an inversion of that principle: It puts the emerging future opportunities at the center and organizes the disciplines and tools around
them. Innovation hubs create spheres of hands-on innovation, a
place for generative conversations that link and mediate between
application-centric action learning projects and head-centric global
classroom sessions. Innovation hubs are about integrating the intelligence of head, heart, and hand, not only for individuals but also for
communities of innovators. Innovation Hubs will look different in
different places. But they will share a blend of the following features:
(a) a space that evokes the mindful simplicity of a Buddhist temple;
(b) the hands-on creative atmosphere of a buzzing artistic community; (c) the high-tech equipment that interconnects all these places
to a functional, global web of co-sensing practices; (d) the clarity of
a well-organized think tank; and (e) the functionality of an avant-
garde theater that can be turned in minutes into a stage for Social
Presencing Theater. In short, an innovation hub would bear little
resemblance to today's campus, and it could in principle be replicated in cities, eco-systems, and urban or rural communities across
the globe.

7. *Individualized lifelong learning journeys.* If the classroom is global,
if the sensing and actualizing of our emerging future are the real

curriculum, and if the possible user base of this school is not tens or hundreds or thousands but millions, hundreds of millions, or billions—basically everyone who is interested in awakening, activating, and strengthening their capacity to be an entrepreneur from this deep place—then the question is: Who is navigating the amazing complexity of such a distributed eco-system? Who is designing your curriculum? The answer is, you are.

Today's educational structure offers you all your training when you need little or none—early in your life and career, when your experience base is small—while offering you very little later, when your appetite for learning and your experience base are much greater. The future of higher education has to be transformed, turning that old standard curriculum into a much more personalized, individualized lifelong learning journey that fits the evolving needs and aspirations of each individual who joins such a community of change-makers and learners.

Looking back, we realize that the journey of the past eighteen years has put us on a path where, together with our PI and MIT colleagues, we have prototyped all seven elements listed above in many systems, sectors, and cultures. Many of these initiatives are small in scale, as we described earlier in this book. What we have yet to do is integrate these seven core elements more intentionally and more fully into a cross-institutional platform that helps the next generation of change-makers connect to this ecology of individuals, institutions, and initiatives that are now starting to pioneer pathways to Society 4.0.

We believe that the time has come to integrate these elements more fully, because if we don't, we will only see more of the same. Just sending students into application projects or putting them through online classes is not creating anything substantially new. In fact, it's a formula for same old thing. It's what most companies and institutions are doing today—they respond to challenges by doing more of the same: cutting costs and becoming more lean and mean, but not reinventing themselves.

In order to facilitate profound innovation like helping eco-systems shift to 4.0, learners and leaders need *practice fields*—that is, new and safe spaces that allow them to prototype new behaviors, new mindsets, and new cultures of collaborating across boundaries. What's missing in today's society are infrastructures that provide new spaces for profound collaborative renewal. Traditional institutions of higher education, many of them teetering on the brink of irrelevance, could become relevant to society again by moving into this space of reinventing themselves in the world of 4.0. In this new world, the potential user base is billions of learners. For the first time in history, universities can operate truly globally. But in order to be relevant to society, they also have to be truly local.

Imagine what our world would look like if we could create a vibrant web of spaces where this living link between local and global could be felt and experienced in creative ways. Where, through co-sensing, people could become aware of the larger emerging movement that their projects already were part of, and become inspired by its evolution. Imagine that we could create these places, that each would integrate the seven above elements in their own way and on a massive scale, enabling local-global communities of practice, of learning, and of knowledge creation, resulting in collaborative online field books that would capture and further disseminate what we are learning, and so on.

We call this slowly emerging networked platform U.school for its emphasis on self-awareness as a core capacity of twenty-first-century leadership, and for its depiction of the inverted pyramid as a holding space for relational transformation. Figure 16 shows how the core activities of the U.school platform could be structured.

The innovation hubs, co-shaped by the U.school's partner institutions from all of society's sectors, hold the space for and interweave all three core activities: (1) the pioneering of hands-on innovation labs; (2) the knowledge creation that emerges from these frontline applications; and (3) the integration of this new knowledge into building collective innovation capacity. Currently we are in the very early stages of "seeding" the U.school initiatives, labs, and programs in Bhutan, China, Indonesia, the Philippines, India, South Africa, Egypt, Brazil, Europe, and North America.

Building on MIT's tradition of generating solutions to some of society's most pressing challenges, the community of awareness-based action researchers in and around PI has been building and road-testing

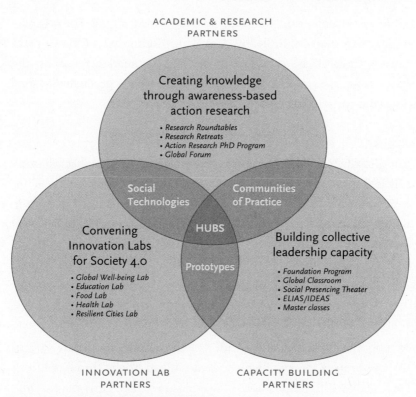

ACADEMIC & RESEARCH PARTNERS

Creating knowledge through awareness-based action research
- *Research Roundtables*
- *Research Retreats*
- *Action Research PhD Program*
- *Global Forum*

Social Technologies

Communities of Practice

HUBS

Convening Innovation Labs for Society 4.0
- *Global Well-being Lab*
- *Education Lab*
- *Food Lab*
- *Health Lab*
- *Resilient Cities Lab*

Prototypes

Building collective leadership capacity
- *Foundation Program*
- *Global Classroom*
- *Social Presencing Theater*
- *ELIAS/IDEAS*
- *Master classes*

INNOVATION LAB PARTNERS

CAPACITY BUILDING PARTNERS

FIGURE 16. U.school: three core activities.

elements of the U.school as a broad societal innovation platform. Some of our first results are summarized below.

AWARENESS-BASED ACTION RESEARCH

The books *Presence* and *Theory U* introduced the U as a language and transformative grammar of profound innovation and systems change.[3] The Matrix of Economic Evolution, introduced in this book, is another cornerstone in our evolving framework of consciousness-based action research. The Presencing Institute also operates a creative commons–based website that shares the further evolution of this framework and its practical methods and tools.[4]

COLLECTIVE LEADERSHIP CAPACITY BUILDING

At PI and MIT, we created and prototyped several high-impact capacity-building environments that embody and blend many of the above-mentioned principles. They include IDEAS China, IDEAS Indonesia, U-Lab (all MIT Sloan), Mel King Community Fellows (MIT CoLab), Global Classroom, the Presencing Foundation Program, and PI's master class offerings. These programs have graduated several thousand participants globally since the early 2000s.

GLOBAL FORUM

The Global Presencing Forums are annual gatherings that bring together leading innovators and change-makers across sectors, systems, generations, and cultures. Launched in 2011 in Boston and in 2012 in Berlin, these regular events are live-streamed to multiple parallel event locations around the world. The program is designed to accelerate and scale the shift from ego-system to eco-system awareness-based action.

Living Examples: Sensing What Wants to Emerge

Among the practical results of our action-research projects are various living examples, many of which are described briefly throughout this book. Here we highlight another two that are in their early stages. Once they are supported by the U.school infrastructure, their impact could ripple throughout the global system and accelerate the global movement to 4.0. As you read these examples, we invite you to reflect on what project in your own local context, if joined with and supported by the U.school infrastructure, could help accelerate profound global change.

A COOPERATIVE INITIATIVE IN THE BRONX

"In the Bronx," says Dayna Cunningham, director of MIT's CoLab, a longtime partner of Presencing Institute, "we see the beginnings of a critical mass of people working across institutions and communities, who, in the face of very challenging conditions, continuously activate a deeper level of humanity in the field."[5]

Dayna is referring to the Bronx Cooperative Development Initiative (BCDI), started by local activists long frustrated by failed development efforts. BCDI has built a broad multistakeholder process over the last two years that includes community-based organizations, businesses and entrepreneurs, labor unions, and Bronx anchor institutions in a comprehensive community planning and development effort. The goal is shared wealth creation, more robust local democracy, and urban sustainability.

Dayna sees these efforts as the seeds of something new, sprouting first through a new generation of young people who are more open-hearted and receptive to the possibility of seeing beyond their narrow self-interest to what might benefit the whole community. Even some larger institutions—hospitals, universities, and cultural organizations—are beginning to see that they might be better off working with, rather than being isolated from, the local community. As of this writing, thirteen anchor institutions have signed on to support the initiative and participate in purchasing analysis and strategic planning for BCDI going forward.

"There is a need to activate a deeper level of humanity in the whole social field," Dayna says:

> And that's why something like the U.school is needed now. We're in the jaws of a crisis. This is the moment when what we need most is enough people with the skill, heart, and wisdom to help us pull ourselves back from the edge of breakdown and onto a different path. Working in social and racial justice, I've seen over and over again that all aspirations to bring deeper humanity into social systems fail because there is no space to hold them.
>
> The Bronx has a long and rich history of organizing and leadership development. Many in the younger generation are predisposed toward the powerfully open-hearted approach to leadership that PI prepares us for. We know there is actually a set of skills you can learn, teach, and share with other people; you can practice, sharpen them, and make yourself a vehicle for this transformation. That's the most powerful and promising thing. The U.school has the potential to institutionalize the teaching and learning of these capacities in a way that could make them available on a scale that is commensurate with the crisis that we face—like the critical mass of people that we're meeting in the Bronx who are ready to shift the terrain of social movements.

THE GLOBAL WELL-BEING AND GROSS NATIONAL HAPPINESS LAB: INNOVATING BEYOND GDP

What we want to see is nothing less than transformative—graduates who are genuine human beings, realizing their full and true potential, caring for others—including other species—ecologically literate, contemplative as well as analytical in their understanding of the world, free of greed and without excessive desires; knowing, understanding, and appreciating completely that they are not separate from the natural world and from others—in sum manifesting their humanity fully. . . . In the end, a GNH-educated graduate will have no doubt that his or her happiness derives only from contributing to the happiness of others.

LYONCHEN JIGME Y. THINLEY, prime minister of Bhutan[6]

The job of Ha Vinh Tho, program coordinator of Bhutan's Gross National Happiness (GNH) Centre in Thimphu, is to put this intention for the future on its feet. "The quote above," says Tho, "is essentially the mandate for the GNH Centre." A graduate of the Presencing Global Masterclass, Tho is developing this example of a U.school-type initiative with an intention that links it directly to a global ecology of like-minded initiatives. To support this intention, Tho is part of another initiative called the Global Well-Being and GNH Lab.

In partnership with the GIZ Global Leadership Academy, the German Ministry for Economic Cooperation and Development, and Bhutan's GNH Centre, the Presencing Institute has initiated a living laboratory to explore new ways of measuring and implementing well-being and progress in societies around the world. The ultimate purpose of the lab is to develop and implement local prototypes like the GNH Centre in multiple contexts and countries, born out of the experience of being and learning together as a group and as individuals on a multilayered U journey.

For many decades, experts have recognized the need to develop metrics other than GDP to measure economic progress. Over the years, countries, communities, and global think tanks have been developing alternative metrics and indices relevant to their own contexts. GNH is one of these, pioneered and exemplified in Bhutan.

Prime Minister Thinley specifies what exactly is meant by "happiness":

We have now clearly distinguished the "happiness" in GNH from the fleeting, pleasurable "feel good" moods so often associated with that term. We know that true abiding happiness cannot exist while others suffer, and comes only from serving others, living in harmony with nature, and realizing our innate wisdom and the true and brilliant nature of our own mind.[7]

The inauguration of the Global Well-Being and GNH Lab in January 2013 brought together some of the leading innovators who are pushing us "beyond GDP"—people in governments, civil society, and the business sector from countries as different as Bhutan, Germany, India, the United States, Sri Lanka, China, Brazil, and Scotland. They include the core team of the GNH Centre in Bhutan, a state governor and First Lady from the United States who seek to increase the social and ecological well-being in their state; key change-makers from Natura (Brazil), Eileen Fisher (United States), BALLE (North America), OECD (Paris), Oxfam UK, and SEWA, the Self Employed Women's Association in India, which, with its 1.7 million members, builds capacity for entrepreneurship and local economies inspired by Gandhian principles.

The lab was launched with a weeklong total immersion journey in Brazil that took the group to the *favelas* in Rio and the communities in the Amazon rainforest in January 2013. The group has worked in peer coaching groups and reconvened in April 2013 for a weeklong immersion visit in Bhutan. The team currently co-creates multilocal prototype initiatives in the contexts of their various institutions. The lab will conclude its initial cycle by sharing the prototyping results in regional forum events in Berlin, Boston, and Asia.

"The process itself feels like it has its own life and momentum," says Marian Goodman, PI's executive director in Cape Town. "It's gathering interest, curiosity, and enthusiastic engagement from all parts of the world—a recognition that we are on the cusp of a future that seems to be unfolding with ease and synchronicity at every step."

A MOVEMENT IN THE MAKING

The Bronx Cooperative initiative is local, while the GNH Lab is global. But both are part of the same larger pattern of an opening that is happening around us now. What do you see in your context? Do you also see some deep structural development issues, as in the Bronx, where people are starting to reach across boundaries to create a future that is different from the past? Do you also see some new constellation of players coming together, as in the Global Well-Being and GNH Lab, that explore new ways of generating and measuring well-being? Where do you see examples like these in your environment—or other places where examples like these could be created?

We believe that the projects and initiatives described in this book matter because they are part of a much larger opening that is happening now in the world. They are part of a crack that is opening, making more and more people aware of what really matters to them. A movement of change-makers is beginning to shift the social field from ego to eco, from me to we. But this movement lacks supporting infrastructures that would help it build its potential power and impact. That is exactly what the U.school can contribute.

Conclusion and Practices

Throughout this book, we have used stories and examples to explain how we are witnessing the death of one civilization and the birth of another. In our institutions, economies, networks, communities, and personal situations, we are experiencing both sides of this transition firsthand. We experience and live through some sort of death and rebirth every single day—particularly on a collective level.

This brings us back to the third question: What strategies can help us to function as vehicles for the future that wants to emerge? We know that we need to

1. *bend the beam of attention* back to its source in order to cultivate generative relationships and advance the movement of institutional inversion as individuals, groups, and organizations;

2. *focus on all eight acupuncture points* to update the economic and societal logic of operating to 4.0; and

3. *shift the global field of entrepreneurship* by creating a multiregional network of "hubs" that support the capacity of the next generation of entrepreneurs to build intentional eco-system economies on a scale that meets the challenges of our time (U.school).

By focusing these on leverage points, we will be stepping into a new space, a space that is formed by different historical streams coming together to form a larger river. There are three specific streams or movements that are beginning to come together now:

- *global civil society*, in the tradition of Gandhi and Martin Luther King;
- *action science*, as represented by Kurt Lewin and Ed Schein; and
- *mindfulness and awareness*, inherent in the essence of all wisdom traditions, as exemplified and articulated by my conversation with Master Nan and Francisco Varela (chapter 4).

So how can we rise to the occasion? How can we meet the challenges of our time at the level that is called for? By bringing these three streams together. And by putting them into the service of transforming and inverting all key institutions of business, government, and education. That's what is starting to happen now.

As Peter Senge put it at the end of our 2012 forum in Berlin: "Obviously, many have been involved in bringing these remarkable accomplishments to reality, but without the vision and commitment [of this community], these many streams would never have come together to form the river we now all see."

It feels as if we all have come a long way to get to the current place of possibility. The door seems wide open. Now it's up to us—*me* and *you*—to cross the threshold from self to Self, from ego to eco, to make the stream join the river—every day, every moment, ever more intentionally, ever more collectively, and ever more aware.

JOURNALING QUESTIONS

What do you see when *you* turn around? What is the seed of the future or the sprout that you see in your field? Here are twelve questions for you to ponder in your personal reflection. Take a journal and a quiet moment to write for a minute or so on each of them:

1. What do you feel is wanting to transform within yourself?
2. What do you want to bring into being?
3. What do you need to let go of?

4. While reading this book, what has been your most important insight?

5. While reading this book, what has been your most important insight about yourself?

6. While reading this book, what has touched you and why?

7. While reading this book, what precious seed of the future (intention) did you become aware of?

8. How can you pull people together from across different systems in order to do something inspiring, fun, and meaningful—your version of a GNH or Society 4.0 Lab?

9. Who is your coaching circle—your circle of five or seven?

10. What practices (moments of stillness) do you use to connect to Source?

11. How do you balance beauty and truth in your life and work?

12. What are your most important next steps? Your action items for the next three days?

CIRCLE CONVERSATION

With other people in your circle, reflect on these points:

1. Each shares where you feel the crack (opening) to a field of the future.

2. Each shares an observation on your own opening over the past few weeks (open mind, heart, or will).

3. Share your observations on a conversational shift in your group that you may have noticed.

4. Share how all these observations relate to the institutional inversion around you.

5. What initiative, if taken on jointly, could help to shift the field of your system to 4.0?

6. Who needs to be involved to make it work?

7. Dialogue on and determine your next steps.

8. Use the www.presencing.com website as a resource to get tools, share stories, and link up with a global community of other circles that are "joining the river." Let's meet at one of the upcoming forum events that will allow us to connect online or in person.

ACKNOWLEDGMENTS

This book emerged from a whole web of collaborative relationships and initiatives with our partners in communities, nongovernmental organizations, business, and government. We would like to thank everyone who has been involved in these initiatives. We also thank our colleagues and students at the Presencing Institute (PI) and at the Massachusetts Institute of Technology (MIT) for many thought-provoking discussions.

We thank Steve Piersanti of Berrett-Koehler, who supported and also challenged us in extremely helpful ways. Thank you for your insights.

Thanks also to all the interviewees and colleagues from our dialogue on leadership project, especially Brian Arthur, Elenor Rosch, the late Master Huai-Chin Nan, and the late Francisco Varela. We thank Joseph Jaworski for co-creating the dialogue on leadership project and for deepening our understanding of sensing and actualizing the emerging future.

Thank you to our good friend Gregor Barnum, who passed away much too early and who greatly contributed to the journey that, among others, resulted in this book.

To our close friend and colleague Dayna Cunningham: You are such an inspiration and motivation. Your tireless work for a just, resilient, and fair society leads by example.

Also thanks to Phil Thompson. Your work and the PhD seminar on transforming capitalism that you initiated and co-taught with us in 2012 at the MIT Department for Urban Studies are an ongoing source of inspiration.

Thank you also to our colleagues at the MIT Sloan School of Management: Deborah Ancona, Rick Locke, Simon Johnson, Wanda Orlikowski, Tom Malone, John Sterman, John Van Maanen, and Ed Schein; to Sandy Pentland, MIT Media Lab; to our close colleagues Rebecca Henderson, Harvard Business School; Marshall Ganz, Kennedy School; and Robert Kegan, Harvard Graduate School of Education; and to Colette Boudreau, MIT Leadership Center.

Thanks to all the participants in the Presencing-in-Action Masterclass, who contributed to this book through their stories, their learning processes, and their feedback on early ideas. Thanks especially to Yishai Yuval, Gail Jacob, and Antoinette Klatzky.

Thanks also to the core group of the Presencing Institute, changemakers who are working to create a world of deep relationships that allow everyone to act from an eco-system awareness: Marian Goodman, Arawana Hayashi, Beth Jandernoa, Dayna Cunningham, Ben Chan, Frans Ade Nugraha Sugiarta, Ilma Pose, Jim Marsden, Julia Kim, Kelvy Bird, Martin Kalungu-Banda, Reola Phelps, Tho Ha Vinh, and Ursula Versteegen.

A special additional thanks to Marian Goodman and Beth Jandernoa, who, with their light-hearted spirit and skillful mastery of how to facilitate change processes, have inspired and enlightened so many of us in cultivating and advancing our use of presencing-based social technologies. And special thanks to Arawana Hayashi for leading the cocreation of Social Presencing Theater at PI. A great thank-you to Kelvy Bird for your leadership from the heart in growing the globally distributed PI community.

Thank you to our good friends Peter Senge, Arthur Zajonc, and Jon Kabat-Zinn, who have been mentors, colleagues, and fellow travelers on our journey of linking science, shifts in consciousness, and social change for many cycles.

Thanks to foundations that have financially supported the Presencing Institute over the past several years: the Nathan Cummings Foundation, the 1440 Foundation, and the Kalliopeia Foundation.

Thank you to Erica Dhawan and Elizabeth Hoffecker Moreno for your early research contributions to this book. And thanks to Karen Speerstra, who helped us with the final part of the book. Thanks to

Peter Teague, who co-created round-table dialogues that inspired the research for this book.

Janice Spadafore: Without you, none of the projects in this book would have happened and the book would not have been written. Thank you from the bottom of our heart!

And a big thank-you to Adam Yukelson, PI's first action-research PhD student: It was so much fun co-creating the final phase of the book together. Thanks for your great energy, focus, and mind.

And, finally, a great thank-you to Janet Mowery, who edited every page of this book from its first to its last iteration, always patient with our delayed deadlines and the sudden rushes at the finish line.

Cambridge, Massachusetts, March 2013

NOTES

Introduction

1. Nicholas D. Kristof, "Equality, a True Soul Food," Opinion, *New York Times,* January 1, 2011, www.nytimes.com/2011/01/02/opinion/02kristof .html?_r=0 (accessed December 14, 2012).

2. Etienne G. Krug et al., "World Report on Violence and Health" (Geneva: World Health Organization, 2002), 185.

3. Lawrence J. Lau, "What the World Needs Is Financial Stability," July 8, 2012, unpublished paper. Lau is Ralph and Claire Landau Professor of Economics, Chinese University of Hong Kong; Kwoh-Ting Li Professor in Economic Development, Emeritus, Stanford University; and chairman, CIC International (Hong Kong) Co., Limited.

4. James B. Davies et al., "Estimating the Level and Distribution of Global Household Wealth," United Nations University, World Institute for Development Economics Research, research paper no. 2007/77, 2007, www.wider.unu.edu/publications/working-papers/research-papers/2007/ en_GB/rp2007-77 (accessed February 28, 2013), 26.

5. C. O. Scharmer, *Theory U: Leading from the Future as It Emerges* (San Francisco: Berrett-Koehler, 2009), 59.

6. These are Bank of America, Citigroup, Goldman Sachs, JPMorgan Chase, Morgan Stanley, and Wells Fargo.

7. Simon Johnson, "The Financial Stability Oversight Council Defers to Big Banks," *Baseline Scenario,* January 20, 2011, http://baselinescenario .com/2011/01/20/the-financial-stability-oversight-council-defers-to-big -banks/ (accessed December 8, 2012).

8. Matt Taibbi, "Obama's Big Sellout," January 15, 2010, video, *Rolling Stone,* www.totalnoid.com/2009/12/14/rolling-stones-matt-taibbi-obamas -big-sellout/ (accessed December 8, 2012); and Simon Johnson and James

Kwak, *13 Bankers: The Wall Street Take-Over and the Next Financial Melt-Down* (New York: Pantheon Books, 2010), 95, 185.

9. Mancur Olson, *The Logic of Collective Action: Public Goods and the Theory of Groups,* rev. ed. (Cambridge, MA: Harvard University Press, 1971).

10. This quote is generally attributed to Einstein, but we could not verify a specific source.

11. Mental models is a term that Peter Senge et al. introduced in *The Fifth Discipline: The Art and Practice of a Learning Organization* (New York: Doubleday, 1990).

12. Garrett Hardin, "The Tragedy of the Commons," *Science* 162, no. 3859 (1968): 1243–48.

13. Wolfgang Münchau, "Peer Steinbrück's grösste Fehleinschätzung," column, *Der Spiegel,* October 3, 2011, www.spiegel.de/wirtschaft/wolf gang-muenchau-peer-steinbrueck-und-seine-groesste-fehleinschaetzung -a-859295.html (accessed December 8, 2012).

14. Reuters, "Euro-Gipfel beschliesst Krisenhilfe für Banken," October 12, 2008, *Der Spiegel,* www.spiegel.de/wirtschaft/einigung-in-paris -euro-gipfel-beschliesst-krisenhilfe-fuer-banken-a-583684.html (accessed December 9, 2012).

15. Eleanor Rosch, "Primary Knowing: When Perception Happens from the Whole Field," interview, October 15, 1999, Berkeley, California, www.presencing.com/presencing/dol/Rosch-1999.shtml#four (accessed February 26, 2013).

16. Donella H. Meadows et al., *Limits to Growth* (White River Junction, VT: Chelsea Green Publishing, 1972).

17. As noted, most of the interviews were conducted by Otto, many of them jointly with his colleague Joseph Jaworski. See also www.presencing .com/presencing/dol (accessed December 9, 2012).

18. See Peter Senge et al., *Presence: Human Purpose and the Field of the Future* (Cambridge, MA: Society for Organizational Learning, 2004); Scharmer, *Theory U.*

19. Scharmer, *Theory U,* 27.

20. See www.democracynow.org/2012/9/12/500_days_author_kurt_ eichenwalds_new (accessed December 19, 2012).

21. Matthew 19:23–24, King James Version.

Chapter 1. On the Surface

1. BBC News, "IMF in 'Global' Meltdown Warning," Business, October 11, 2008, http://news.bbc.co.uk/2/hi/7665515.stm (accessed December 8, 2012).

2. You can see it here: www.youtube.com/watch?v=SgjIgMdsEuk.

3. World News, December 6, 2012, http://news.linktv.org/videos/hero -of-egyptian-revolution-holds-teach-in-for-occupy-wall-street-protestors (accessed December 8, 2012).

4. Democracy Now!, "Asmaa Mahfouz & the YouTube Video That Helped Spark the Egyptian Uprising," February 8, 2011, www.democracy now.org/2011/2/8/asmaa_mahfouz_the_youtube_video_that (accessed December 8, 2012).

5. Paul O. Hawken, *Blessed Unrest: How the Largest Movement in the World Came into Being and Why No One Saw It Coming* (New York: Viking, 2007), 4.

6. Simon Johnson, "The Quiet Coup," *Atlantic,* May 2009, www.the atlantic.com/doc/200905/imf-advice (accessed December 9, 2012).

7. Johan Galtung, *Peace by Peaceful Means: Peace and Conflict, Development and Civilization* (Thousand Oaks, CA: Sage, 1996), 197.

8. Thomas Johnson, *The Battle of Chernobyl* (Brooklyn, NY: First Run/ Icarus Films, 2006), DVD.

9. Ibid.

10. Chernobyl Forum 2003–2005, *Chernobyl's Legacy: Health, Environmental and Socio-Economic Impacts, and Recommendations to the Governments of Belarus, the Russian Federation and Ukraine,* 2nd rev. ed., www.iaea .org/Publications/Booklets/Chernobyl/chernobyl.pdf (accessed December 9, 2012).

11. Johnson, *The Battle of Chernobyl,* 1:26.

12. In January 1986, Gorbachev proposed the elimination of intermediate-range nuclear weapons in Europe and outlined a strategy for eliminating all nuclear weapons by the year 2000; this is often referred to as the January Proposal. He also began the process of withdrawing troops from Afghanistan and Mongolia on July 28, 1986. On October 11 of that year, Gorbachev and Ronald Reagan met in Reykjavik, Iceland, at Höfði to discuss reducing intermediate-range nuclear weapons in Europe. To the immense surprise of both men's advisers, the two agreed in principle to the removal of their countries' intermediate-range nuclear forces (INF) from Europe and to a global limit of one hundred INF missile warheads each. They also agreed in principle to eliminate all nuclear weapons in ten years (by 1996), instead of by the year 2000 as Gorbachev had originally proposed. In 1987, this would culminate in the signing of the Intermediate-Range Nuclear Forces Treaty.

13. www.abc.net.au/news/2011-08-25/three-planets-resources-popula tion/2854812 (accessed March 2, 2013).

14. United Nations Environment Programme (UNEP), "At a Glance:

Millennium Issues," www.unep.org/ourplanet/imgversn/III/glance.html (accessed December 9, 2012).

15. L. R. Oldeman, "Impact of Soil Degradation: A Global Scenario," International Soil Reference and Information Centre, working paper no. 2000/01 (2000), 2, www.isric.org/isric/webdocs/docs/ISRIC_Report_2000 _01.pdf (accessed February 27, 2013).

16. David Pimentel, "Soil Erosion: A Food and Environmental Threat," *Environment, Development, and Sustainability* 8, no. 1 (2006): 119–37.

17. UNEP, "At a Glance: Millennium Issues"; Food and Agriculture Organization of the United Nations (FAO), *Land Degradation Assessment,* www.fao.org/nr/land/degradation/en/ (accessed December 9, 2012).

18. Intergovernmental Panel on Climate Change (IPCC), "Working Group I: The Physical Science Basis," *IPCC Fourth Assessment Report: Climate Change 2007,* www.ipcc.ch/publications_and_data/ar4/wg1/en/spm sspm-direct-observations.html (accessed December 9, 2012).

19. World Bank, "New Report Examines Risks of 4 Degree Hotter World by End of Century," November 18, 2012, www.worldbank.org/en/ news/2012/11/18/new-report-examines-risks-of-degree-hotter-world-by-end -of-century (accessed December 19, 2012).

20. Millennium Eco-System Assessment, *Eco-Systems and Human Well-Being: Synthesis* (Washington, DC: Island Press, 2005), 1. www.millen niumassessment.org/documents/document.356.aspx.pdf (accessed December 9, 2012).

21. Achim Steiner, "Rehabilitating Nature-Based Assets Generates Jobs, Wealth and Restoration of Multi-Trillion Dollar Services," press release, UNEP, June 3, 2010, www.unep.org/Documents.Multilingual/Default.asp ?DocumentID=628&ArticleID=6596&l=en (accessed December 9, 2012).

22. The richest 1 percent of the world's adult population have incomes higher than US$500,000; Davies et al., "Estimating the Level and Distribution of Global Household Wealth."

23. Branko Milanovic, "Global Income Inequality: What It Is and Why It Matters," UN Department of Economic and Social Affairs, working paper no. 26 (2006), www.wds.worldbank.org/servlet/WDSContentServer/ WDSP/IB/2006/03/02/000016406_20060302153355/Rendered/PDF/wps 3865.pdf (accessed December 9, 2012), 9.

24. FAO, *The State of Food Security in the World,* Executive Summary, Rome, Italy, 2012, www.fao.org/hunger/en/ (accessed December 9, 2012), 2.

25. World Bank, "World Bank Sees Progress against Extreme Poverty, but Flags Vulnerabilities," press release no. 2012/297/DEC, Washington, DC, February 29, 2012, http://web.worldbank.org/WBSITE/EXTERNAL/

NEWS/0,,contentMDK:23130032~pagePK:64257043~piPK:437376~theSite
PK:4607,00.html (accessed December 9, 2012).

26. Navteij Dhillon and Tarik Yousef, eds., *Generation in Waiting: The Unfulfilled Promise of Young People in the Middle East* (Washington, DC: Brookings Institution, 2009); Michael Kumhof and Romain Rancière, "Inequality, Leverage and Crises," International Monetary Fund (IMF), working paper no. 10/268 (2010), www.imf.org/external/pubs/ft/wp/2010/ wp10268.pdf (accessed February 27, 2013); and Isabel Ortiz and Matthew Cummins, "Global Inequality: Beyond the Bottom Billion: A Rapid Review of Income Distribution in 141 Countries," UNICEF Social and Economic Policy, working paper (April 2011), www.networkideas.org/featart/apr2011/ Ortiz_Cummins.pdf (accessed December 9, 2012).

27. International Labour Organization (ILO), "*World of Work Report 2008*—Global Income Inequality Gap Is Vast and Growing," press release, October 16, 2008, www.ilo.org/global/about-the-ilo/newsroom/news/WCMS _099406/lang--en/index.htm (accessed December 9, 2012).

28. Income inequality has increased particularly in the following countries since the 1990s: China, India, and English-speaking countries such as the United Kingdom, Australia, the United States, and, to a lesser degree, Canada. See Anthony B. Atkinson et al., "Top Incomes in the Long Run of History," *Journal of Economic Literature* 49, no. 1 (2011): 3.

29. The National Institute of Mental Health's Epidemiological Catchment Area studied a "large and representative sample of Americans from catchment areas in the U.S. and Canada" and found that people born around 1910 had a much lower chance of having experienced a "major depressive episode" in their lives than did people born after 1960. The study also showed that "each succeeding cohort in each area had a higher rate of depression than cohorts before it. There were huge differences in the rates of depression across cohorts, suggesting a roughly 10-fold increase in the risk of depression across generations." See Ed Diener and Martin E. P. Seligman, "Beyond Money: Toward an Economy of Well-Being," *Psychological Science in the Public Interest* 5, no. 1 (2004): 16.

30. www.who.int/mental_health/prevention/suicide/suicideprevent/ en/ (accessed February 28, 2013).

31. Barry Schwartz, *The Paradox of Choice* (New York: HarperCollins, 2004), 209.

32. www.who.int/mental_health/prevention/suicide/suicideprevent/ en/ (accessed February 28, 2013).

33. Vandana Shiva, *Earth Democracy: Justice, Sustainability, and Peace* (Cambridge, MA: South End Press, 2005).

Chapter 2. Structure

1. Lau, "What the World Needs Is Financial Stability."

2. See the description of archetypes in Senge et al., *Presence;* and Senge et al., *The Fifth Discipline.*

3. Richard Wilkinson and Kate Pickett, The Spirit Level: Why Equality Is Better for Everyone (New York: Penguin, 2009), 7.

4. Joseph Stiglitz, *The Price of Inequality: How Today's Divided Society Endangers Our Future* (New York: W. W. Norton, 2012), 8.

5. Ibid., 17.

6. Arnold J. Toynbee, *A Study of History,* abridgement of vols. I–VI by D. C. Somervell (Oxford: Oxford University Press, [1946] 1987).

7. We owe this idea to Johan Galtung.

8. Thomas L. Friedman, "The Virtual Middle Class Rises," *New York Times,* February 2, 2013, www.nytimes.com/2013/02/03/opinion/sunday/friedman-the-virtual-middle-class-rises.html?ref=thomaslfriedman (accessed March 3, 2013).

9. Karl Polanyi, *The Great Transformation: The Political and Economic Origins of Our Time* (Boston: Beacon Press, [1944] 2010).

10. Paul. J. Crutzen et al., "N_2O Release from Agro-Biofuel Production Negates Global Warming Reduction by Replacing Fossil Fuels," *Atmospheric Chemistry and Physics* 8 (2008): 389–95.

11. Adam Smith, *An Inquiry into the Nature and Causes of the Wealth of Nations* (Chicago: University of Chicago Press, [1904] 1976), 18.

Chapter 3. Transforming Thought

1. Ernst Haeckel, *Generelle Morphologie der Organismen. Allgemeine Grundzüge der organischen Formen-Wissenschaft, mechanisch begründet durch die von Charles Darwin reformirte Descendenz-Theorie,* Band 2 (Berlin: G. Reimer Publ., 1866), 286.

2. Presentation by Johan Galtung in fall 1989 at University Witten/Herdecke, Germany, personal notes.

3. Johnson, "The Quiet Coup."

4. Johnson and Kwak, *13 Bankers,* 10.

5. Simon Johnson, "Tunnel Vision, or Worse, from Banking Regulators," *New York Times,* "Economix," January 20, 2011, http://economix.blogs.nytimes.com/2011/01/20/tunnel-vision-or-worse-from-banking-regulators/ (accessed February 25, 2013).

6. The West also continues to ignore indigenous sources of wisdom, adding attentional violence through cultural disrespect. *Attentional violence* refers to the damage that is done when one's personal potential and

future possibilities are ignored or not seen. This form of violence can be even more insidious than physical, structural, and cultural violence. Otto Scharmer, "Attentional Violence," blog entry, August 24, 2009, www.blog .ottoscharmer.com/?p=18 (accessed December 9, 2012).

7. Max Weber, *The Protestant Ethic and the Spirit of Capitalism* (New York: Scribner, 1951), 181–82.

8. Juliet B. Schor, *Plenitude: The New Economics of True Wealth* (New York: Penguin, 2010), 43.

9. UN News Center, "Restoring Damaged Eco-Systems Can Generate Wealth and Employment—UN Report," June 3, 2010, www.un.org/apps/ news/story.asp?NewsID=34906 (accessed December 9, 2012).

10. One notable exception is the economic school of thought of the physiocrats; however, this stream of thinking began in the preindustrial era.

11. A few great exceptions prove the rule. See Polanyi, *The Great Transformation*.

12. Janine Benyus, *Biomimicry: Innovation Inspired by Nature* (New York: HarperCollins, 2009); Fritjof Capra, *Hidden Connections* (New York: Anchor Books, 2002); and Karl-Henrik Robert, *The Natural Step Story: Seeding a Quiet Revolution* (Gabriola Island, BC: New Society Publishers, 2008).

13. Ernst Ulrich von Weiszäcker et al., *Factor Five: Transforming the Global Economy through 80 Percent Improvements in Resource Productivity* (London: Earthscan Publishing, 2009).

14. William McDonough and Michael Braungart, *Cradle to Cradle: Remaking the Way We Make Things* (New York: North Point Press, 2002).

15. See Bill McKibben, *Deep Economy: The Wealth of Communities and the Durable Future* (New York: St. Martin's Griffin, 2008).

16. See www.dannwisch.de/ (accessed December 9, 2012).

17. Polanyi, *The Great Transformation*.

18. ILO, "*World of Work Report 2008*—Global Income Inequality Gap Is Vast and Growing." See also World Bank, "Jobs Are a Cornerstone of Development, Says World Development Report 2013," press release, October 1, 2012, www.worldbank.org/en/news/2012/10/01/jobs-cornerstone-develop ment-says-world-development-report (accessed December 9, 2012).

19. Daniel H. Pink, *Drive: The Surprising Truth about What Motivates Us* (New York: Riverhead Books, 2009).

20. Steve Jobs, Apple founder and late CEO, commencement speech, Stanford University, 2005, www.youtube.com/watch?v=D1R-jKKp3NA (accessed December 9, 2012).

21. Communities in Vermont operated with such a shared bond after the storm-caused flooding in 2011. See Nina Keck, "Neighbors Help Each

Other Deal with Vermont's Flood," NPR, September 14, 2011, www.npr
.org/2011/09/14/140458332/neighbors-help-each-other-get-past-vermont
-flood-waters (accessed December 9, 2012).

22. See www.bignam.org/BIG_pilot.html (accessed December 9, 2011).

23. Ibid.

24. There is an earlier use of the term that referred to the heads of animals in a herd. In the Middle Ages, the term *capital* entered the vocabulary of business when it was used in *summa capitalis* to mean the sum of a calculation in business.

25. Larry Neal, *The Rise of Financial Capitalism: International Capital Markets in the Age of Reason: Studies in Monetary and Financial History* (Cambridge: Cambridge University Press, 1990).

26. Stiglitz, *The Price of Inequality*, 61.

27. Diana Farrell et al., "Mapping Global Capital Markets," Fourth Annual Report, McKinsey Global Institute, January 2008, 7.

28. Robert Kimmitt, "Public Footprints in Private Markets," *Foreign Affairs* 87, no. 1: 121.

29. Sally Kohn, "Profit on Wall Street, Recession on Main Street," *Guardian*, Wednesday 24, 2011, www.guardian.co.uk/commentisfree/cifamerica/2011/aug/24/profit-wall-street-recession (accessed December 9, 2012).

30. Johnson and Kwak, *13 Bankers*, 13, 61.

31. Ibid., 115.

32. Johnson, "The Quiet Coup."

33. Kimmitt, "Public Footprints in Private Markets."

34. Lau, "What the World Needs Is Financial Stability."

35. Bernard Lietaer, "Erhöhte Unfallgefahr," interview, *Brand Eins* magazine, January 2009, www.brandeins.de/magazin/-afc796490a/erhoehte-unfallgefahr.html (accessed February 27, 2013).

36. According to former Treasury secretary Larry Summers in a speech at the Brookings Institution, Washington, DC, March 13, 2009, *Wall Street Journal*, http://blogs.wsj.com/washwire/2009/03/13/remarks-by-lawrence-summers-at-the-brookings-institution/ (accessed December 9, 2012).

37. "Global Job Losses Could Hit 51m," *BBC News*, January 26, 2009, http://news.bbc.co.uk/2/hi/7855661.stm (accessed December 9, 2012).

38. Joseph A. Schumpeter, *Capitalism, Socialism and Democracy* (New York: HarperCollins, [1942], 1975).

39. Ibid., 205.

40. Tobi Baxendale, "Public Attitudes to Banking," a student consultancy project by ESCP Europe for the Cobden Centre, June 2010, www.cobdencentre.org/?dl_id=67 (accessed December 9, 2012).

41. Rudolf Steiner, *Nationalökonomischer Kurs und Nationalökonomisches Seminar: Vierzehn Vorträge* (Dornach: R. Steiner Verlag, 1904/05).

42. BRAC Bank was founded in 2001 and had almost seven thousand employees and a loan volume of US$926 million in 2011. At least 51 percent of its loans are small and medium-sized ones.

43. Margrit Kennedy et al., *Regionalwaehrungen* (Munich: Riemann, 2004); Phillipp Jebens, *Komplementaerwaerhungen/Regionalgeld: eine Antwort auf die Globalisierung* (Norderstedt: Grin, 2008).

44. Jürgen Habermas, *The Theory of Communicative Action,* vol. 2: *Lifeworld and System: A Critique of Functionalist Reason* (Boston: Beacon Press, 1987; Frankfurt: Suhrkamp Verlag, 1981).

45. Jürgen Habermas, *The Theory of Communicative Action, vol. 1: Reason and the Rationalization of Society* (Boston: Beacon Press, 1984; Frankfurt: Suhrkamp Verlag, 1981).

46. Jeremy Rifkin, *The Third Industrial Revolution: How Lateral Power Is Transforming Energy, the Economy, and the World* (New York: Palgrave Macmillan, 2011).

47. Bill Joy, "Why the Future Doesn't Need Us," *Wired* 8, no. 4 (April 2000), www.wired.com/wired/archive/8.04/joy.html (accessed December 9, 2012).

48. Erik Rauch, "Productivity and the Workweek," http://groups.csail.mit.edu/mac/users/rauch/worktime (accessed December 9, 2012); John de Graaf, "Affluenza Cure Calls for Political Action: Different Standards for Workweek an Opportunity," special to the *Denver Post,* October 29, 2001.

49. For a more artistic way of saying pretty much the same thing, see the Flobots' "Handlebars" video at www.youtube.com/watch?v=HLUXoy4EptA (accessed December 9, 2012).

50. Naomi Klein, "Geoengineering: Testing the Waters," *New York Times,* Opinion, October 27, 2012, www.nytimes.com/2012/10/28/opinion/sunday/geoengineering-testing-the-waters.html?pagewanted=all&_r=1& (accessed December 9, 2012).

51. Division for Science Policy and Sustainable Development at UNESCO, "UNESCO Science Report: The Current Status of Science around the World," Executive Summary (UNESCO Publishing, 2010), http://unesdoc.unesco.org/images/0018/001898/189883e.pdf (accessed December 9, 2012).

52. Global Forum, "90/10 Gap," www.globalforumhealth.org/about/1090-gap/ (accessed December 9, 2012).

53. http://en.wikipedia.org/wiki/History_of_Wikipedia (accessed December 9, 2012).

54. www.linuxfoundation.org/news-media/blogs/browse/2011/08/ what-we-know-sure-linux's-20th-anniversary (accessed March 2, 2013).

55. Julius Pokorny, *Indogermanisches etymologisches Wörterbuch* (Tübingen: Francke, 1994), 672.

56. "Und kennst du nicht dies stirb und werde, so bist du nur ein trüber Gast auf Erden."

57. Steve Jobs, "You've Got to Find What You Love," *Stanford News*, Commencement Address, June 12, 2005, http://news.stanford.edu/news/ 2005/june15/jobs-061505.html (accessed December 9, 2012). Italics added.

58. Quoted in Senge et al., *Presence*, 158.

59. Jorge Majfud, "The Pandemic of Consumerism," *UN Chronicle* 46, nos. 3–4 (2009): Research Library Core, 87.

60. See www.lohas.com (accessed December 9, 2012).

61. Johan Galtung coined the term *Weltinnenpolitik*.

62. Albert Hirschman, *Exit, Voice, and Loyalty* (Cambridge, MA: Harvard University Press, 1971).

63. We thank Philip Cass, chief executive officer, Columbus Medical Association and Affiliates, for sharing this observation.

64. http://creativecommons.org/ (accessed December 9, 2012).

65. Allmende can be still found in southern Germany; Gotland, Sweden; and Switzerland, among other locales.

66. Manfred Brocker, *Arbeit und Eigentum. Der Paradigmenwechsel in der neuzeitlichen Eigentumstheorie* (Darmstadt: Wissenschaftliche Buchgesellschaft, 1992), 33.

67. Hardin, "The Tragedy of the Commons."

68. Peter Barnes, *Capitalism 3.0: A Guide to Reclaiming the Commons* (San Francisco: Berrett-Koehler, 2006).

69. Article 14, paragraph 2, German Constitution.

70. http://data.worldbank.org/country/china (accessed December 9, 2012).

71. Andrew Malone, "The GM Genocide," *Mail Online*, News, November 2, 2008, www.dailymail.co.uk/news/article-1082559/The-GM-geno cide-Thousands-Indian-farmers-committing-suicide-using-genetically -modified-crops.html; and Anthony Gucciardi, "Monsanto's GMO Seeds Contributing to Farmer's Suicide Every 30 Min," *Natural Society*, April 4, 2012, http://naturalsociety.com/monsantos-gmo-seeds-farmer-suicides -every-30-minutes/ (accessed December 9, 2012).

72. Barnes, *Capitalism 3.0*.

73. Mark Levine, "Share My Ride," *New York Times Magazine*, March 5, 2009, www.nytimes.com/2009/03/08/magazine/08Zipcar-t.html?page wanted=all&_r=0 (accessed December 15, 2012).

74. Rachel Botsman, presentation at TEDx Sydney, May 2010, www .ted.com/talks/rachel_botsman_the_case_for_collaborative_consumption .html (accessed December 15, 2012).

75. Rachel Botsman and Roo Rogers, *What's Mine Is Yours: The Rise of Collaborative Consumption* (New York: HarperBusiness, 2010).

76. Kerstin Bund, "Käufer werden Nutzer," interview with Robert Henrich, *Die Zeit* 51, December 15, 2011, www.zeit.de/2011/51/Car2go-Car sharing-Daimler (accessed February 26, 2013).

77. Vincent Graff, "Carrots in the Car Park. Radishes on the Roundabout. The Deliciously Eccentric Story of the Town Growing *All* Its Own Veg," *Daily Mail*, December 10, 2011, www.dailymail.co.uk/femail/article -2072383/Eccentric-town-Todmorden-growing-ALL-veg.html#ixzz1n6xu JwWzCitizens (accessed December 15, 2012).

78. www.mondragon-corporation.com/ENG.aspx (accessed December 15, 2012).

79. Raymond Saner et al., "Cooperatives—Conspicuously Absent in Trade & Development Discourse," CSEND Policy Brief no. 8, Geneva, November 2012, www.csend.org/site-1.5/images/files/20121117_Cooperatives %20conspicoulsly%20absent.pdf (accessed December 15, 2012).

80. See http://en.wikipedia.org/wiki/Internet (accessed December 15, 2012); and www.ietf.org/ (accessed December 15, 2012).

Chapter 4. Source

1. Peter Senge, "Closing the Feedback Loop between Mind and Matter," privately recorded interview, March 15, 1996, www.presencing.com/ presencing/dol/Senge.shtml (accessed December 14, 2012).

2. Confucius, "The Great Learning," trans. Ken Pang, October 2006, based on James Legge's translation and inspired by Huai-Chin Nan's interpretation. Unpublished paper.

3. Master Nan Huai-Chin, "Entering the Seven Meditative Spaces of Leadership," private interview, October 25, 1999, www.presencing.com/ presencing/dol/Huai-Chin.shtml (accessed December 14, 2012).

4. Francisco Varela, "The Three Gestures of Becoming Aware," private interview, January 12, 2000, www.presencing.com/presencing/dol/Varela .shtml (accessed December 14, 2012).

5. Ibid.

Chapter 5. Leading the Personal Inversion

1. He referred to this self with the somewhat problematic term *Übermensch*—Superman.

2. Friedrich Nietzsche, *Thus Spake Zarathustra,* trans. with a preface by Walter Kaufmann (New York: Random House, [1883] 1995), 126–27.

3. Quoted in Roberta Grossman et al., *Hannah Senesh: Her Life and Diary* (Woodstock, VT: Jewish Lights Publishing, 2004), 304, trans. from Hebrew by Yishai Yuval.

4. Email, Yishai Yuval to authors, November 13, 2012.

5. Email, Antoinette Klatzky to authors, November 13, 2012.

6. Reprinted from *Call Me by My True Names: The Collected Poems of Thich Nhat Hanh* (1999), with permission of Parallax Press, Berkeley, California, www.parallax.org.

7. Email, Dayna Cunningham to authors, November 8, 2013.

8. Email, Gail Jacobs to authors, November 29, 2013.

9. Ibid.

10. Martin Buber, *I and Thou* (New York: First Scribner Classics Edition, 2000), 65.

11. Jon Kabat-Zinn, foreword, Donald McCown et al., *Teaching Mindfulness: A Practical Guide for Clinicians and Educators* (New York: Springer, 2011), x.

12. Personal conversations with authors.

13. Ibid.

14. Quoted in Scharmer, *Theory U,* 416.

15. Brian Arthur, interview, Palo Alto, California, April 16, 1999, www .presencing.com/presencing/dol/Arthur.shtml (accessed February 28, 2013).

16. For examples, see www.presencing.com/presencing/dol/C07.shtml.

Chapter 6. Leading the Relational Inversion

1. See http://climateinteractive.org/ (accessed December 16, 2012).

2. William Isaac, *Dialogue and the Art of Thinking Together* (New York: Doubleday, 1999).

3. See http://wwf.panda.org/what_we_do/footprint/water/dams_initia tive/dams/wcd/ (accessed December 19, 2012).

4. Personal conversations with authors.

5. Quoted in ibid.

6. See http://just-energy.org/ (accessed December 16, 2012).

7. See www.worldwildlife.org/what/wherewework/coraltriangle/ (accessed December 16, 2012).

8. Recently, for example, we received three new inquiries about developing country-level tri-sector innovation and leadership platforms using the IDEAS/ELIAS model in Brazil, Zambia, and the Philippines.

9. Methods and tools for collective sensing sessions include voices from

the field, personal storytelling, systems thinking, scenario thinking, modeling, constellation practices, world café, and social presencing theater. See,
for example, www.theworldcafe.com/ and www.presencing.com/embodi-
ment (accessed December 17, 2012).

Chapter 7. Leading the Institutional Inversion

1. For example, in a special report for *Time* magazine, author Steven
Brill wrote a stinging expose about the health industry, revealing that there
exists "nothing rational . . . about the costs [hospital patients] faced in a marketplace they enter through no choice of their own." Examples range from
US$1.50 for one Tylenol pill (Amazon sells 100 for US$1.49) to US$49,237
for a piece of medical equipment that costs "about $19,000." Steven Brill,
"Bitter Pill: Why Medical Bills Are Killing Us," *Time*, "Health and Family," February 20, 2013, http://healthland.time.com/2013/02/20/bitter-pill
-why-medical-bills-are-killing-us/?iid=sci-main-mostpop2 (accessed March
3, 2013).

2. Harry G. Summers, On Strategy: A Critical Analysis of the Vietnam
War (Novato, CA: Presidio Press, 1982), 1.

3. For examples, see http://inovacao.enap.gov.br/index.php?option=
com_content&task=blogcategory&id=50&Itemid=53 (accessed December
16, 2012).

4. Personal conversations with authors.

5. Personal conversations with authors in Brazil; and http://en.wiki
pedia.org/wiki/Participatory_budgeting (accessed March 3, 2013).

6. "Northern Lights: Special Report: The Nordic Countries," *Economist*,
February 2, 2013, 1–16.

7. Authors' personal notes.

8. Quotes here and in the remainder of the section from authors'
notes.

9. For details on the case clinic process, see http://presencing.com/
tools/u-browser (accessed December 10, 2012).

10. Email exchange with authors, February 2013.

11. Uwe Schneidewind, "Towards a Transformative Literacy," *Rural
21*, December 11, 2012, www.rural21.com/nc/english/news/detail/article/
towards-a-transformative-literacy-0000559/ (accessed March 3, 2013).

12. Nietzsche, *Thus Spake Zarathustra*, 25–27.

13. Robert Kegan, *The Evolving Self: Problem and Process in Human
Development* (Cambridge, MA, and London: Harvard University Press,
1982); Robert Kegan and Lisa Laskow Lahey, *How the Way We Talk Can
Change the Way We Work* (San Francisco: Jossey-Bass, 2000); and Robert

Kegan and Lisa Laskow Lahey, *Immunity to Change: How to Overcome It and Unlock the Potential in Yourself and Your Organization* (Boston, MA: Harvard Business Press, 2009).

14. We thank MIT student Elizabeth Hoffecker Moreno for valuable background research on this section.

15. See www.whitedog.com/ (accessed December 15, 2012); and Judy Wicks, *Good Morning, Beautiful Business: The Unexpected Journey of an Activist Entrepreneur and Local Economy Pioneer* (White River Junction, VT: Chelsea Green, 2013).

16. Judy Wicks, "Good Morning, Beautiful Business," lecture addressing the E.F. Schumacher Society, Stockbridge, Massachusetts, October, 2004; interview with Judy Wicks, August 23, 2011; and "About Judy," www.judywicks.com/Bio.html (accessed December 14, 2012).

17. Judy Wicks, interview with Elizabeth Hoffecker Moreno, August 23, 2011.

18. Ibid.

19. Wicks, *Good Morning, Beautiful Business*, 24.

20. Robert G. Eccles et al., "Natura Cosméticos, S.A.," Harvard Business School case no. 9-412-052 (Boston: Harvard Business School Publishing, 2011).

21. Pink, *Drive*.

22. Susan Sweitzer, "Sustainable Food Laboratory: Learning History," unpublished internal document provided by the author, 2004.

23. Hawken, *Blessed Unrest*.

24. World Wildlife Fund remains WWF's official name in Canada, the United States, and the United Kingdom.

25. Banks also hold a competitive advantage over nonbanks through what is called fractional-reserve banking, which allows banks to invest more than they hold as deposits.

26. See www.gabv.org/ (accessed December 10, 2012).

27. On the distinction among purchase, lending, and gift money, see Rudolf Steiner, *Rethinking Economics: Lectures and Seminars on World Economics* (Great Barrington, MA: SteinerBooks, 2013).

28. Matthew Valencia, "Storm Survivors," *Economist*, special report on offshore finance (February 16–22, 2013): 4.

29. Fritz Andres, "Alterndes Geld im Mittelalter," *Info* 3 (June 1994): 17.

Chapter 8. Leading from the Emerging Future

1. Bill Torbert, "The Practice of Action Inquiry," in Peter Reason and Hilary Bradbury, eds., *Handbook of Action Research: Participative Inquiry and Practice* (Thousand Oaks, CA: Sage, 2001), 250.

2. For more information on edX, see https://www.edx.org (accessed February 3, 2013).

3. Senge et al., *Presence*; Scharmer, *Theory U*.

4. See http://presencing.com/tools/u-browser (accessed December 10, 2012).

5. Personal conversations with authors.

6. Lyonchen Jigme Y. Thinley, "Keynote Address," Karen Hayward and Ronald Colman, *Educating for Gross National Happiness Workshop*, December 7–12, 2009, prepared for the Ministry of Education, Royal Government of Bhutan, Thimphu, Bhutan, January 2010.

7. Lyonchen Jigmi Y. Thinley, Thimphu, December 7, 2009.

INDEX

74t, 75, 126, 138, 239–241
reading the, 75–76
Matrix of Social Evolution, 146–147,
148t, 149, 239–241, 247
reintegrating the, 149–151
McDonough, William, 81–82
Mead, Margaret, 168
Mental models, outmoded
giving rise to systemic bubbles and
disconnects, 3–4, 11
producing intellectual bankruptcy, 11
sources that give rise to, 16–17
terminology, 11
Meridians. *See* Acupuncture
points of economic and social
transformation
Michels, Rinus, 124
Mind
and matter, 142–143
shutting down the open, 23
Mindfulness, 253
moments of madness and, 33–36
Mindfulness-based stress reduction
(MBSR), 163–167
research publications on, 164f
MIT Center for Organizational Learning, 17
MIT IDEAS Indonesia program,
198–201
Mondragon Corporation, 136
Money
"aging," 235
does not equal money, 99–100
flows the wrong way, 9
function of all, 97
intentional, for the realization of community, 97
is not a commodity, 96–99
is not capital, 95–96
myths about, 86, 102
options for using, 233
transfer of, 99
types of, 233
Mubarak, Hosni, 28, 31, 32, 51
Multitasking, 106

Namibia, 88, 203–207

Nan Huai-Chin, 141–146
Natura, as shifting the field of busi-
ness, 219–223
Natural resources, disconnect between
infinite growth imperative and
finite, 6
Nature, 75, 77, 241
diversity in, 81
relinking economy with, 78–82
as zero-waste system, 81
Nazis, 32, 153, 155, 158. *See also*
Holocaust
Neoliberal Reagan-Thatcher revolution,
58, 64
New York City Housing Authority
(NYCHA), 41
Newman, Kate, 229
Nhat Hanh, Thich, 159–160
Nietzsche, Friedrich Wilhelm, 213,
214, 221
"Man is a rope," 152–153
Nike, 112
Nongovernmental organizations
(NGOs), 112
NGOs 4.0, 227–228
Now, connecting and staying with the,
170. *See also* Presencing
Nuclear disarmament, 261n12

Obama, Barack, 10, 59
O'Brien, Bill, 18
Observation, 169
bending the beam of, 161, 240 (*see
also* Self-reflection)
Occupation theory of ownership,
130–131
Occupy Wall Street movement, 28
Oikos, 2, 67, 69–70, 83
Olson, Mancur, 10
One Truth (ideology/closed mind), 32,
33
One Us (closed heart/rigid collectiv-
ism), 32, 33
One Will (closed will/fanaticism), 32,
33
Open-door policy, 200
Open heart, shutting down the, 23

ABOUT THE AUTHORS

 **DR. C. OTTO SCHARMER,** author of *Theory U* and co-author of *Presence,* is a senior lecturer at the Massachusetts Institute of Technology (MIT) and the founding chair of the Presencing Institute. He also is faculty chair of MIT's IDEAS program.

In 2012 he co-founded the Global Well-Being and Gross National Happiness (GNH) Lab, which links innovators from Bhutan, India, China, Brazil, Europe, and the United States in order to prototype profound innovations in government, business, education, and civil society. He has worked with governments, UN organizations, companies, and NGOs in Africa, Asia, the Americas, and Europe, and he has delivered award-winning leadership and innovation programs for clients including Alibaba, Daimler, Eileen Fisher, Fujitsu, Google, Natura, and PriceWaterhouse.

Scharmer is currently a vice-chair of the World Economic Forum's Global Agenda Council on New Leadership Models. He holds a PhD in economics and management from Witten-Herdecke University in Germany. He lives with his family in the Boston area. More information about Scharmer and his work can be found at www.presencing.com and www.ottoscharmer.com.

DR. KATRIN KAUFER is co-founder and research director at the Presencing Institute and research fellow at the Community Innovators Lab (CoLab) at MIT's Department of Urban Studies and Planning. Her research focuses on leadership, social transformation, and socially responsible banking.

She has consulted with midsized and global companies, nonprofit organizations, the World Bank, and the United Nations Development Programme. She currently works with the Global Alliance for Banking on Values, a network of twenty financial institutions that focus on relinking finance with a shared intention for positive social change. She also co-developed the Global Classroom concept at the Presencing Institute, an online learning platform that links live-streamed virtual classroom interaction with small-group dialogue and local action.

Kaufer earned her MBA and PhD from Witten-Herdecke University in Germany. Her dissertation focused on socially responsible banking. She lives with her family in the Boston area. More information can be found at www.presencing.com.

ABOUT THE PRESENCING INSTITUTE

The Presencing Institute (PI) is an awareness-based action-research community that creates social technologies, builds capacities, and generates holding spaces for profound societal renewal. This community tries to contribute to shifting the economy from ego to eco, and toward serving the well-being of all.

A ten-year research project that we started in 1996, conducted by Otto and his colleagues, including Joseph Jaworski and Peter Senge, at MIT resulted in a consciousness-based framework of leadership and change. That framework, referred to as presencing or Theory U, says that the quality of the results that a system creates is a function of the awareness from which the people in that system operate. The findings have been published in the books *Theory U* (by Otto) and *Presence* (coauthored by Otto with Peter Senge, Joseph Jaworski, and Betty Sue Flowers).

The second phase focused on many applications that resulted in a global ecology of laboratories, projects, programs, and initiatives that link partners in business, government, and civil society. The delivery of these projects and programs occurred directly through PI or its partner institutions, including MIT, Synergos, the Sustainable Food Lab, United in Diversity (UID), the GIZ Global Leadership Academy, Tsinghua University, FGV and FDC (Brazil), SoL (the Society for Organizational Learning), and others. Throughout this period, the online community of PI grew to over ten thousand members.

The third phase starts now, with this book, which introduces the 4.0 framework and the concept of the U.school as a global platform for helping a new generation of 4.0 eco-system entrepreneurs to act more creatively and intentionally and to be more connected.

More information can be found at www.presencing.com.

Also by Otto Scharmer

Theory U
Leading from the Future as It Emerges

In this groundbreaking book, Otto Scharmer invites us to see the world in new ways and in so doing discover a revolutionary approach to leadership.

What we pay attention to and how we pay attention is key to what we create. What prevents us from attending to situations more effectively is that we aren't fully aware of and in touch with the inner place from which attention and intention originate. This is what Scharmer calls our blind spot. By moving through Scharmer's U process, we consciously access the blind spot and learn to connect to our authentic Self—the deepest source of knowledge and inspiration—in the realm of "presencing," a term coined by Scharmer that combines the concepts of presence and sensing. Based on ten years of research and action learning and interviews with over 150 practitioners and thought leaders, *Theory U* offers a rich diversity of compelling stories and examples and includes dozens of exercises and practices that allow leaders, and entire organizations, to shift awareness, connect with the best future possibility, and gain the ability to realize it.

Paperback, 560 pages, ISBN 978-1-57675-763-5

PDF ebook, ISBN 978-1-57675-866-3

Berrett–Koehler Publishers, Inc.
www.bkconnection.com

800.929.2929

Berrett–Koehler
Publishers

Berrett-Koehler is an independent publisher dedicated to an ambitious mission: *Creating a World That Works for All*.

We believe that to truly create a better world, action is needed at all levels—individual, organizational, and societal. At the individual level, our publications help people align their lives with their values and with their aspirations for a better world. At the organizational level, our publications promote progressive leadership and management practices, socially responsible approaches to business, and humane and effective organizations. At the societal level, our publications advance social and economic justice, shared prosperity, sustainability, and new solutions to national and global issues.

A major theme of our publications is "Opening Up New Space." Berrett-Koehler titles challenge conventional thinking, introduce new ideas, and foster positive change. Their common quest is changing the underlying beliefs, mindsets, institutions, and structures that keep generating the same cycles of problems, no matter who our leaders are or what improvement programs we adopt.

We strive to practice what we preach—to operate our publishing company in line with the ideas in our books. At the core of our approach is stewardship, which we define as a deep sense of responsibility to administer the company for the benefit of all of our "stakeholder" groups: authors, customers, employees, investors, service providers, and the communities and environment around us.

We are grateful to the thousands of readers, authors, and other friends of the company who consider themselves to be part of the "BK Community." We hope that you, too, will join us in our mission.

A BK Currents Book

This book is part of our BK Currents series. BK Currents books advance social and economic justice by exploring the critical intersections between business and society. Offering a unique combination of thoughtful analysis and progressive alternatives, BK Currents books promote positive change at the national and global levels. To find out more, visit **www.bkconnection.com**.

Berrett–Koehler
Publishers

A community dedicated to creating
a world that works for all

Visit Our Website: www.bkconnection.com

Read book excerpts, see author videos and Internet movies, read our authors' blogs, join discussion groups, download book apps, find out about the BK Affiliate Network, browse subject-area libraries of books, get special discounts, and more!

Subscribe to Our Free E-Newsletter, the *BK Communiqué*

Be the first to hear about new publications, special discount offers, exclusive articles, news about bestsellers, and more! Get on the list for our free e-newsletter by going to **www.bkconnection.com**.

Get Quantity Discounts

Berrett-Koehler books are available at quantity discounts for orders of ten or more copies. Please call us toll-free at (800) 929-2929 or email us at **bkp .orders@aidcvt.com**.

Join the BK Community

BKcommunity.com is a virtual meeting place where people from around the world can engage with kindred spirits to create a world that works for all. **BKcommunity.com** members may create their own profiles, blog, start and participate in forums and discussion groups, post photos and videos, answer surveys, announce and register for upcoming events, and chat with others online in real time. Please join the conversation!